the complete gu

QUICKEN
5 - UK

JEAN MILES

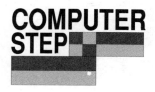

COMPUTER
STEP

Revised edition (version 5), 1996
First published (version 4), 1996

Computer Step
5c Southfield Road Southam
Warwickshire CV33 OJH
England

Tel. 01926 817999
Fax. 01926 817005

Notice of Liability
Every effort has been made to ensure that this book contains accurate and current information. However, Computer Step and the author shall not be liable for any loss or damage suffered by readers as a result of any information contained herein.

Trademarks
Quicken is a registered trademark of Intuit Inc. All other trademarks are acknowledged as belonging to their respective companies.

Printed in England

ISBN 1 874029 55 5

ABOUT THE AUTHOR

Jean Miles is a journalist who specialises in financial software. She contributes to the Financial Times and other financial publications, and writes on more general topics for the computer press. This is her fifth book.

FOREWORD

Being financially organised is more and more challenging in this day and age, as our financial lives become increasingly complex. Multiple banking relationships, including credit cards and store cards, standing orders and direct debits, mortgages or loans with variable interest rates - any or all of which may be shared with others - make the task more complicated still. For small businesses these difficulties are compounded by the requirement to keep detailed, accurate records, to monitor VAT and to project cashflow for business planning purposes. For all of us, the information required to make the best financial decisions can be difficult to come by, and is often out-of-date when finally received.

And yet the need for financial control has never been greater. With recent moves towards financial deregulation in the UK, provision for one's own future is the only sure way to financial independence in later life. There are any number of financial advisers willing to assist us with the task of planning ahead, but until we have a close understanding of our current financial situation, planning ahead remains a somewhat intangible pursuit.

Quicken, now in its fourth incarnation as the UK's best-selling finance software, is designed to alleviate the hassle of financial management, and to provide a clear insight into one's financial situation. The software is designed to be easy enough for everyone to use, and to automate the chore of maintaining a complete, accurate and up-to-date set of financial records. The flexibility of Quicken is key to its widespread usage throughout the world by householders and small business people alike. Quicken has now sold in excess of 11 million copies world-wide.

Jean Miles is a self-confessed 'Quicken-addict', having used UK versions of the program since its introduction in this country in 1992. The program improves with each new release, as it incorporates suggested enhancements from thousands of Quicken users. Some of Jean's own pet-features have gone into making *Quicken 5 for Windows*, the Best Quicken Ever!

This book provides personal insights from the author into getting the most out of your software. The hints and tips are based on her own usage of the program, and as such complement the Quicken User Guide well. Moreover the author's uncomplicated writing style and humour throughout the book provide further substantiation of her opening claim:

"It's easy; it's fun; right from the beginning, you'll take charge of your finances in ways you wouldn't have imagined possible".

Ian Yarlott
Managing Director
Intuit Ltd.

TABLE OF CONTENTS

CHAPTER
1

Getting Started

So – you've bought *Quicken 5*, or you're thinking about it. This chapter is your introduction to the program – to its philosophy, and to more mundane matters such as its hardware requirements. You'll also find here a list of improvements and additions to earlier versions of the program. The installation process is described, and there is a final section for business users. If you are familiar with earlier versions of the program or with other accounting programs, you may be tempted to move briskly through this chapter. Don't go too fast: there are a lot of new things in *Quicken 4* and *Quicken 5*. The new forecasting and graphic features are particularly good. And there are dozens of small improvements to the program all-too-easy to overlook if you are familiar with an earlier version.

1.1 How to Use this Book

The *Quicken* phenomenon is one of the biggest stories of recent years in the world of computer software. First this accounting program for home and small business users took America by storm. Then it came to Europe and did the same thing here. The reasons for its success are obvious as soon as you start to use it:

- it's easy;
- it's fun;

- right from the beginning, you'll take charge of your finances in ways you wouldn't have imagined possible.

There is an extra reason for its European success – the software house Intuit has taken a lot of trouble to get things right. They realised from the start that there was more to it than just changing all the $s into £s. We do things very differently here.

It is quite possible that *Quicken* has been put through a process of Europeanisation such as no program has ever undergone before. The result is a program thoroughly at home with many UK financial practices that are rare or unknown in America, from VAT to standing orders to endowment mortgages. This book is concerned entirely with the UK version of the program.

Nor did Intuit sit back and relax after the first highly successful version of *Quicken* was introduced to Britain in 1992. *Quicken 4 for Windows* contained major improvements in specifically European areas – multi-currency Investment accounts, to mention one impressive example. *Quicken 5* has made the program vastly easier to use.

Quicken 5 for Windows, like its predecessor *Quicken 4*, is sold as a separate program, and also as part of *Quicken Deluxe*, which includes the separate programs *Home Inventory* and *QuickInvoice*. Both of these additional programs are discussed in this book. *Home Inventory* is in Chapter 6, on Asset accounts. *QuickInvoice* is in Chapter 10, the business chapter.

If you're upgrading from an earlier version of *Quicken*, you might want to start by looking at Section 1.3 later in this chapter, What's New in *Quicken 4* and *5*? The major new functions are listed with brief descriptions. You will also find there references to other parts of the book where these features are discussed at length.

If you plan to use *Quicken* for business accounting, you will be particularly interested in Chapter 10, which is entirely devoted to that subject. But it is important for you to have a look at the rest of the book as well. For one thing, you are likely to decide to use *Quicken* for your domestic accounts – surveys have shown that many *Quicken* business users do that. For another, there are tips throughout the book of potential interest to business users.

On the other hand, if this is your first venture into bookkeeping or perhaps even into computing, you will want to pay careful attention to the sections in this first chapter on installing *Quicken* and setting up your first account; and then to read the following chapter, First Steps in Finance, which will tell you the rest of what you need to know to get started. Chapter 3 will introduce you to the financial planning features that are a powerful feature of *Quicken*. Chapter 4 is a round-up of *Quicken*'s special effects, which let you tailor the program to your own outlook on finance and on life. After that, you can pick and choose from the other topics as they affect you.

If your computer has a CD-ROM drive, you probably bought *Quicken* on CD-ROM. In that case, you will find the complete manual available on-line, with hypertext links. If you have *Quicken Deluxe* you will also be able to view six different 5-6 minute videos in which the staff of Intuit demonstrate the use of the program and point out some of its features. It's a lot of fun to get started that way.

Quicken is full of choices, of ways you can adapt the program to your own way of thinking and working. Throughout this book I will mention, from time to time, the way I have set *Quicken* to work for me. I do not mean for a moment to suggest that my way is best. I only want to start you thinking about how you would like your *Quicken* to work.

1.2 A Word about Operating Systems

The illustrations in this book show *Quicken* running under *Windows 95*, the new operating system from Microsoft. It runs just as well under *Windows 3.1* or *Windows 3.11*, and there are no differences in the behaviour of the program. So don't worry if you have the older system and your screens look slightly different from the ones you see here. The illustrations are taken from the latest version of the program, *Quicken 5 for Windows*. Users of *Quicken 4* will see a lot that looks strange, but the way the program works has not changed and you will have no difficulty using this book. If you have an even earlier version of *Quicken*, you should think of upgrading. *Quicken 4* really was a great leap forward; *Quicken 5* continues the good work.

As everybody knows by now, computers with any version of *Windows* are operated by means of mice. Using these electronic pointing devices, you move the cursor to different parts of the screen and click a button on the mouse for action. It is also possible to steer your way through *Windows*, and through a program like *Quicken*, using the keyboard only. Some people prefer to, and *Quicken* is particularly good at making keyboard navigation easy. But this book assumes you're using a mouse.

1.3 What's New in Quicken 4 and 5?

The principal changes in *Quicken 4 for Windows* made the program a powerful financial planning tool, with new graphical features to help you get an overview of your financial situation. *Quicken 5* has taken the process further. The new EasyAnswers feature gives instant answers to your most frequent questions about your finances – such as, "Where did all the money go?" Chapter 3 of this book is dedicated to the subjects of cashflow prediction and financial planning. In it you will find:

The **Snapshots** page, probably the single most impressive addition to *Quicken 4*. You can choose and arrange screens, each consisting of up to six graphs or short reports, which show you at a glance the important things you want to know about your finances.

The **Forecast graph**, which uses your budget and your standing orders in a new way to predict future account balances. Business users should become familiar with this feature as soon as possible, as cashflow is, if anything, even more important in business than for the rest of us. *Quicken 5* lets you formulate and save up to three separate budgets, allowing you more scope than ever before to try out "what if" scenarios.

Savings Goals, which help you set money aside for the important things you want out of life.

Progress bars, which can be set to monitor your progress towards your most important budget or savings goals. You can have two Progress bars on screen at all times if you choose.

And there are plenty of other improvements:

Quicken 5 is vastly friendlier and more helpful than earlier versions of the program. You can use the improved HomeBase screen as a springboard for all features. You can choose to be guided through the procedure for setting up a new account, step by step. The Qcards which offer advice at potentially difficult points are more helpful than ever. See Chapter 2.

Supercategories provided a whole new way of organising your income and expenses in *Quicken 4*. In *Quicken 5* their use has been extended. You can now use them to organise Cash Flow reports and Summary reports. Supercategories are explained in Chapter 2. Their use in reports is covered in Chapter 5.

Quicken's Reminders have become friendlier and more effective. See Chapter 4.

Quicken 4 made major changes and improvements in the handling of investments. You can now enter Tax Credits in *Quicken* for a more accurate calculation of the total return on your investments. And you can now have Investment accounts in any currency, all in one *Quicken* file. *Quicken 5* has added further refinements. See Chapters 7 and 8.

Quicken can provide more help than ever before with preparing your income tax return. See Section 9.3.

Quicken 5 has made navigation among the program's many features even easier than it was.

You can now suppress – without removing – inactive accounts. You can also hide columns in reports, and tell *Quicken* to print any report, however wide, on one sheet of paper.

1.4 Installing Quicken

The *Quicken Deluxe* package demands a lot of your computer. You'll need:
*   a 100% IBM-compatible computer with a 486 processor or better and a minimum of 8 MB of RAM;
*   *Windows Version 3.1* or above, including *Windows 95 – Windows 3.0* won't do;
*   at least 8 MB of disk space on your hard disk.

The tricky one in that list is the 8MB of RAM – even if you bought your computer recently, you might have less. Check the details with your software dealer, or phone Intuit on 0800 585058, if you're not sure. You may need to content yourself with the plain-vanilla version of *Quicken 5*, or even fall back on *Quicken 4*, which demands only 3 MB of RAM. Don't worry: it's an excellent program.

Once you're satisfied on these points, you're ready to start. If you're upgrading from an earlier version of *Quicken*, the installation process will locate your data files, make a copy of them for you in a new directory called OLDFILES, and then convert the files for use with *Quicken 5*. You won't be able to use *Quicken 5* files with earlier versions of the program.

Put Install Disk No. 1 in your floppy disk drive. In *Windows 95* you then click the Start button, point to Settings and click Control Panel. Choose "Add/Remove programs" by double-clicking, and follow the instructions that appear on your screen. For older versions of *Windows*, open the File Manager and click on File; from the File menu, choose Run. In the Run window, type A:INSTALL (or B:INSTALL if you are using drive B). From there on, *Quicken* will take over, although you can, if you prefer, override the default settings of the installation program.

When you start the program for the first time, you'll see the New User Setup window. It will walk you through the process of setting up your first account and loading a list of categories. The assumption is that you will want to start with your Current account – a very good idea.

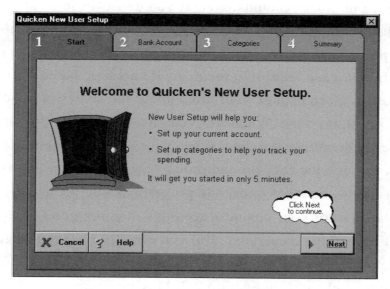

FIGURE 1.1 THE NEW USER SETUP WINDOW

The New User Setup window makes the process absolutely painless. If you'd rather not have your hand held like this, click on the Close button in the upper right-hand corner of the window to go straight into the program. Assuming you stick with New User Setup, and have decided to set up your Current account first, you'll be asked a series of simple questions.

The New User Setup window will ask you what categories you want to start with – the choices are Home, Business, or Both. On the subject of categories, see Section 2.1, and remember that any decision you make now can easily be changed or adjusted later. That's one of *Quicken*'s great merits.

When that decision has been recorded, the New User Setup window is ready to say goodbye. Click Done, and you'll find yourself at the Create New Account window, ready to add more accounts to your setup.

But again, *Quicken* lets you relax. You can start making entries in the Transaction Register of one of your new accounts right now, and worry about categories and other accounts later. If you don't fill in a category for a particular transaction, you can always go back and add one. If you decide you've put something in the wrong category, you can change it – or use a wonderful *Quicken* feature to recategorise a whole batch of transactions at once. And you can change your mind about the names of the categories themselves at any time. Whenever you alter a category, perhaps by changing its name, or demoting it to be a subcategory of something else, *Quicken* will go back through the register and redo every transaction that is affected. You can learn how you want to use the program as you go along. (If you are using *Quicken* for your business accounts, it is not good practice to leave a transaction without a category. But you can still change category names and promote or demote subcategories like anyone else.)

In the next chapter, in Section 2.2, Making Entries in the Register, you will find a full description of a Transaction Register, where actual entries are made of money in and money out.

If you're not a new user but an upgrader, pause a moment here to look at the new *Quicken* screen. A lot of it will be perfectly familiar, of course. But notice the list of active windows towards the upper left. Click on any one to bring it to the top. This is usually the easiest way, in *Quicken 5*, to switch from one frequently-used account to another. At the lower left, you'll see a

"To Do" notice – click on that to go straight to the Reminders window (Section 4.2 in this book). And notice that the buttons you may need when you are making an entry in a register, Record, Edit, and Splits, are now right there where you want them, in the Spend and Receive columns in the register.

1.5 A Foreword for Business Users

If you are about to start using *Quicken* for business accounting, you may be feeling a little nervous. Perhaps you have never kept formal accounts before, trusting like many of us to instinct, the bottom line of the bank statement, and the steadying advice of an accountant. Now you want to take control of your finances. Can *Quicken* help? Or perhaps you are operating a formal double-entry bookkeeping system, either by hand or on your computer. It takes a lot of time, and you often feel bogged down in rules that are hard to understand. You wonder if *Quicken* would make life any easier.

The answer, to either question, is almost certainly yes. As you will see in Chapter 10, *Quicken* can do everything a small business needs (except stock control), including payroll transactions, accrual accounting and helping you fill out the dreaded Value Added Tax return for HM Customs and Excise. It is suitable for any business where the boss keeps the accounts – whether the boss is a dentist, a newsagent, the owner of a country cottage for rent; or just about anything else you could name.

You may be anxious precisely because *Quicken* is so easy to use. Can you be keeping "proper" accounts with so little anguish? The answer, again, is yes. *Quicken* is, in fact, operating a full-scale double-entry bookkeeping system behind the scenes. All the necessary safeguards are in place. Talk it over with your accountant: that is a good idea anyway when you are contemplating a change as important as this. More and more accountants know about *Quicken*. You are likely to encounter enthusiastic encouragement. If you don't, try keeping accounts in *Quicken* for a month in parallel with your present system. Then print out some of *Quicken*'s business reports and take them in for your accountant to inspect.

If your business involves sending out a lot of invoices, you might think of adding *Quicken*'s sister program *QuickInvoice*. It works with *Quicken*, and makes it easier for you to keep a record of your dealings with your customers. You can start out with *Quicken* alone, and add *QuickInvoice* later if you decide to. *QuickInvoice* is sold with *Quicken* as part of *Quicken Deluxe*. It is described in Section 10.7.

Don't be too quick to turn to Chapter 10. *Quicken* is all one program, and the best way to learn how it can help you in business is to grasp the idea of the way the whole program works. You will need a lot of the general techniques, starting with the basic ones like setting up accounts and entering transactions. And some of the special features, especially the Forecasting and the Financial Calendar (Chapter 3), will be of considerable use to you. You may well want *Quicken* to write your cheques (Section 9.1). You will certainly need to know how to reconcile a bank statement (Section 9.2).

In Chapter 10, you will find a discussion of the difference between *Quicken* and traditional business accounting methods. You will also find the two important concepts mentioned above which do not appear in the rest of the book, or in the rest of *Quicken* for that matter: accrual accounting, and VAT accounting. If your business is too small to be registered for VAT, and if you do almost everything on a cash basis, you may not need to be introduced to either of these ideas. If you do need them, you probably know it already, even if you don't quite understand as yet what is going to be involved. There is no doubt that these two subjects are more difficult than anything a non-business user of *Quicken* will ever encounter. They are not so difficult that you need to be apprehensive. But it is important to read Chapter 10 carefully, and the relevant parts of the *Quicken* manual as well, before you start.

CHAPTER 2

First Steps
in Finance

This is the nitty-gritty chapter, the one about how to set things up and how to take your first steps in *Quicken*. It starts with the basic idea of separating your income and expenditure into "categories" – the foundation of all accounting systems. *Quicken* has some elegant variations on the theme, which you will also find described here. This chapter then walks you through the process of making the first real entries in your *Quicken* accounts.

2.1 Income and Expense Categories

Before we start, here are some tips on how to find your way around.

You can navigate through *Quicken*, as through any *Windows* program, by choosing an item from the menu bar at the top of the screen, and then choosing again from the drop-down menu. But in almost every case, *Quicken* has provided you with an easier and more obvious way to get where you want to go.

- All the facilities of the program can be approached through the improved HomeBase screen. Click on Activities in the menu bar, then choose HomeBase. Simpler yet, just choose HomeBase from the top of the list of open windows, towards the upper left of your screen.

- As just mentioned, the windows you currently have open in *Quicken* are listed to the left of the screen, near the top. Click on one of them to bring it to the top of the pile.

- All your accounts are listed at the bottom of the register of each account. Click on one to open it. You can rearrange those buttons so that your most frequently-used accounts are always visible. This feature, the Account Selector, has been improved in *Quicken 5*. See Section 4.4.

- Many windows in the program have their own Help button, offering specific guidance about whatever is going on at the moment.

- If you hold the cursor for a moment over one of the buttons or icons in the program, you'll see a "bubble" explaining what that particular button or icon is for. This is a new feature in *Quicken 5*.

- Look for the helpful yellow Qcards which pop up from time to time. If you close one of them, *Quicken* will ask whether you want that particular Qcard to be closed permanently. Turn them all off (or on again) by clicking on Help on the menu bar and then clicking on "Show Qcards".

- Like many *Windows* programs, *Quicken* now starts each session by offering you a tip. You can turn this feature off if it irritates you, but I'd suggest that you leave it alone for a while. Of course most days it'll tell you something you know all about. But once in a while it might surprise you.

Let's get to work.

Categories are the headings under which you receive and pay out money. "Salary" and "Child Benefit" would be examples of the former; "food", "clothes", "mortgage" and "car", of the latter. Getting your categories right is one of the most important aspects of account-keeping. And it's pretty well impossible to get them right first time, especially if you're new to the whole

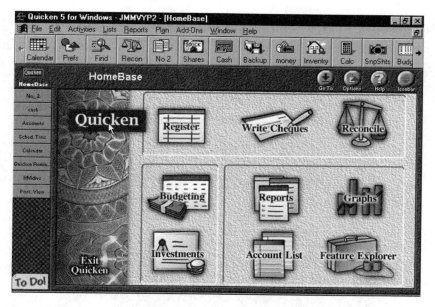

FIGURE 2.1 THE HOMEBASE SCREEN

business of bookkeeping. Furthermore, things change. You might get married (or divorced); move from a rented flat to a house with a garden and a mortgage; who knows? you might even have a baby. New categories would be needed for each of those events. You'll want to keep going back to the Categories list and tinkering with it. The great thing about *Quicken* is, you can.

Traditional accounting systems do not allow such freedom. With them, once you have made an entry under a particular heading, you're stuck with that category for life – or at least until you reinstall the program. *Quicken* allows you to change anything, any time. It also allows you to set safeguards, such as a password, so that your data is safe if you want to rule out the possibility of change.

Quicken comes supplied with lists both of domestic and of business categories. When you first used the program after installing it, you chose whether to load the business list as well as the domestic one. You're not stuck with the *Quicken* lists, even after you've loaded them. You can delete categories, change their names, group them, mark them as tax-related – and you can go on making these changes as long as you like.

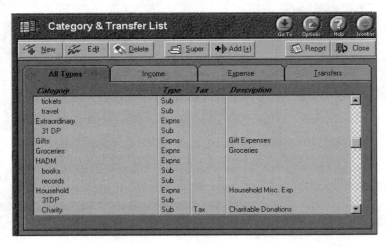

FIGURE 2.2 CATEGORY & TRANSFER LIST WINDOW

To see your Category List, click Lists from the Menu Bar, and choose Category & Transfer. Notice the row of buttons along the top of the Category & Transfer List window. Using them, you can:

- add new categories of your own;
- edit the ones already in the list, perhaps by changing the name or adding a description;
- delete any category you don't need;
- group your categories together as supercategories.

The other option, the invaluable QuickReport, doesn't come into play until you have entered some financial data.

Have a look at *Quicken*'s list of categories. There are four columns in the window: Category, Type, Tax, and Description. If you're tracking VAT in your business accounts, there will be a column for that as well.

- **Category** is the current name of the category. If you want to change it to something snappier, select the category and click the Edit button. If it is one of *Quicken*'s category suggestions that you know you'll never use, select it and click Delete. And if *Quicken* has failed to include a category that you think you are going to want, click New to add it.

- The **Type** of a category can be Inc, for Income; Exp, for Expense; or Sub, for Subcategory. A subcategory takes on the type of its parent. If you set up "AA" as a subcategory of your expense category "Motor", "AA" will automatically be an expense category. Read on to learn more about subcategories.

- The **Tax** column indicates whether or not you have designated the category as tax-related. *Quicken* can give you a lot of help with the preparation of your tax return. It's worth setting your categories up from the beginning to take full advantage of this feature. There is more on this painful subject below, and in Section 9.3.

- The **Description** column allows you a few words to identify the category for yourself. Business users who want to keep the numbers from their old Chart of Accounts as the category names can use the Description to specify the contents of the category, and can have the Descriptions printed on their reports if they choose.

- If you are tracking VAT, there will be a column headed "**VAT**", showing which VAT codes have been assigned to your various categories. See Section 10.5.

Before you start work on your categories, it would be a good idea to choose Options from the Edit menu (the one on the menu bar at the top of your screen, not the one on the Category & Transfer window itself), and then click on International in the Options window. Make sure that "United Kingdom" is the selected country, if that's where you are; and also make sure there is a tick in the box labelled "Use Tax Return with Categories". You'll see why in a moment.

Start with your income categories. There won't be so many of them (alas). Later on you will probably want to fill in estimates of how much you receive under each heading, so that you can take advantage of *Quicken*'s facilities for forward planning. For now, though, just list the categories themselves. You won't have any trouble thinking of them. Be hopeful: include things like your Christmas bonus, even though it isn't a certainty.

If you can't bear to think about tax at the moment, there's no harm in just listing your income categories. With *Quicken*, it's never too late to go back and make changes and improvements. When you're feeling strong enough, here's how to set things up with tax-time in mind:

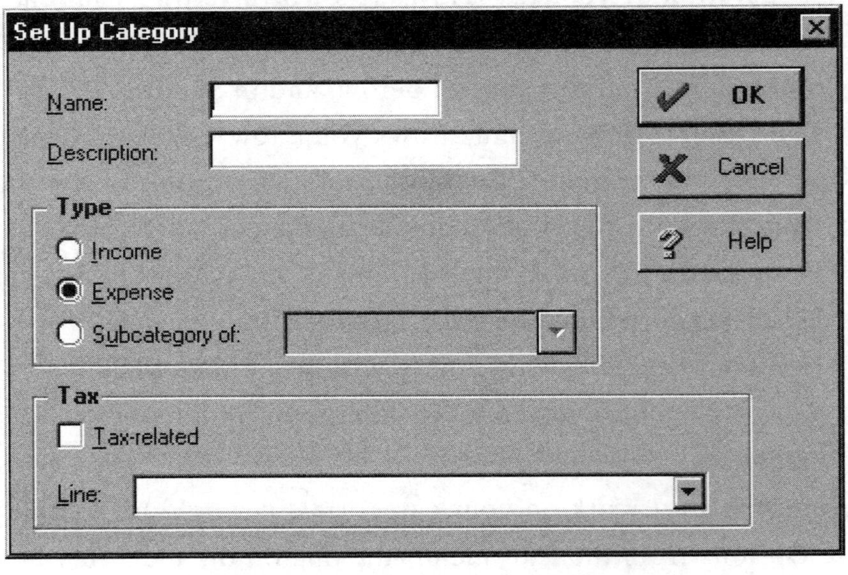

FIGURE 2.3 SET UP CATEGORY WINDOW

Almost all income categories will be tax-related, so you'll probably put a tick in the "Tax-related" box in the Edit Category or Set Up Category window. If you have used the Preferences window as just suggested to indicate your interest in relating categories to tax returns, you will see a field called "Line". Click on the button beside the field to see what *Quicken* means by that. You'll see a list of the headings the Inland Revenue uses on the tax return form. Choose the appropriate one for the category you are working on.

In most cases, the choice will be perfectly straightforward. Your salary, for instance, is declared to the Inland Revenue as "Wages, salary, fees, bonuses, etc.". *Quicken* lists this as "Employment – salary and wages". So choose that line for your income category Salary. More than one category can be assigned to the same line – the hoped-for Christmas bonus, for example, is also "salary and wages" in the eyes of the Inland Revenue.

Income from interest is a bit more complicated. If you have a Tax-Exempt Savings Account (a TESSA) or a Personal Equity Plan (a PEP), you will have income which is not taxable and which doesn't need to be included on a tax return. So you'll need a separate income category, not tax-related, for that income. Your normal bank and building society interest can go in a tax-related category assigned to the line "Banks, building societies, etc. – tax deducted". *Quicken* has already provided you with one category called "Int Inc". You'll have to think of a name for the other one – perhaps Taxfree Int.

That's not the end of the possible complications, by any means, nor of the help *Quicken* can offer in straightening things out. See Section 9.3, Preparing a Tax Return, for more.

With income out of the way, take a look at the expense categories. *Quicken*'s list will give you some ideas. The major ones will be obvious (food, rent or mortgage, car, clothing, holidays). Notice that you are allowed subcategories: they can be extremely useful. By way of example, look at the three subcategories under "Motor" in *Quicken*'s standard list: Fuel, Loan, and Service. You can even have sub-subcategories if you like.

A lot will depend on your circumstances. If you have finished paying for your car, the subcategory "Loan" under "Motor" can be deleted to start with. Everyone will approach this subject differently, and *Quicken*'s list is only a suggestion. There are no right answers – the whole point of *Quicken* is that you can do it your way.

Notice that either sort of category, income or expense, can in fact accept either sort of transaction, in or out. For instance, if you have minor freelance earnings as a spin-off from some interest or hobby, breeding tropical fish or repairing your friends' computers, you could set it up as an income category but enter expenses, too, as they occurred, to help you with your tax return. For more serious earnings of that sort, see Chapter 10 on Using *Quicken* in Your Business.

Likewise, if you enjoy a flutter on the ponies or the National Lottery from time to time, you could put in Gambling as an expense category – or, indeed, as an income category, but that would be tempting fortune. Both lost stakes and your winnings could then be entered in the same category, and would soon form a record which might lead you to mend your ways.

Quicken also lets you group your categories into supercategories – a wonderful feature. More about them in a moment. I would still suggest that you try to limit the number of expense categories to something between 12 and 15, but spread yourself on subcategories, and on sub-subcategories if you find them useful. When you're looking at your spending in a *Quicken* report, subcategories can be suppressed, so that all the expenditure appears under the heading of the category itself. That way, you get a good general view of your situation without getting bogged down in detail. A couple of clicks is all it will take to let you see the same report with spending assigned to subcategories and sub-subcategories.

Some of your expense categories will be tax-related – payments made under a court order to your child or former spouse would be one example, charitable payments under deed of covenant another. Treat these categories in exactly the same way as tax-related income, marking them as tax-related and assigning them to the appropriate line on the income tax form.

Don't hesitate to have some subcategories, such as Road Tax or AA Subscription under Motor, which will attract only one entry a year. It is best to be as precise as possible. You always can classify something as "Other" – or leave it unclassified, in which case *Quicken* will classify it as "Other" for you. But it's better to have a category for everything. In business accounting you have no option: everything must be classified.

It is also worth noting that *Quicken* can reverse subcategories in its reports on your financial position. If, for example, you have a country cottage with a telephone, you could enter the bills as Dunroamin:telephone, and your home bills as Household:telephone. You could then specify "reversed subcategories" on a report, to see all the telephone bills together. So when you are planning subcategories, try to use the same word as the subcategory name in cases where you might want to reverse the order one day.

Remember, you can always change things. You can rename categories, demote them to subcategories or merge them with other categories. Subcategories can be transferred from one category to another, or promoted to full category status. In the Category & Transfer List, move the highlight to the category you are interested in, and click Edit. To rename a category, to add a description or to change the description that's already there, just type your new information in the Name or Description field. To demote a category to subcategory or sub-subcategory status, click "Subcategory of", instead of "Income" or "Expense". The category list will then (and only then) be available in the next field. Type in the category or subcategory name you want, or click the button on the right of the field to see the category list, and make your choice from that.

Promoting a subcategory to full category status is even easier. Just click Income or Expense instead of "Subcategory of", and the job is done. To transfer a subcategory so that it is dependent on a different category, change the name in the "Subcategory of" field.

The best course is probably not to spend too much time at the beginning thinking about categories at all: list the obvious ones, delete the obvious duds from *Quicken*'s suggested list, and then plunge boldly in and use the program, especially if you're new to the whole business of account-keeping. Start entering some actual transactions (see Section 2.2, Making Entries in the Register, later in this chapter) and feel your way forward from there. You'll soon begin to have ideas of your own about how to manage your categories. You can even add new categories "on the wing", while you are entering transactions – you don't need to come back to the Category & Transfer List. And remember that *Quicken* will reclassify all your data as often as you like. So even if you're using *Quicken* for business accounting, you needn't hesitate to experiment until you find the set of categories that suits your purposes best.

You can group your categories together into supercategories. You will find when you start using the program that *Quicken* suggests Discretionary and Non-Discretionary for expense categories, and Salary Income and Other Income for income categories. That may give you some ideas about how supercategories can be used. This is another feature you should come back to when you are more familiar with the program.

To set up your own supercategories, click on the Super button at the top of the Category & Transfer List window. You will see the Manage Supercategories window. Discretionary and Non-Discretionary, Salary Income and Other Income are already listed as supercategory names. When you click New in that window you will be invited to give a name to a new supercategory. As soon as you have done so, the name appears in the

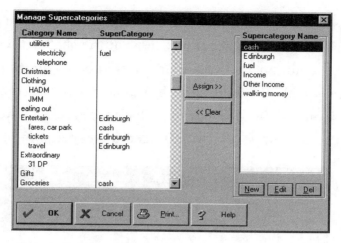

FIGURE 2.4 THE MANAGE SUPERCATEGORIES WINDOW

Supercategory list. When naming is complete, use this same window to assign your categories to supercategories. Just highlight a category in the list on the left and a supercategory in the list on the right, and click Assign.

Using supercategories makes it much easier to get a bird's-eye view of how things are going, as you will see in Chapter 3. In earlier versions of *Quicken*, it could be difficult sometimes to see the wood for the trees.

Tip

If you make a habit of closing windows like the Category & Transfer List when you're finished with them — windows you don't use every day — the pile of open windows listed in the upper left-hand corner of your screen will be even more useful, because you'll be able to spot the one you want next more quickly.

2.2 Making Entries in the Register

You're probably keen to get started on the program. There's no better way to learn more about *Quicken* than to start using it. So find your cheque book, your latest bank statement and anything you can muster in the way of cash withdrawal vouchers and Switch receipts.

Click Lists in the Menu Bar. Choose Accounts from the drop-down menu. Move the highlight to the account you want to use. That will be easy, since so far you have not opened very many accounts in *Quicken*, perhaps only one. If there is a choice, highlight the name of your Current account and double-click on it. You will see soon that there are easy ways in *Quicken* to move between accounts. You won't need to keep coming back to this list.

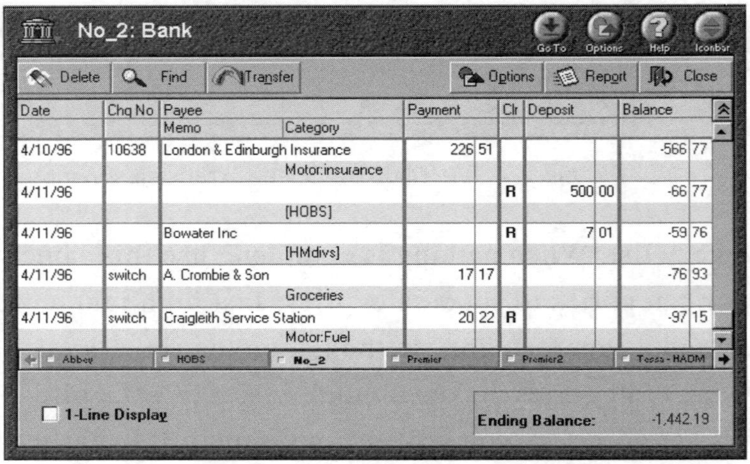

FIGURE 2.5 A TRANSACTION REGISTER WINDOW

You're now at the Transaction Register window for your Current account. You will spend a lot of your working time at this window. If you have upgraded from an earlier version of *Quicken*, the register will look familiar. It's not identical, however. Changes have been made in order to put you in easy reach of things you often want to do while you are making entries in a register. So even if you're an old *Quicken* hand, take a fresh look at the Transaction Register. You're in danger of missing something useful if you assume too quickly that you know it all already.

First of all, we'll make some entries. When you set up the account, you told *Quicken* the balance as it appeared on your most recent bank statement.

Now you are going to bring yourself up to date by typing in what has happened since.

What follows may look like an alarmingly long-winded account of a process that you could almost certainly waltz through without any help at all. Here again, don't be in too much of a hurry. Of course it's easy – that's the whole point of *Quicken*. But there are some interesting things to think about along the way. You might as well get this program working the way you want it to work as soon as possible.

Start with the cheque book. You're going to type in the details of all the cheques you've written since the date of your last bank statement. You also need to include at some point the ones you wrote before that date which hadn't yet found their way home to roost when the statement was issued. They can be harder to identify, especially if your pre-*Quicken* record-keeping was less than perfect. Don't worry: as a last resort, you can add them when the next statement arrives. Incidentally, you don't need to worry about entering cheques and other debits in order – *Quicken* will arrange them in date order for you.

When you're ready to roll, type the date of your first cheque in the register's Date field. *Quicken* will have started things off by filling in today's date. For this first session, that's probably not right. Just type over it.

Notice the button to the right of the field – it only appears while your insertion point is in the Date space. If you click on the button, you will see a little calendar. You can, if you like, enter the date for your cheque by finding it on the calendar and clicking. The blue arrows on the calendar let you move forward or backward in time. It's probably quicker just to type the date, but the calendar is fun, occasionally really useful, and typical of the thoughtful detail with which this program is packed.

Once you have safely entered a date, press the Tab key to move on to the next field, namely "Chq No" for "cheque number". Depending on your computing past, you might find it more natural to hit the Enter key. If you really can't stand the Tab key, or can't remember to use it, click on the Options button at the top of the register. In the Register Options window, choose the Miscellaneous tab. Put a tick in the checkbox labelled "Enter key moves between fields". That's not an easy sentence to parse, but never mind. Click OK, and you'll find that the Enter key now works the way you are used to. You can click on Options as often as you like to change that or any of the other preferences listed.

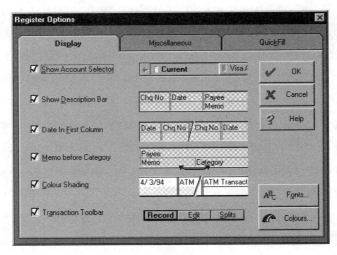

FIGURE 2.6 THE REGISTER OPTIONS WINDOW

You don't have to put a cheque number in the Cheque Number field. In fact, you don't have to put anything. *Quicken* makes life as easy as possible by keeping the amount of required information to a minimum. Nor does the "cheque number" have to be a number – various things happen to a Current account which require a word, or nothing at all, in this column. *Quicken* can list the cheques in numerical order when asked without being thrown off its stride by the entries that don't have numbers. There's a drop-down list for this field, too: to see it, press the Alt key and the down-arrow at the same time. *Quicken* will fill in the next cheque number for you or let you choose from a few other possibilities. You'll see the word "Print" on this list. That concerns *Quicken*'s cheque-writing feature – see Section 9.1. "Switch" is a new addition to the preset list in *Quicken 5*. You can add your own entries to the Chq No list by clicking on "<NEW>". I use the Bank of Scotland's on-line Home and Office Banking system, so I have added HOBS to my list.

Tip

I always enter a cheque by choosing "Next chq. no." from this list, instead of typing the number in. That way, Quicken automatically reminds me of any cheques I have forgotten to enter when I wrote them. This cuts down on mistakes, too.

Tab on, and the next field is Payee.

If your transaction is a cash deposit or withdrawal, or a payment towards your credit card or store card, leave it out for the moment. Such transactions are really transfers of money from one place to another. Soon you will make some decisions that affect how such transactions are entered. See Section 2.3 in this chapter, How Much Detail?

I have been keeping accounts in *Quicken* since it was first introduced to Britain in the latter part of 1992. I used to adopt a fairly happy-go-lucky approach to payees. I would put "window cleaner" one month and "Mr. Hocking" the next; or even put "cardigan for Helen" instead of "Marks and Spencer". After all, I was keeping accounts for my own information. Budgeting and reporting are done by category – Household:Cleaning for the windows; Gifts for Helen's cardigan. I could see no particular reason to standardise payees.

But the QuickReport feature, first introduced with *Quicken 3*, has taught me to change my ways. With QuickReport, you can select any entry in the register and click on the QuickReport button – it's the one on the Register window itself, on the top towards the right, labelled "Report". The

QuickReport will then list all your dealings with that payee for the current year. Once you've seen the list, you can change the date range. QuickReport is very useful, but it does depend on consistency. It can't show you how much you're spending on train travel if you put "BR" one day, "British Rail" the next, and "trip to London" the time after that.

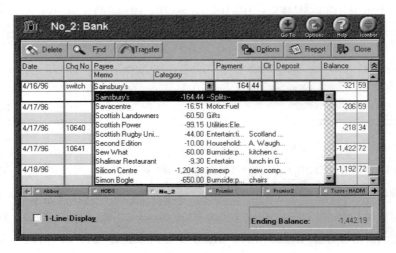

FIGURE 2.7 THE DROP-DOWN LIST OF PAYEES

For the sake of QuickReport, it is important to be long-winded and specific as you enter a payee's name: "British Rail", not "BR". That is because, if you asked for a QuickReport on "BR", you would get every transaction that included those two letters together. "London Library", "British Diabetic Association" and my optician "Clive Brooks" would all make the "BR" list.

(QuickReport has many other uses, besides listing transactions by payee. It is one of the most useful features of *Quicken*, and you will meet it again and again. See Chapter 5, Facing Facts, for more information.)

Quicken itself will help you be consistent in your naming of payees, if you like. This is particularly useful for business users, who have lists of suppliers and clients and can't afford to be careless about how they spell entries in the Payee field.

Quicken has a feature called QuickFill which will memorise every entry as you make it. Then the next time you start to type in the name of a payee it already knows, it will finish the typing for you if you like. If you let it, it will finish entering the whole transaction, exactly as you entered it the previous time. You can change the amount, or any other part of the entry, before you click Record.

I've never used the full-scale QuickFill. I find it just gets in the way. But I do let QuickFill finish typing the name of a payee when it can, as an aid to consistency. The moral is, as so often, that *Quicken*'s features are there to be used, to be adapted, or to be turned off – as it suits you.

To change the way QuickFill works, choose the Options button at the top of the Register window again. From the Register Options window, click on the QuickFill tab if it isn't already on top. There are now six choices you can make.

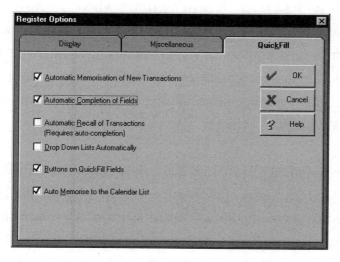

FIGURE 2.8 THE REGISTER OPTIONS WINDOW, WITH *QUICKFILL* SELECTED

I have set my own preferences with a tick in the first box, so that all transactions are memorised; and a tick in the second box, "Automatic Completion of Fields", so that as soon as I have typed "Sai...", *Quicken* will fill in the word "Sainsbury's". There is no tick in my third box, because "Automatic Recall of Transactions" means that *Quicken* will fill in the whole transaction, using the previous entry for that payee, and that's exactly what I don't want. I also have no tick in the fourth box – I don't want to see the drop-down lists until I ask for them. But there is a tick in the fifth box, so that there will be buttons visible for clicking as a reminder whenever a drop-down list is available; and in the sixth, so that a list of past payees will be available when I am using the Financial Calendar. See Section 3.3 for The Financial Calendar, and Section 4.3 for more about Memorised Transactions.

Of course you will have your own feelings about how you want QuickFill to work for you. And as with all of *Quicken*'s preferences, you can change your mind and come back to this window whenever you like.

If you set QuickFill to finish typing the payee for you as soon as you have typed the initial letters, there will be times when you have several payees on your list that start in the same way. In that case, *Quicken* starts off with the one that comes first alphabetically. If that's not right, you'll have to go on typing until you have provided enough information to let *Quicken* distinguish. This system can occasionally cause problems, or at least irritation. With a little thought, you can usually find a way around the difficulty.

We make payments to British Rail quite often, British Telecom quarterly, the British Diabetic Association once a year. You see the problem – the least-wanted payee name comes up first in *Quicken*, and stays there until I finish typing "British" and start on the next word. I solved this one by inserting the word "The" in front of "British Diabetic Association". So if you find that *Quicken* is driving you mad with its preference for a rare payee, stop and think. There'll probably be something you can do about it. But bear in mind that one of the things you can do when you are creating a report on your data in the future, is to sort transactions alphabetically by payee. If that feature is at all likely to be of use to you, you may want to put payees' surnames before their given names, and put up with the fact that the British Diabetic Association comes ahead of British Rail in the alphabet.

It does happen from time to time that I buy something or pay someone and really don't want *Quicken* to clutter up my payee list with the name – I might buy petrol in unfamiliar territory, for instance. In that case, I just leave the Payee field empty, and fill in any necessary information in the Memo field on the next line. On the other hand, I'm often sorry, as I look back through my records, that I have adopted this technique. What was the name of the woman who re-caned the dining room chairs? If I'd filled in that transaction properly, I'd know.

With the payee's name at last entered, tab on to the Payment or Deposit field. Since you are making a start by filling in transactions using the stubs in your chequebook, you'll almost certainly have a Payment to record, not a Deposit. The button on this field, and on Deposit, puts a mini-calculator at your disposal. As you use it, the figures that would be displayed on a real calculator appear in the Payment or Deposit field. When the answer to your calculations is the amount you want to enter, just tab away from the field.

The field between Payment and Deposit is called Clr, for "cleared". Normally, you will leave that one for *Quicken* to deal with. The program will put an "R" in that field when you have reconciled your bank statement. (It was an "X" in *Quicken 4.*) The "R" means that the payment or deposit has been through the hands of your bank and is debited or credited to your name in the bank's records as well as your own. There are circumstances when you will mark an item as "Cleared" yourself, but they are rare.

Quicken won't let you make an entry in the final column on the right – the Balance. The program brings that figure up to date every time you deposit or spend money. If you're new to computer budgeting, you'll soon discover that that simple feature is one of the most useful of all. From now on, you'll always know how much you have in the bank. If funds are available, you can move them in at the last moment to avoid an overdraft. You can at least try to slow your spending down if you see disaster looming.

Tab on, and you'll come to the Category field. Here you put a classification for the transaction you have just entered. See the preceding section of this chapter if you haven't yet thought about categories. Most transactions will probably fit neatly enough into one of *Quicken*'s standard categories or one of the ones you have already added to the list. The button on this field, as by now you would expect, provides you with a drop-down list of the categories. You can enter the right one by finding it in the list and clicking on it.

Eventually – and probably sooner rather than later – you'll come to an entry that doesn't fit anywhere. You'll have to think of a new category for it. There's no need to leave the Transaction Register and go back to the category list. Just type in your new category and tab away from the field. *Quicken* will recognise that the name is new, and take you straight to the Set Up Category window.

This is another field where you don't have to put anything at all if you don't want to. Leave Category blank, and *Quicken* will define your transaction as "other" in reports and graphs. However, you miss a great deal of the benefit of account-keeping if you let transactions slip through as "other". And business users really have no choice: all transactions must be properly categorised. If you like, you can ask *Quicken* to remind you if you fail to make an entry in the Category field. Click on the Options button and then on the Miscellaneous tab in the Register Options window. Make sure there is a tick in the checkbox next to "Warn Before Recording Uncategorised Transactions".

Finally, the Memo field. You don't need to put anything here. You'll probably often leave this field blank. Other times, it's useful for making notes – perhaps to jot down what you actually bought at the department store or car boot sale; to say who a gift was for; or to remind yourself what bill you were paying with a cheque to "Post Office Counters". Note that you have a bit more space for your Memo than you can see on the screen. Your words will scroll off to the left as you write, but don't worry; *Quicken* hasn't lost them.

By the way, if you'd rather have the Memo field before the Category field, as in earlier versions of *Quicken*, just click Options, choose the Miscellaneous tab, and tell the program to do it that way.

When you have finally got your first transaction as you want it, click Record or press Return. *Quicken* will give a little confirmatory beep. The transaction is recorded.

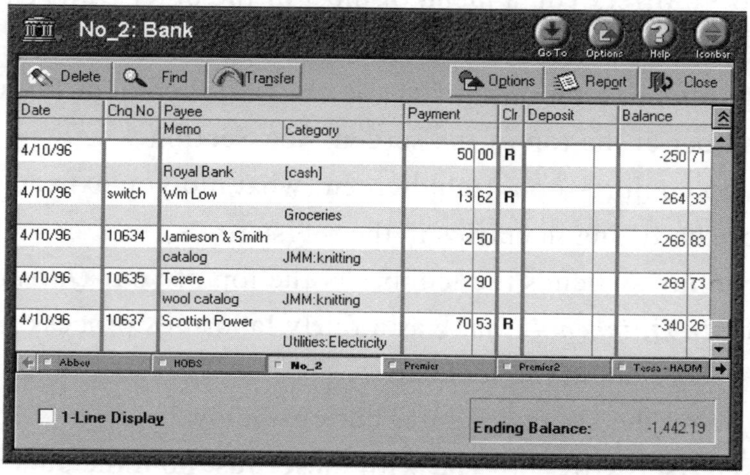

FIGURE 2.9 TRANSACTION REGISTER WINDOW

Furthermore, it is recorded on your computer's hard disk. You don't need to do anything else about saving your data. You don't need to worry that someone will trip over the electric cord and wipe out an afternoon's work. You do, however, need to make sensible provision for backing up your increasingly valuable data files: that's a fact of life where computers are concerned. See Section 11.1.

Enter a few more transactions from your chequebook stubs until you begin to feel confident about the process. Then stop and take a look at the buttons and icons around the Transaction Register window.

There are four round button-like buttons above the register itself, in the title bar of the account register window. Below them, immediately above the register entries, are another six rectangular buttons. The layout of buttons in *Quicken 4* was somewhat different. Some of the functions mentioned below therefore must be invoked rather differently in *Quicken 4,* but nothing has been added which you can't achieve somehow in the older program.

First, the four round buttons:

- **Go To** offers you a menu of most of the other *Quicken* features. Use this one to hop effortlessly around the program.
- **Options** has the same effect as clicking Prefs (for Preferences) on the iconbar at the top of the screen. See Section 4.4.
- **Help** conjures up a Help Screen (what did you expect?), starting with help on filling in entries in the register.
- **Iconbar** switches the iconbar at the top of your *Quicken* screen on or off. In *Quicken 4*, that was a fairly laborious process. See Section 4.1 for more about the iconbar.

What about the six rectangular buttons below?

Quicken itself will help you with these. Just hold the cursor over the button for a moment, and you'll see a brief description of its function.

- **Delete** will delete the current transaction, but only after *Quicken* has asked you to confirm your decision.

- **Find** opens a window you can use to search for a particular transaction in the register. It works like the Find function in your word-processor. As your data builds up through the months and years, you'll use this one more and more.

- **Transfer** opens a window to assist you with the business of transferring funds from one of your accounts to another. The concept can be slightly confusing at first, and you may be glad of *Quicken*'s help here. Later on, you'll save time by entering a transfer like any other transaction. Just put the name of the account where the money is going to wind up, in place of a category name. See Section 2.3 later in this chapter for more on the subject of transfers.

- **Options** lets you make a number of changes in the way the register itself is displayed (whereas the Options button above lets you make more general changes in the way *Quicken* works).

- The invaluable **Report** feature was described above, earlier in this section.

- And **Close** closes the window.

Three buttons which *Quicken 4* users found elsewhere in this window have now been moved to exactly the point where they're wanted, on the Transaction Register itself.

- Click on **Record** to save your transaction when you've entered it to your satisfaction.

- To change a transaction you have already made and recorded, you don't have to click on **Edit** at all. Just put the insertion point anywhere in the transaction, make your change, and click Record again. The Edit button provides a menu with further possibilities:

–   **New Transaction** moves you to the first empty place at the end of the Transaction Register.

–   **Insert Transaction** creates a space for a transaction above the transaction currently selected. You don't really need to insert transactions, since *Quicken* automatically arranges them in date order as soon as they are recorded.

–   **Delete Transaction** does just what it says, but again *Quicken* will make sure first that that's what you really want to do.

–   **Void Transaction** marks the current transaction as Void. It allows you to keep a record of a transaction, while at the same time ensuring that it does not affect your bank balance. This procedure is often preferable to deleting a transaction.

–   **Memorise Transaction**. For this one, see Section 4.3. Like "Insert" I regard it as a feature that has been largely superseded by other things the program can now do. QuickFill does most of my memorising for me.

–   **Copy Transaction**, **Paste Transaction**. You're probably familiar with copying and pasting from your work with a word-processor. Use these when you realise you've made some entries in the wrong register. Once the transaction is safely copied where it belongs, go back and delete it from the register where it was wrongly put in the first place.

–   **Go To Transfer**. This is a really useful feature, introduced in *Quicken 4*. When you have entered a transfer from one of your accounts to another, select Go To Transfer and go immediately to the other end of the transaction. See Section 2.3 later in this chapter for more about transfers.

–   **Go To Date**. You'll use this one to travel back in time. This was another of the new features in *Quicken 4*, and it's a good one. I used to spend a lot of time scrolling through my Transaction Registers. Now I can Go To the right date immediately.

- When you first look at the Edit drop-down menu, you'll notice one other feature, at the top of the list, faded out: **Restore**. Use this one when you're halfway through entering a transaction and realise to your horror that what you have achieved is to mess up a previously-entered transaction and, worse, you can't remember how it used to be. Click Restore and *Quicken* will put it back for you the way it was. You have to use Restore before you press Record, however. When you need this feature, you'll find that it isn't faded any more.

• There's one more button, next to Record and Edit. It's called **Splits**, and it's invaluable. It will come in handy again and again as you use *Quicken*. In business, the program will use it automatically to divide a transaction into Net and VAT elements. For now, we'll cover the basics.

Use Splits whenever one transaction needs to be divided into two or more for account-keeping purposes. Perhaps you buy clothes as well as food at the supermarket, or you want to put part of your telephone bill down as a business expense. You could enter two separate transactions – in some accounting programs, you would have to. But that would make it hard to reconcile your bank statement. The *Quicken* way is better.

Start the transaction off with the date, cheque number and payee as usual. You can go ahead and put the amount in the payment or deposit field, or you can leave it blank for the moment. Click on Splits. Several lines are visible in the Splits window, and more are available out of sight, enough to allow for some really complicated splitting. There are three fields: Category, Memo, and Amount. On the first line, if you put an amount in the Transaction Register, the Amount field has already been filled in with that sum. The insertion point is poised in the Category field of that first line.

Assume as an example that you want to divide your supermarket bill between your categories Groceries and Household, and make a cash withdrawal at the till as well. Put one of those categories on the first line, add a memo if you like, and type over the figure in the Amount field with the amount you spent on that category. *Quicken* will instantly calculate the remainder and enter it for you in the Amount field on the second line.

If you are dividing this transaction between only two categories, all you need to do now is fill in the second category name and click OK. If you didn't enter an amount in the Transaction Register in the first place, *Quicken* will now ask whether this is a payment or a deposit. You'll then find yourself back at the Transaction Register window. You still need to click Record to tell *Quicken* to store the information.

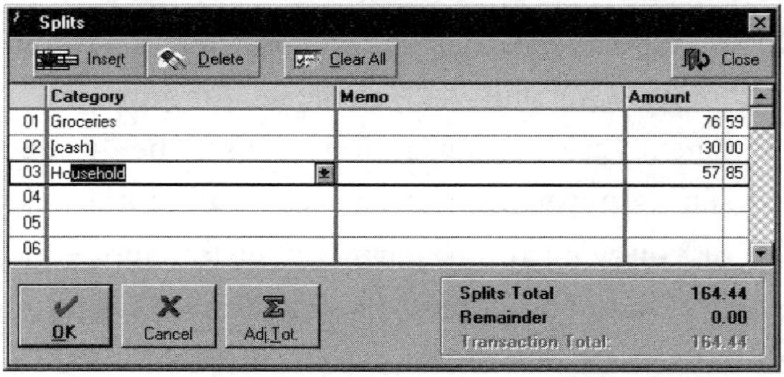

FIGURE 2.10 A SPLITS WINDOW

If you want to divide your transaction up into more pieces, stay in the Splits window and add as many lines as you need to. If you find that you somehow did your arithmetic wrong in the first place, you can click Adj Tot (for Adjust Total) and *Quicken* will adjust the total in the register to correspond to the total of all the separate entries you have made in the Splits window.

Note

*In the Amount field, you can enter, if you prefer, not an amount but a percentage —
Quicken will fill in the figure for you. If, for example, you work from home, you might
claim, say, 35% of each of your telephone bills as a business expense. When the bill
comes in, enter the full amount in the register and then click Splits. In the first
Category field, put the budget category you use for your business expenses. In the
Amount field, put "35%". Quicken will work out 35% of your telephone bill, and enter
the amount. The balance of your telephone bill will immediately appear on the next
line. All you have to do is fill in the expense category you use for domestic telephone
bills in the Category field on the second line. Quicken can memorise this percentage
split for future use — see Section 4.3.*

Notice that there is now a Clear All button on the Splits window, so that
you can scrub everything clean and start again.

Below the register is one further feature, a checkbox labelled "1-line
Display". If you put a tick there by clicking on it, *Quicken* will display the
register with only one line for each transaction. That means you can get a lot
more of the register on-screen. (And don't forget you're working in
Windows – you can resize the Transaction Register window itself by
grabbing hold of its top or bottom edge and moving it; and you can maximise
it to fill the entire screen by clicking on its Maximise Button.) In the one-line
display, you can no longer see anything of the Memo field, or enter anything
in it. But *Quicken* hasn't forgotten your memos. They will all still be there
when you switch back to a two-line display.

A taskbar with the names of other *Quicken* accounts (if you have set up
any others so far) appears immediately below the register entries. Click on
one of them to go directly to that account. *Windows 95* users will be familiar
with this useful idea already – but, in fact, *Quicken* got there first. An
accounting session, just like a day in town, is likely to involve your Current
and your Cash accounts, and perhaps your credit card and a store card as
well. It's convenient to be able to move quickly from one to another. In

these early days, you may not have any other accounts, but you will soon. There's more about the account selection bar in Section 4.4, on Some of Quicken's Other Tricks.

By the time you have entered a few transactions and explored the features available from the Transaction Register, you have mastered the basics of *Quicken*. It's time to start thinking about some of the fundamental questions, starting with your accounts: how detailed do you want your records to be?

2.3 How Much Detail?

Perhaps you have been wondering about the Category & Transfer List – what are transfers? There is a button on the Transaction Register window labelled Transfer, remember. And perhaps you noticed that the Bank account (or accounts) you set up when you first used *Quicken* appears in the Category & Transfer List, at the end. It's in the Account List as well, of course. But why should a Bank account be listed with the categories?

You will often transfer money from one of your accounts to another, especially if you set up a Cash account – more about that in a moment. You can, if you like, enter such a transaction directly in the Transaction Register of the account you're taking the money from. Instead of a category name, you will put the name of the account the money is going to. *Quicken*, which knows all about double-entry bookkeeping, will make the entry in the register of the other account automatically. That's why categories and transfers are considered together; and that's why account names are given with the Category List.

Quicken 4 added an easier way of doing the same thing. Click on the Transfer button on a Transaction Register to see the Transfer Money Between Accounts window. Fill in the details, including an optional description. Then click OK. In your early days with *Quicken*, you may find this approach an easier way to make transfers than entering them directly in the register.

Obviously, transferring money between accounts doesn't really change your financial situation. *Quicken* understands that, and transfers are excluded from reports unless you particularly want to include them. But if you want to know how much you spent as cash last year – that is, how much you transferred from your Bank accounts to your "Cash" account, i.e., your pocket – *Quicken* is equally ready to tell you. The simplest way is to call up the Category & Transfer List, move the highlight to the name of your Cash account – at the end of the list, remember – and click on our old friend, the QuickReport button. At first, the QuickReport will be a simple list of all your cash withdrawals since the dawn of history – or at any rate since you started using *Quicken*. But once the report is on your screen, you can customise it: change the date range, if you like, or subtotal the report by month. See Chapter 5 for further information on reports in general and QuickReport in particular.

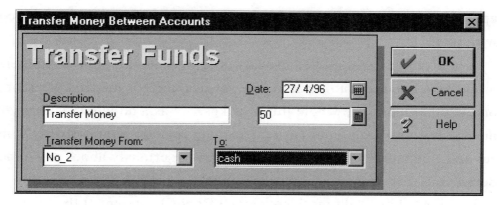

FIGURE 2.11 THE TRANSFER MONEY BETWEEN ACCOUNTS WINDOW

By now, you're ready to set up some more accounts. To do so, click on Activities in the Menu bar and then choose Create New Account from the Activities menu, or select Accounts from the Lists menu to open the list of accounts, and then click New. *Quicken* will hold your hand and walk you through account-opening with a process called EasyStep. It's a new feature in *Quicken 5*, and it means that opening an account couldn't be easier.

There are eight types of account in *Quicken*: Current, Deposit, Credit Card, Cash, Building Society, Investment, Asset and Liability. (The types were slightly different in *Quicken 4*. "Money Market" has been eliminated, and "Savings" divided into "Deposit" and "Building Society".) You probably opened a Current account as your first *Quicken* account. For practical purposes, you can have as many accounts as you want in *Quicken*. The limit is 255, if you're interested.

Eventually, you will want to bring all your financial affairs together under *Quicken*'s roof. In Chapters 6 and 7, you can read about Liability accounts for your mortgage and other major debts; and, on the brighter side, Asset accounts for your National Savings Certificates and other valuable possessions, and Investment accounts for your unit trusts and share portfolio. But you don't need all that detail at the beginning. Of course, if you're upgrading from an earlier version of *Quicken*, all your accounts will come with you.

If you're feeling at all bemused by account-keeping or by computers, it might be a good idea to stick to just one account for the first week or so. If, on the other hand, the whole thing strikes you as a doddle now that you have made a few entries in your Current account register, you probably want to set up some more accounts now, and to think seriously about how much detail you want in your account-keeping.

If you have any savings accounts – a Deposit account at the bank, a National Savings Ordinary or Investment account, perhaps a bank TESSA –

you can go ahead and set them up in *Quicken* right away. In the Create New Account window, choose Deposit.

Quicken needs a few, easy pieces of information to start off with – the name of the account, as it will appear in the Account List; the account number in the Description field, if you like; the balance, as of a particular date. *Quicken*'s EasyStep system will walk you through the process. If you prefer, click on the Summary tab, No. 4 in the Account Setup window, and just fill in all the information there. You can then put a tick in the Start with Summary box on that screen, and go straight there in the future.

Use the balance and date of your last statement, or the last time your passbook was brought up to date. Don't worry if the date is different, even very different, from the starting date of other accounts. *Quicken* can handle that. You can add a description – it can be handy to put the account number here.

You can add more information about the account, for your own records, by saying Yes at the third screen. You will also notice a Track VAT checkbox on the final, Summary screen. That is for business users. If you are keeping domestic accounts in *Quicken*, be sure that checkbox is clear.

That's all there is to it. You can now make entries in the registers of your new accounts as you have already learned to do. And you'll find buttons bearing the names of the accounts you just opened on the taskbar at the bottom of each register. Click on one of the names to go at once to the register for that account.

At this point there are two decisions to be made: what about cash? and, what about credit cards and store cards? As with all other decisions in *Quicken*, it is a comfort to remember that you can change your mind later.

When you were making your first few entries in the Transaction Register of your Current account, you may have followed my advice and left out cash withdrawals and payments to your credit card company. Now it's time to decide what to do about them. You could just set up budget categories called Cash and Visa, and enter cash withdrawals like any other payment. Or you could set them up as separate accounts.

One important factor in the decision will be your knowledge of your own temperament. You couldn't stand having to account for every penny? Forget about a Cash account. That's the solution most long-term budget keepers go for. You spend a lot of money as cash even in these days of plastic cards, and you want to know what happens to it all? Set up a Cash account in *Quicken*. It's easier than you may think to keep track of cash expenditure. See below for a discussion of the options.

Another factor may be your use of your computer. If you use it almost every day, as I do, you can tailor *Windows 95* or *Windows 3.1* to start *Quicken* every time you boot your computer. If you know that you are only going to face *Quicken* once a week or even more rarely, you won't want to worry too much about most of the money that trickles through your fingers. One budget-keeper I know assigns that sort of cash to a category called "walking money".

Whatever you decide to do about cash, I would strongly advise setting up a separate account for each of your credit cards and store cards, and making some effort to keep them updated. The reason: mistakes do happen. You might as well take advantage of the ease and accuracy of *Quicken* to keep an eye on the people who are, in effect, looking after your money. From the Create New Account window, choose Credit Card.

If you have a charge card for use at a particular store or group of stores, set it up in *Quicken* as a Credit Card account. Use your most recent statement to determine the opening balance – *Quicken* understands that the balance in a Credit Card account is a negative amount, an amount you owe. If you can remember any uses you have made of the card since the last statement, or if you have any vouchers lying around, enter them in the Transaction Register.

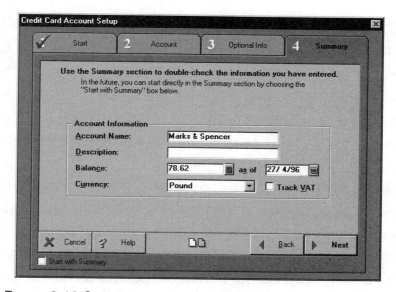

FIGURE 2.12 SETTING UP A STORE CARD ACCOUNT (SUMMARY TAB)

When you are filling in the purchase in the Transaction Register of your store card account, there's no need to put the name of the store as the payee every time. That would get tiresome. Just leave that field blank. Fill in the item you bought in the Memo field, and of course assign it to a category. When you get your monthly statement, you will need to reconcile it to your own records – see Section 9.2, Balancing Your Bank Statement. You'll probably find that a few uses of the card have slipped through the net: you can easily add them now, if you're satisfied that they represent purchases you actually made.

The procedure for a Credit Card account is exactly the same, except that here you will want to fill in the name of the payee.

What about cash? Here are the choices:

- Set up a Cash account and try to track every penny you spend.
- Set up a Cash account, enter as many transactions as you conveniently can, and let *Quicken* call the rest "Other".

- Set up a Cash account and use it from time to time. The rest of the time, choose one of the two following options:
  - Forget it: assign all cash withdrawals to a budget category called "cash", and never mind what happens to the money after that.
  - Assign cash withdrawals to a category called "cash", but use *Quicken*'s Split Transaction window to catch and categorise the important cash transactions.

Tracking every penny – It's not as hard as it sounds. Choose Cash in the Create New Account window. Fill in the details in the usual way. The simplest procedure is to set the opening balance at "£0.00" as of the date of your most recent bank statement for the account from which you draw your cash. Then, using the Transfer button on the Transaction Register of either your Current account or your new Cash account, record each of the cash withdrawals you have made since the date of that last bank statement.

Now go to the Transaction Register of the Cash account. Enter any cash transactions you can remember since the starting date. You will probably be able to do some shrewd estimating. You might be able to calculate the amount you spend every week on fares, or cigarettes, or lunches, or newspapers, and make an appropriate entry.

When you have entered all the transactions you can think of, count the money in your pocket. It will certainly be less than the Closing Balance of your Cash account, as given by *Quicken* in the lower right-hand corner of the cash account Transaction Register window. From the Activities menu, choose Update Balances, then Update Cash Balance. The Update Account Balance will offer you the opportunity to assign the "missing" money to a category. This is where I use the category Balance Adjustment – see the section on categories earlier in this chapter.

In the future, update the balance in your Cash account in this way from time to time.

Tip

To avoid a separate entry in the register for every postage stamp and Mars bar, I keep a running total each month for the commonest cash items. I date these running totals to the first of the month, so that Quicken will keep them all together, and give them names in the Payee field such as "Cash:journalism" and "Cash:stamps and stationery".

To add to the total when I pay another paper bill or buy another envelope later in the month, I use the Go To A Specific Date choice in the Edit menu on the register window, to travel back to the first of the month. To add in the new amount, I click on the Amount field of the "Cash:journalism" or "Cash:stamps and stationery" entry in the register. All I have to do then is type, or click, "+" (which produces the mini-calculator), the new amount, and "=". *Quicken* enters the new total in the Amount field. I click Record, and the job is done. (And if I make a hash of it, the Restore option on the Edit drop-down menu puts the entry back the way it was so that I can try again.)

Laid-back cash accounting – Set up your Cash account and make the first entries exactly as described above. But don't bother with running totals for postage stamps and newspapers. Keep the receipts for your larger cash purchases and enter them in the Transaction Register of your Cash account. If you have regular cash outlays that can be accurately estimated, such as bus fares or lunches, include them. You can always find out how much a day at the zoo or a night on the tiles costs by counting your cash before and after. Then update the balance as just described and assign the money that isn't there to a category such as "Walking Money". You'll probably find after several months that your outlay on Walking Money is fairly constant (although it may be alarmingly high).

Intermittent cash accounting – A new *Quicken 5* feature makes this option more attractive than it used to be. You could set up a Cash account and make use of it from time to time, to figure out where all the money is going. You might try a fortnight's strict accounting every six months, for instance. The rest of the time, cash withdrawals would be assigned to categories like "walking money" or "David's cash". *Quicken 5* offers you the option of hiding obsolete or zero-balance accounts so that they don't appear in the Account List. To use this feature, open the Account List, select the account you want to hide, and click the Hide button at the top of the Account List window. So you could, if you wanted to, set up a Cash account, use it strictly from time to time, and hide it from view the rest of the time.

The easy way – Don't bother with a Cash account. When you draw cash out from your Current account, assign it to your Walking Money category right away. You'll probably find that cash withdrawals are fairly steady, although the total may be a good deal higher than you expected.

The best of both worlds – Don't set up a Cash account, but do keep receipts or make notes for sizeable cash outlays that you would like to include in your records. The next time you use *Quicken*, find a cash withdrawal in your Transaction Register large enough to cover the cash items you want to enter. Click Splits, and then divide the transaction as described in the previous section of this chapter. Assign your cash items to their proper categories. Any leftovers can remain as Walking Money. This approach works very well; it is described in detail in the chapter on Tracking Cash Transactions in the *Quicken* manual.

I find, however, that there are two important advantages to running a Cash account. Consider them for a moment, even if the idea doesn't attract you:

- Having a Cash account provides a check on cash withdrawals from your Current account. The banks keep telling us that cash machines are absolutely reliable. The financial press tells a different story. Whatever the truth, I like to keep an eye on things. If I didn't have a Cash account, I know I would often forget to enter cash withdrawals.

- In these days of plastic cards, I find I don't write many cheques. I prefer to use Switch whenever I can. If I didn't have a Cash account, I might be tempted not to bother with *Quicken* for a week or so, and then everything would depend on whether or not I could still find the Switch vouchers. With a Cash account, I have an incentive to update my accounts almost every day. Not only the Cash account but all my other *Quicken* records benefit from regular attention.

If you do set up a Cash account in *Quicken*, you may want to mark each transaction as Cleared when you enter it. In accounts of all other types, you leave the little field called Clr, for Cleared, strictly alone most of the time. *Quicken* itself will enter an "R" in that field when the transaction has been reconciled with your bank statement – see Section 9.2. Cash accounts, of course, never get reconciled. They just get brought up-to-date with balance adjustments. To mark a transaction as Cleared, click on the Clr column. First, *Quicken* will put a small "c" in the space. Click again to get an "R". (The "c" is normally used by the program when you are part of the way through a reconciliation process, to indicate a transaction which you have marked as clear. When you have finished reconciling your account you'll click on Done and the "c"s will all change to "R"s.)

The reason you might want to mark cash transactions yourself is that perhaps, in the distant future, you may want to archive some of your data to reduce the number of transactions in your active file. *Quicken* performs that operation by making a copy of your data, and then weeding out all cleared transactions before a date that you specify. See Section 11.3 for details of this procedure. You won't be using it for a long time, and may never use it at all. But if you think you might, then you should consider marking cash transactions as Cleared. If you use my system of running totals for small cash expenditure, don't put the "X" in the Clr column until the end of the month. *Quicken* will fret, and reasonably so, if you try to change a transaction after it has been marked as Cleared, although you will be allowed to do it if you insist.

Whatever system you choose, there are going to be times when life gets on top of you and your accounts are neglected. It happens to me every year during the last two weeks of December. *Quicken*, as I have said, is easy and fun. You'll enjoy using it so much that the crunch may not come for months or even years. But one day it will. And when it does, you will find that, once having fallen behind, you feel less and less inclined with every day that passes to sit down to the job and straighten out the mess.

Like most messes, it'll be easier to manage the sooner you face up to it. If you're keeping Cash accounts, you'll probably have to enter a largish sum as a Balance Adjustment. For other accounts, you may have to rely on the accuracy of your bank and credit card statements for once, instead of the more usual approach of letting *Quicken* verify them. But the blip is not likely to be as serious as it seems at the time. Your well-kept records from before and after the lapse will continue to give you an accurate picture of your financial position.

2.4 Using Classes

By now you should be beginning to see the benefits of using categories, supercategories and subcategories to classify your income and expenditure. The idea of still more pigeon-holes, *Quicken*'s classes and subclasses, may seem, at first sight, a bit odd. Whatever do we need them for?

Your surprise may be justified. You may never need them at all. In your first weeks as a *Quicken* user, you probably won't want to bother with them. But they can be extremely useful in a wide variety of situations. In fact, here is a good general rule: if you can't think of how to get *Quicken* to do something you want, try using classes.

A class provides a way of gathering together under one heading income and expense that take place in a variety of categories. For example, if you own several holiday cottages available for letting, each one can have a class of its own. Then your expenditure for furnishing, repairs, Council Tax, decoration, and anything else that comes along, can be classified according to which cottage was involved. The rental income can be assigned to the same classes. And QuickReport works with Classes just as it does with Payees and with Categories. From the Lists menu, click Class. From the Class List window, select the class you are interested in and click the QuickReport icon. You will get a report showing all transactions of whatever category that fall into that class.

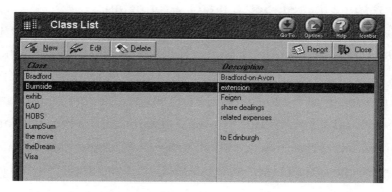

FIGURE 2.13 CLASS LIST WINDOW

I am currently involved in an arrangement of potentially hideous complication whereby I collect rent for a friend, pay from my own account the mortgage on the rented property, and transmit the balance to the friend's account. Money flies in all directions. But I assign every relevant transaction to a class called Bradford (the location of the house in question), and QuickReport produces instant, reassuring accounts of exactly where we all stand.

I have an expense category called Extraordinary to cover the events in life that really don't happen every year. If you like that idea, you could use classes to distinguish different sorts of extraordinary expenditure. When we moved house recently, I put the estate agents' and solicitors' fees, the bill from the removers, and the actual sale and purchase transactions for the two houses into my Extraordinary category, using "themove" as the Class name. Needless to say there were many other related expenses, from light fittings to tins of paint to train fares. Each of those went into an appropriate budget category, but each was also tagged with the Class name "themove". From the Class List window, I can call for a QuickReport that gathers together the finances for the entire saga.

Some events might be better handled by creating a subcategory under Extraordinary to take advantage of the financial planning features which are so powerful in *Quicken*. See Chapter 3 for details.

As far as the technicalities go, classes are much like categories. You can access the Class List window from the Lists menu, and add a new one by clicking New. Or you can put a forward slash, "/", after the category name as you are typing in a transaction, and make up a class name on the spot. *Quicken* will take you straight to the Set Up Class window. For future transactions, type the forward slash after the category name, and the first letter or so of the class name, and QuickFill will finish the job for you as usual.

It is a good idea to keep class names fairly short, as they have to fit into the space allocated for categories and subcategories.

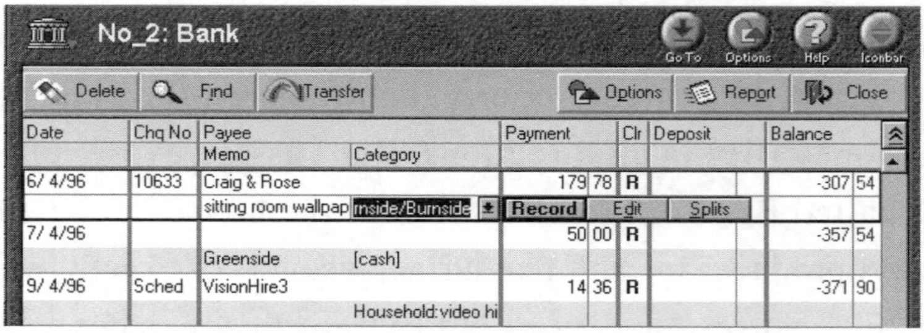

FIGURE 2.14 ENTERING A CLASS IN THE TRANSACTION REGISTER

2.5 Standing Orders and Direct Debits

You are likely to have some transactions which happen regularly without any direct action on your part. Your salary or Child Benefit is paid into your bank account, for example, and your mortgage and perhaps quite a few other things are paid out. *Quicken* can enter these transactions in your accounts automatically.

That being the case, you may at first be surprised to see that Standing Orders is not one of the options on the drop-down menu of Lists. What you will find instead is a list of Scheduled Transactions. And, no, Standing Orders and Scheduled Transactions are not quite the same thing.

Caution

Keep Standing Orders and Scheduled Transactions separate in your accounts.

Choose Scheduled Transactions anyway, from the Lists drop-down menu, and you will see the Scheduled Transaction/Standing Order list. Click New to start setting up your automatic receipts and debits. The fields in the Create Scheduled Transaction window will lead you gently through the process.

First of all you specify the next scheduled date for your payment. If you have just paid your once-a-year subscription to the Automobile Association, the date you put in this field will be a whole year in the future. In most cases it will be nearer. When the program enters a Standing Order in your Transaction Register, it updates the "next scheduled" date automatically. You can come back to the Scheduled Transaction window to check up on when subsequent payments are due, or just look for them on the Financial Calendar – see Chapter 3. Next, you tell *Quicken* which account the payment will be made from.

In the Type field you will choose between Payment, Deposit, and Print Cheque. That third choice refers to *Quicken*'s own cheque-printing facility –

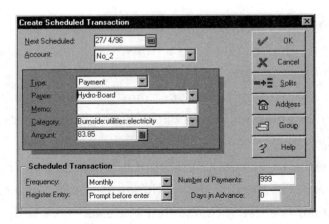

FIGURE 2.15 THE CREATE SCHEDULED TRANSACTION WINDOW

see Section 9.1. It doesn't apply to Standing Orders and Direct Debits anyway, since cheques aren't involved.

Next you fill in the details, exactly as you would if you were entering the transaction directly in the register: Payee, Memo, Category, Amount. A Splits button is provided if you want to divide the amount among different categories – your mortgage payment, for example, may contain an amount for insurance. The Address button is for Scheduled Transactions, not Standing Orders, in cases when you are going to use the *Quicken* cheque-printing facility to pay a bill: again, see Section 9.1. The Group button allows you to group several transactions together after you have set them up. For example, an employer might want to group all the payroll cheques together. For more about groups of transactions, see Section 9.1 on Writing Cheques, and Section 10.3, Doing Your Payroll.

The drop-down list in the Frequency field offers a great variety of time-intervals. "Every two weeks" and "Every four weeks" are there as well as "Twice a month" and "Monthly" – and a good many others as well. I have a lot of Standing Orders of various sorts, and have never yet caught *Quicken* out with an impossible time-interval. This is one of the many areas where *Quicken* is miles ahead of any other budget program I have seen.

If the payments are to go on more or less forever, like your mortgage or AA subscription, leave "999" in the Number of Payments field. Otherwise, enter the actual number of future payments to be made.

There are three more fields. Register Entry allows you to choose whether *Quicken* is to enter the transaction automatically or ask your permission to enter it. Former *Quicken 3* users will notice that the third choice, For Planning Only, is no longer available. That is because the remarkable new planning features which were introduced in *Quicken 4* rendered it unnecessary – again, see Chapter 3. I think that Automatically Enter is the appropriate choice for Standing Orders and Direct Debits. The bank is going to debit your account without asking you every time. *Quicken* might as well do so too. That way, your account balance will be kept up to date.

Quicken then asks how many days in advance to enter the transaction. If you're new to the program, this question seems slightly odd. It's bad enough paying your bills, without paying them in advance.

Relax. All *Quicken* has in mind is a post-dated entry. It will appear at the end of the Transaction Register, below a heavy line which separates past from future. In the lower right-hand corner of the register, you will see that, in such a case, your Current Balance is different from your Ending Balance. The Current Balance is what you have in the bank right now; the Ending Balance is what will be there when all the post-dated entries have been paid in or out.

So when *Quicken* makes the entry a few days in advance, the program is simply warning you that the payment is nearly due – or, in the happy instance of your paycheque, reminding you that relief is at hand. When I first met *Quicken*, I indignantly declined to have entries made early. I soon saw how convenient it was, and now usually choose to have entries made automatically, five days in advance – longer for the once-a-year payments because it is so easy to forget all about them.

When, on the other hand, you want *Quicken* to remind you to pay a bill at the last possible moment, use Scheduled Transactions. See Section 3.3.

Enter Direct Debits in the same way as Standing Orders. In this case, you may have to change the actual amount of the transaction when the day comes. When your payee notifies you of the exact amount, choose the appropriate transaction from the Scheduled Transaction/Standing Order list. Click the Pay button. You will see the Record Scheduled Transaction window in which you can fill in the revised details, including the actual date when the money will leave your account. In this window, the Num Field is available. Put "DrDeb". It's easy to forget which payments are Standing Orders and which are Direct Debits; a reminder comes in handy.

When you have entered the details of a few Standing Orders and Direct Debits, take a look at the list in the Scheduled Transaction/Standing Order List window. Notice the field at the bottom of the window which allows you to sort the list according to the next payment date, the size of the payment (Amount), or alphabetically by Description.

Notice, however, that there is one Direct Debit that you can leave out of your list in *Quicken*. That is: the Direct Debit you may have set up to pay all or part of your monthly credit card or store card bill. When you receive your monthly statement, check it over. If you have set up a Credit Card account in *Quicken* for each of your plastic friends, as recommended earlier, you will have *Quicken*'s help with the checking process. When it is complete, the program will ask you how much you want to pay, and will then make the entry for you in the appropriate Transaction Register. And even if you are just going to assign the whole bill to a category called Visa, it is a good idea to check the statement first, and only then to make the entry in your accounts.

CHAPTER 3

The Bottom Line: Predicting Cashflow

This is the chapter in which you begin to harness *Quicken*'s power. You learned in Chapter 2 how to arrange your income and expenditure into categories, and how to make entries in a Transaction Register. Here, you move on to budgeting, and to all the ways *Quicken* can help you make sober predictions about your financial future once you have a budget up and running. The financial planning features of *Quicken 4* and *5* are among the most exciting of the program's capabilities. This chapter will help you make the maximum use of these powerful tools.

3.1 Quicken's Financial Planning Aids

Monitoring and predicting your cashflow is surely the single most important reason for keeping accounts in *Quicken* or by any other system. All right, it's useful to know how much money you've got in the bank; and it's nice to be able to spot the bank's mistakes (they do happen). But the big questions are the ones connected with cashflow – are we living within our means? Can we afford a second holiday this year? How large a mortgage could we take on? Where can we find money for school fees? How comfortable will we be in retirement?

Quicken 3 was good at financial planning. *Quicken 4* was superb. *Quicken 5* carries on the good work by making the business of planning even easier. Prepare to be impressed.

Budgeting is budgeting – the first section of this chapter is devoted to that familiar but still important subject. Once you've put a budget in place, you're ready to use the rest of *Quicken*'s powerful tools.

- The **Financial Calendar** lets you jot down upcoming bills and reminds you to pay them.
- The **Accounts Balance Graph** lets you see the projected level of your cash reserves for the month ahead. You can use it to monitor the level of your Current account, so that it always gets topped up just in time to prevent an overdraft; or you can bring in your Savings accounts and keep an eye on the overall level of your funds.
- A **Forecast Graph** can show you projected cash balances up to two years ahead. This one is really magic – worth the price of the program by itself.
- You can help yourself on the way to cherished goals by setting up **Savings Goal accounts**.
- **Progress bars** monitor your success at keeping to your budget or reaching your savings goals. You can arrange to have Progress bars visible wherever you are in *Quicken*.
- The **Snapshot page** provides an instant, up-to-date view of graphs and reports to show you exactly where you stand. You can choose the individual graphs and reports to be included among your own particular snapshots.
- Finally, *Quicken*'s **Financial Planning Calculators** help you to visualise and plan for the more distant future, your children's higher education and your own retirement.

These powerful tools make the prediction of future cashflow easier and much more visual than it has ever been before. You'll need to have a budget in place before you can make full use of them, but if you have already accumulated some data, *Quicken* can use it to do the budgeting for you. If the whole subject of cashflow weren't so grim, you could even say that in *Quicken*, it's fun.

3.2 Setting Up a Budget

Before *Quicken* there was only one way to set about answering life's big financial questions (other than by closing your eyes and hoping for the best):

- You set up a budget, by going through your income and expense categories and estimating an amount for each.

- You kept careful accounts, and compared the results with your budget. You probably found that you were spending more than you thought on several categories. Food, entertainment, running the car, and miscellaneous cash are notorious categories for surprises of that sort.

- You revised your budget estimates, or your expenditure, or both, in the light of experience.

- You looked (literally) at the bottom line: was your budgeted income at least as much as your budgeted expenditure? Could you spot a few "good" months coming up in which you could build up some savings?

Drawing up a budget remains the foundation. But *Quicken* has given a new slant to the entire problem. Read all of this chapter before you decide how to proceed.

Budgeting is hard work the first time. You can take some comfort from the fact that you only have to do it once. After that, it's just a matter of "tweaking" from time to time as individual items need to be changed. And some further comfort can be drawn from the fact that *Quicken* has done everything possible to make the process easy, if not exactly painless.

To get started, choose Budgeting from the Plan menu, or the Budget icon from the iconbar. If you know your way around computers, you may recognise the screen you see next as a spreadsheet, with your categories listed down the left-hand side of the screen and the months of the year across the top. A grid of zeros awaits transformation into your budget estimates.

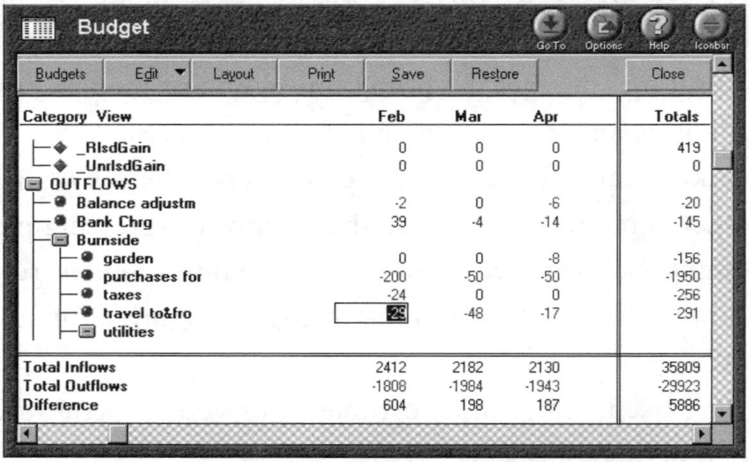

FIGURE 3.1 THE BUDGET WINDOW

Obviously, this isn't going to work until you've got your categories the way you want them, at least roughly. See Section 2.1. But you don't need to wait until your categories have reached a state of final perfection. Just as *Quicken* can recategorise old transactions in the register when you change your mind, so it can move budget amounts around.

When you begin, you will see the names of your categories – but not supercategories or subcategories – listed down the left-hand side of the screen. You will notice that some categories have a little button showing a plus-sign next to the category name. Those are the categories with subcategories under them. Click on one of those plus-signs to see the subcategories. Once you've done that, you can reverse the process. Now you will see a button with a little minus-sign next to the category name. Click on it to hide its subcategories again. When you have budgeted amounts for individual subcategories, this clicking process allows you to see the entire amount gathered together next to the category name, when the subcategories are hidden; or distributed to the individual subcategories, when they are displayed.

And there's more. Click on the Layout button, which you will find at the top of the Budget window. The options on offer allow you to see your supercategories displayed; to budget for transfers of money between accounts; and to suppress from view any categories for which there is no budget amount. You won't want to make use of that last option until you've done your preliminary work on the budget, of course. From this Layout Budgets window, you can also choose to have the time-interval columns display quarters or a whole year, instead of months.

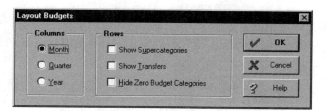

FIGURE 3.2 THE LAYOUT BUDGETS WINDOW

It's always easiest and pleasantest to start with income. For all regular monthly sources of income, enter the amount at the appropriate spot in the January column. Click the Edit button and choose Fill Row Right. *Quicken* will enter the same amount in that category for each of the other eleven months.

There are lots of sources of income (and of expense) that are calculated weekly and therefore don't fit neatly into months. Some possible examples, among many, would be Child Benefit, the state retirement pension, and rent payments. You could just pretend that four weeks is the same as a month, but of course that's not quite true. And it turns out that *Quicken* has a neat trick to help you here.

Enter, in the January column, the amount you receive in Child Benefit (say) every two weeks. Click Edit in the Budget button bar and choose "2-Week...". In the Set Up Two-Week Budget window, check that the correct category, Child Benefit, is displayed; and that the amount shown is what you receive every two weeks. For "Every two weeks starting:" put the first date in January of the current year on which you will have amassed two weeks' entitlement to Child Benefit. Click OK. *Quicken* does the rest, for the whole year.

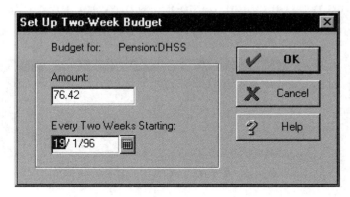

FIGURE 3.3 BUDGETING A PENSION PAYMENT

You can use this system to budget for an amount that is actually paid into your Bank account every four weeks. To take the state retirement pension as an example that can easily be converted to other purposes: your notification from the DHSS will have told you how much you receive per week, and which day of the week you are paid on. Look at a calendar to find the second occurrence in January of your pension day. Then proceed to set up a two-week budget, as before. Of course, back in the real world, at the Create Scheduled Transaction/Standing Order window, you will have set up the actual transaction as it is actually paid to you – a Standing Order at four-weekly intervals. See Chapter 2.

Those who think in months but receive or pay out substantial sums by the week may already realise that there is one glorious month in each year with two pay-days. Or one hideous month with two pay-outs, as the case may be. That's because there are 52 weeks in a year, and 52 divided by 4 is 13, not 12. If you budget this way, *Quicken* finds your bonus month for you.

If a budgeted amount changes during the year – you get a rise in salary, or your Child Benefit goes up because you've had another baby – enter the first occurrence of the new amount in the appropriate place. Click Edit and Choose Fill Row Right if it's a monthly amount. If it happens every week, enter it as a two-week budget as described above.

Some forms of income arrive irregularly. Dividend income is a good example, and a writer's earnings are another. Here's what to do. Click Layout and choose Year. Under the appropriate category for your irregular income, put the total amount you expect in a year – you must have added it up for last year's income tax return. Don't be too optimistic – the golden rule of budgeting is pessimism. Then click Layout again and go back to a column for each month. You will find that *Quicken* has averaged your income out through the year.

With your income in place, work on down through your expense categories, putting in an estimate for a month's expenditure in the January column where you can and filling in the other months automatically as before. Your first attempts to guess what to put will probably be wide of the mark in some cases. Never mind: experience will soon teach. You can and should come back to this budget screen and try again.

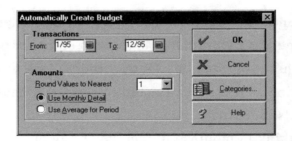

FIGURE 3.4 THE AUTOMATICALLY CREATE BUDGET WINDOW

If you have arranged to pay some of your big bills by monthly Direct Debit (gas, electricity, telephone, etc.), it will be easy to fill in a monthly amount. Let *Quicken* "fill row right" as it did for your income. If you pay these bills quarterly, dig out last year's bills and use them as a basis both for the amount and for finding the right month for the entry. Move through the rows and columns until you find the spot. It's always a good idea to assume, for budget purposes, that this year's bills will be higher than last year's.

You can move around the Budget window by using the arrow keys on your computer keyboard. You will also find in the *Quicken* manual a list of key combinations to make things go faster. And there's a nice trick concerned with scrolling. As you drag the scroll box in the scroll bar on the right, in the usual *Windows* way, the view will not change as long as you hold the left-hand mouse button down. Instead, you will see a box in which the names of categories appear and disappear. When you have found the one you want, release the mouse button. The category named in the box now appears at the top of the Budget window.

Next, try to think of as many items as possible in the Big and Predictable league – insurance bills; Road Tax; Council Tax and water rates; higher-rate income tax; television licence. Enter them in the appropriate place, using last year's bills for guidance. If you have a separate category or subcategory for Christmas, put in something for that. That's another one where reality may surprise you. For some things like clothing it may be easier to make a quarterly or an annual guess, as described above for dividend income, and let *Quicken* strike an average. Don't forget to take some account of your weakness, be it beer, computer magazines, or knitting wool. Again, it may be costing you more than you think.

If you're working month-by-month, you won't be able to see the whole year on your computer screen at one time. Notice, however, that you can always see the total for the row you are working on, and the other nearby ones (that is, the yearly totals for your categories and subcategories) at the right of the screen; and the totals of both income and expense for the current month and its neighbours at the bottom of the screen. Keep an eye on those totals at the bottom of the screen: there are bound to be good months and bad months, but you are laying up trouble for yourself if expense exceeds income too often in the year. And leave yourself some leeway. Especially in your early attempts at budgeting, you are almost inevitably going to spend more than you think you will. I had been at it for 15 months before I brought a month in under-budget.

If you click on the Layout button and then put a tick in the Show Transfers checkbox, you can include transfers between accounts in your budgeting. Transfers don't make any difference to the bottom line. But if, for instance, you budget to move a certain amount every month from your Current account into a Building Society account, you have given *Quicken* some information that can be useful when it comes to forecasting. See Section 3.4.

When the Show Transfers checkbox is selected, you will see the list of your accounts in the budget spreadsheet – twice. In the top section, where your income is planned, each of the account names is preceded by FROM. At the bottom of the list, each name appears again, preceded by TO. To budget a transfer amount, you must enter it twice, in the account that is to give the money, and again in the account that will receive it.

There's one transfer you almost certainly will want to include – your mortgage. You could treat mortgage payments like any other expense, and simply create a budget category for them. But you could also set up your mortgage as a Liability account – see Chapter 6 for details. If you do that, your monthly outgoings will take the form of a transfer to that account, and they will certainly have to be included in your budget.

Earlier versions of *Quicken* had room for only one budget. *Quicken 5* lets you save three. In the future, you may want to look back and find out, not just how much you spent but how much you expected to spend. When you come back to this screen to modify your budget because the Chancellor has put up Road Tax again, or because you are spending twice as much on groceries as you thought you would, click on the Budget button and choose Create Budget from the Manage Budgets window. In the Create Budgets window, choose Copy Current Budget. You can then make any changes you like, and save your new budget as Budget 2. Later on, as data builds up, it is interesting to keep a previous year's budget to compare with this year's reality.

If you really can't face budgeting, you can wait until you have at least a month's data, and let *Quicken* do it for you. From the Budget screen, click the Budgets button. In the Manage Budgets window, choose create. In the Create Budget window, choose Autocreate Budget. *Quicken* will do its best. This technique gets really useful when you have a year's figures to work with. At the beginning, it's worth making the effort yourself.

What are all those buttons for at the top of the Budget window?

- You know about the Budgets button already. That's the one that lets you load an old budget, if you have one, or create a new one, with or without *Quicken*'s help. You can use the Autocreate feature selectively for some categories but not others. It is particularly helpful for categories such as clothing that involve large but not regular expense. For categories like that, the best plan is probably to click Use Average for Period rather than Use Monthly Detail in the Automatically Create Budget window. If you are including transfers in your budget, don't let *Quicken* create a budget for them automatically. That will just confuse things.

- We have already used some of the options available under Edit. Of the others, Clear Row and Clear All do just what you might expect. Using them, you can replace all the figures in the current row with noughts, or wipe the whole budget clear ready to start again. Fill Columns allows you to make a budget for one month (or quarter) and then have *Quicken* copy it to the other months (or quarters). Supercategories takes you to the Manage Supercategories window, so that you can create supercategories and assign budget categories to them while you're in a budgeting frame of mind. Copy All copies the entire budget to the *Windows* clipboard, ready for you to import it into another program such as your word-processor or spreadsheet.

- The Layout button is the one you used to specify whether the columns should represent months, quarters, or years; and whether supercategories, transfers, and unbudgeted categories should be shown.

- The Print button tells your printer to make a permanent copy of a completed budget. There isn't room on one sheet of paper for the budget, just as there isn't room on your computer screen. *Quicken* takes charge and arranges things sensibly on several pages.

- When you're satisfied with your budget – or just tired of tweaking it – click Save.

- But if you decide that you've done it all wrong and wish you'd let well enough alone, click Restore instead and everything will be as it was when you started the current session.

- Close, of course, closes this Budget window. If you haven't yet saved your work, *Quicken* will ask whether you want to.

Once you have drawn up a budget, you'll be able to use it regularly to monitor your financial progress. You will want to create budget reports and budget variance graphs frequently – see Section 5.2. All you need for your first report or graph is a budget and one month's accounts. You can also view various financial scenarios based on your budget – see Section 3.4 in this chapter.

3.3 The Financial Calendar

The Financial Calendar is a *Quicken* feature like no other – you'll love it. Click the Calendar icon on the iconbar, or choose Financial Calendar from the Activities drop-down menu. You will see a calendar of the current month, occupying more than half the screen. Click on Prev (for previous) or Next to go backward or forward in time. On the calendar are noted all the Standing Orders and Direct Debits you have set up; all transactions, both past and post-dated future ones, from your Transaction Register; and any cheques you have "written" in *Quicken*, but not yet printed and dispatched. For cheque-writing as a *Quicken* activity, see Section 9.1.

If it doesn't look right, click Options near the top of the Financial Calendar window. You can then choose which of your accounts should appear on the calendar.

Tip

The Financial Calendar works best if you confine it to your Current account: more precisely, to the account or accounts from which your Standing Orders are paid and with which the business of life is conducted. You don't need your Deposit accounts and Building Society accounts here.

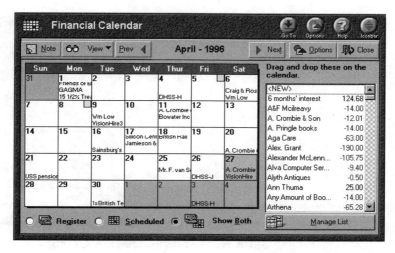

FIGURE 3.5 THE FINANCIAL CALENDAR

You can add notes, just as you might to a wall calendar. Select the required date, and click Note on the Financial Calendar button bar. Write the note in the Note window, select a colour for it and click OK. A little square in your chosen colour will appear on the Calendar on that date. To read the note again, click on the little coloured square. It does sometimes happen, in this peculiar world, that a bill arrives so long in advance of the date when it is due that there is every danger of its being permanently lost before the day ever comes. I use *Quicken*'s notes to remind myself of where I have put such bills. Sometimes it works. You can use the note for any purpose at all – it needn't be financial: wash socks, write to mother.

These notes can be made to appear automatically in a reminder window that opens every time you start the program. Then when you click on the words "To Do" at the bottom left of the *Quicken* window, you'll see the current batch of notes. And you can include them in a Snapshot page. For reminders, see Section 4.2; and for Snapshots, Section 3.6 later in this chapter.

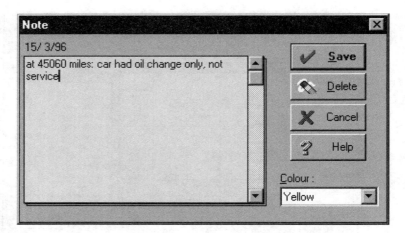

FIGURE 3.6 A NOTE FOR THE *QUICKEN* CALENDAR

The Standing Order display is useful, the notes are useful and fun, but the best is yet to come. The main function of the Calendar is to allow you to pencil in, electronically speaking, future financial events that are not Standing Orders. The car has to go in for a service some time next month; you pay your Council Tax in two instalments, one now, one in October; school fees will be due in September – that sort of thing. This is, in fact, where Scheduled Transactions come in.

You will have noticed on the right of the calendar a list of the payees QuickFill has memorised. If the list isn't there, click View at the top of the Calendar window and select Show Memorised Txns.

To schedule a transaction, find a payee on the list. Hold the right-hand mouse button down and drag the payee to a day on the calendar when you expect to owe that payee more money. When you let go of the mouse button, you will see the Drag and Drop Transaction window, with details already filled in from your most recent encounter with that payee. All you have to do is change anything that needs changing and click OK. The new transaction appears on the calendar, marked with a little "1x" to distinguish it from the Standing Orders.

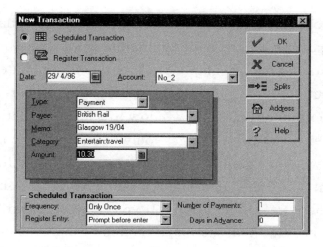

FIGURE 3.7 SCHEDULING A TRANSACTION ON THE CALENDAR

As with Standing Orders, you can tell *Quicken* whether or not to make the entry in the register in advance, and whether to make it without further instructions from you. When you are scheduling a transaction that will not be made automatically by your bank, I would strongly suggest that you choose Prompt Before Enter. How many days in advance you specify depends on how regularly you use the program. When the days-in-advance period arrives, you will be reminded when you start the program that a scheduled transaction is pending. Click on the Record button in that window to see the details of the transaction again, and to carry on with actually paying it if that's what you intend to do. If you decide to postpone the awful moment for another day or so after all, just click on Done and *Quicken* will drop the subject for now.

Caution

DON'T let Quicken make the entry in the register until the bill is actually paid in real life. The merit of this system is that the program is nudging you, but not fooling you into thinking you've paid a bill when you haven't.

You can schedule transactions on the Financial Calendar for payees who don't yet appear on the list by dragging the word <NEW> from the top of the Payee list. Or you can simply click on the desired date: that produces a list of transactions already scheduled for that day, if there are any. Just click New at the bottom of that little window to add a transaction.

If you do either of those things, you will see the Drag and Drop Transaction window again. You can use it to pencil in a forthcoming payment, that is, a Scheduled Transaction. You can also use it to set up your Standing Orders and Direct Debits. If you select Register Transaction instead of Scheduled Transaction at the top of the Drag and Drop Transaction window, you can use this window to enter a transaction in the register. The opposite approach is equally possible: you can set up a Scheduled Transaction just as you did your Standing Orders, from the Scheduled Transaction/Standing Order list, as described in Section 2.5.

Often, you will add a Scheduled Transaction to the calendar on a particular day without knowing, in fact, exactly when you will pay the bill. If it comes in earlier than expected, just open the Scheduled Transaction/ Standing Order list, select the transaction, and click the button labelled Pay at the top of the window. You'll see the details of the transaction again, and you can make any alterations you like before it goes into the register.

I would strongly advise keeping Scheduled Transactions and Standing Orders separate in your thinking and in your approach to *Quicken*. Use Standing Orders and Direct Debits so that *Quicken* will make automatic entries in your accounts to correspond with money that is automatically paid to you and taken from you in the real world. For such transactions, choose Automatically Enter and let *Quicken* make the entry in the register a few days early if you feel you want to be reminded in advance of what your bank is going to do. Use Scheduled Transactions for bills or receipts that you can see coming up, but which will not be paid automatically. For them, choose

Prompt Before Enter and only add them to the register when money has actually changed hands.

I find it a great help psychologically to deal with bills – especially the nasty ones – as soon as they arrive, by scheduling their payment on the *Quicken* calendar. When I have done that, I feel I have faced up to things. It cuts down the worry by a surprising amount. Writing cheques in *Quicken* (but not sending them immediately) works even better in this respect – see Section 9.1.

And the wonders of the Calendar are still not exhausted. All the information you and *Quicken* have entered goes to shape the Account Balances Graph. To see it, click the View button at the top of the Financial Calendar window, and select Show Accounts Graph. Below the calendar you will see a bar graph, with one bar for each day of the current month and a bit beyond. It represents, day by day, the balances in the account or accounts you have selected for the calendar. Today's bar is green, the past is yellow, the future blue. If you schedule a large bill and don't tell *Quicken* where you're going to find the money, you'll find that the future deficit shows up in red. You can see at a glance how close to the edge you are skating, and how bad things are going to get before pay-day comes around again.

You may (rightly) think this a very useful feature, and wonder why the Account Balances Graph will display balances only for the month ahead. Wouldn't it be nice to be able to estimate balances even further ahead? Well, have a look at the Forecasting window, described in the next section.

3.4 Forecasting

This is the point, in my opinion, where *Quicken* really takes flight. This feature is easy to use and enormously useful. It'll tell you a lot about your finances.

Before you can profitably use it, you need to set up your Standing Orders and Direct Debits (see Section 2.5) and to schedule any other predictable recurring receipts and payments as described in the previous section of this chapter. And you need either a budget or several months' data – preferably a budget. For that, see Section 3.2 earlier in this chapter.

To see the Forecasting window, click on Plan in the menu bar and choose Forecasting. You'll see the Forecasting – Base Scenario window. *Quicken* is going to forecast your financial future, using information you have already provided. Click Create to get started.

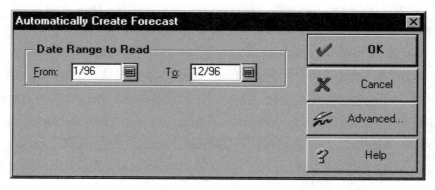

FIGURE 3.8 THE AUTOMATICALLY CREATE FORECAST WINDOW

When you click on Advanced in this window, you will see that *Quicken* will create a forecast based on your scheduled transactions, your budget, your past financial behaviour as reflected in your Transaction Registers – or all three. For estimated items, those not locked into Standing Orders, *Quicken* can use either your budget or the Transaction Registers to form the estimate. What's really clever here is that the program understands that the monthly Direct Debit to British Gas "fixes" that sum. No further estimate is needed for your category Utilities:Gas. My own choices in this window are Create Both (under Forecast Items to Create) and From Budget Data (under Create Estimated Amounts). Click Accounts to limit the forecasting to certain of your accounts only, if you like. I think it works best to stick to the accounts that hold your cash balances, and to leave Asset, Liability and Investment accounts out of the picture.

Finally, you can select income and expense categories for inclusion. I leave out my Extraordinary category (see Chapter 2).

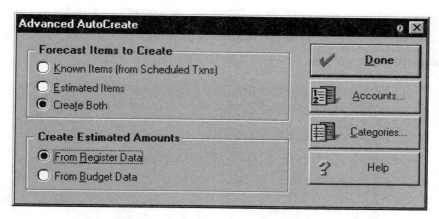

FIGURE 3.9 THE ADVANCED AUTOCREATE WINDOW

Now click Done. You'll see the Forecasting – Base Scenario window. The balances in the accounts you have selected are shown as a line graph, with a gently rising tendency (we hope) from left to right. In the bottom left-hand corner of this window you can change the time-scale from one year to one month, six months, or two years. In the lower right-hand corner you will see the figures for *Quicken*'s forecast of your average monthly income and expenditure. Very interesting, this. Your budgeted and your actual income and (especially) expense probably vary a good deal from month to month – mine certainly do. But underlying all the flux of actual life there must be an average, and here you will discover *Quicken*'s calculation of exactly what it is.

At this point it is a good idea to click first on the Income button and then on the Expense button at the bottom of the window, next to the estimated monthly figures. You will then be able to see exactly how *Quicken* has worked out your forecast. If you have told the program to use your own data for the forecast, you may find as you go through the list that some of last year's unusual financial events are distorting the picture. Or you may decide that some categories of income or of expenditure "don't count" and you'd rather rule them out.

Notice that there is a button labelled Accounts at the top of the Forecasting window. You have another chance to choose which accounts to include on your graph.

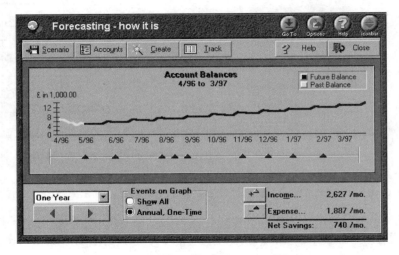

FIGURE 3.10 THE FORECASTING WINDOW

When you have everything in place, you can save your scenario. If you choose to do that, you can come back whenever you like and find out how reality compares with your hopes and fears of today. Click on Scenario, at the top of the window where your Forecast graph is displayed. In the Manage Forecast Scenarios window, select Show How Forecast Looked On, and click Update. You will then see that today's date appears after the words "Show How Forecast Looked On...". In the future you can come back to this window, select that phrase again – the date of the scenario you saved will still be there – and see a graph consisting of two lines: the forecast you saved, and the current forecast starting from the actual state of your account balances now. It's depressing, but salutary, to see the current line running along underneath the hopes of only a couple of weeks ago. I would strongly recommend getting to know the Forecasting feature and making good use of it.

You can do more:

- You can try out different scenarios by going back to the Income and Expense buttons on the Forecasting window and changing the figures for any of the estimates. And notice that there is a button labelled New at the bottom of the Forecast Income (or Expense) Items window. If you click on that, you can add items and see at once their future effect on your balances. What if you or your partner took on a part-time job? What if you started paying school fees? Or payments on a new car? You can see the answer at once.

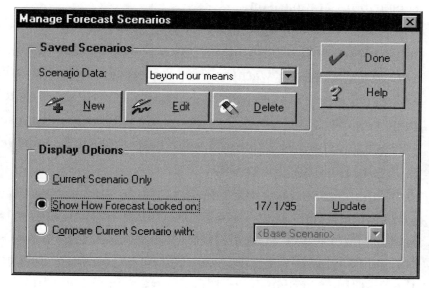

FIGURE 3.11 THE MANAGE FORECAST SCENARIOS WINDOW

- You can save any scenario that looks interesting. From the Forecasting window, click Scenario, and then from the Manage Forecast Scenarios window, click New. In the Create New Scenario window, you must give your scenario a name, and make sure that the checkbox labelled Copy Current Scenario is selected.

- You can retrieve a scenario and compare it with any other scenario. To retrieve a scenario you have saved, click on the button beside the Scenario Data field in the Manage Forecast Scenarios window. Then select a scenario from the list. While the Scenario Data field is selected, you can also use the Edit button just beneath to change the name of one of the scenarios in your list, or the Delete button to get rid of one.

- To compare scenarios, retrieve the first one as just described and then select Compare Current Scenario With... in the same Manage Forecast Scenarios window. From the list of your previous efforts, choose a scenario for comparison.

- You can create a budget based on any scenario that seems to offer a hopeful way forward. From the Forecasting window, click Track. *Quicken* will – after warning you – create a new budget from the estimated items in your current scenario. It will also create a Snapshot page consisting of Progress bars for the six largest expense categories in your budget. See Section 3.6 for both Snapshots and Progress bars – they're fun as well as useful.

- And finally, you can always start again. In the Forecasting window, click Create. You'll go back to the Automatically Create Forecast window where you started. Here, you can ask *Quicken* to do the forecast again. If you used your budget as the basis for the estimates the first time, perhaps you'd like to try using actual figures from your Transaction Registers. Or click on Advanced and try including all your categories this time, instead of ruling out the ones that "don't count".

3.5 Savings Goals

It may seem odd, in a program so devoted to helping you face facts, to find *Quicken* encouraging you to deceive yourself. It's all in a good cause.

Savings Goals allow you to set a target and monitor progress. As you mentally set aside amounts towards your goal, *Quicken* will "hide" the money, if you choose, from the balances actually in your accounts. To see how it works, click on Plan in the menu bar and choose Savings Goals from the drop-down list. You'll see the Savings Goals window.

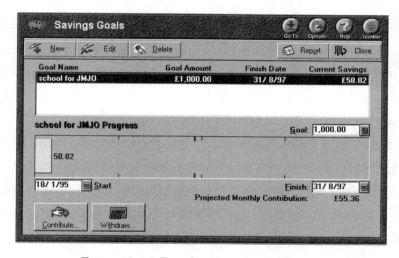

FIGURE 3.12 THE SAVINGS GOAL WINDOW

Think of something worth saving for – that shouldn't be hard. Click on New at the top of the Savings Goals window and you'll find yourself at the Create New Savings Goal window. The work you have to do here is short and simple – give your goal a name, a target amount, and an end date.

When you click OK, you'll go back to the Savings Goal window. The information you have just supplied is presented in the upper part of the window. Below, you can see how much progress you have made towards your goal – none at all, so far, probably. In addition, *Quicken* has worked out how much you need to save every month in order to reach your target in the time specified. There it is, just under the finish date. Right away, your dream seems more possible.

Now let us suppose you have £573 in a building society, and you decide that you could afford to earmark £200 of that money towards your savings goal. Click on the Contribute button at the bottom of the window. The Contribute to Goal window shows in its title bar the name you have given to your savings goal. In the field labelled From Account, select the Building Society account you have in mind. As soon as you do that, *Quicken* will remind you, at the bottom of this window, how much there is in the account at the moment – not counting any amounts you may have previously designated towards savings goals. In the Amount field, *Quicken* will suggest a contribution equal to the monthly target it has worked out for you. It's only a suggestion. You're free to type in any amount.

As soon as you do that, and click OK, you will see some changes in the Savings Goals window. There is now a bar graph showing how far along you are towards your goal. If you have contributed more or less than the suggested monthly amount, *Quicken* has worked out a new monthly amount for you. And the amount you have just set aside appears under "Current Savings" at the top of the window.

Now go to your Building Society account and see what's happened there. Nothing has really happened, of course. There is still £573 in the account. But a new checkbox has appeared at the bottom of the account window, labelled Hide Sav. Goal.

The idea is this: if there is a tick in the box, the amount you have set aside is hidden, and so the account register shows the actual, real-world state of affairs. It tells you that you have £573 in your Building Society account, just as you had at the start of this exercise. If you clear the checkbox, you will see your contribution to your savings goal appear in the Transaction Register

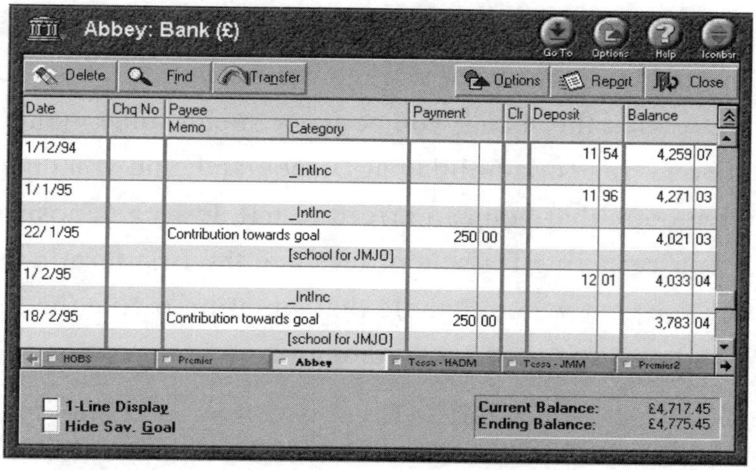

Date	Chq No	Payee		Payment	Clr	Deposit	Balance	
		Memo	Category					
1/12/94						11 54	4,259 07	
			_IntInc					
1/ 1/95						11 96	4,271 03	
			_IntInc					
22/ 1/95		Contribution towards goal		250 00			4,021 03	
			[school for JMJO]					
1/ 2/95						12 01	4,033 04	
			_IntInc					
18/ 2/95		Contribution towards goal		250 00			3,783 04	
			[school for JMJO]					

Abbey: Bank (£)

Go To   Options   Help   Iconbar

Delete   Find   Transfer   Options   Report   Close

HOBS   Premier   Abbey   Tessa - HADM   Tessa - JMM   Premier2

☐ 1-Line Display
☐ Hide Sav. Goal

Current Balance: £4,717.45
Ending Balance: £4,775.45

FIGURE 3.13 HIDE SAVINGS GOAL IN ACTION

like any other payment. And the figure for the Ending Balance will go down. In our imaginary example, you will see that you only have £373 left in the building society now that you have set £200 aside towards your savings goal. Pretending, in this way, that the actual balance is lower than it really is should help concentrate your mind.

What if one of life's crises turns up and you have to spend some of the money you had hoped was set aside towards your dream? The central heating boiler gives up the ghost in January, perhaps, or your dentist tells you he's not doing National Health work any more. Well, it happens. In that case, go back to the Savings Goal window and click on Withdraw. Take back the money you need, returning it to the appropriate account. That will be, of course, the account where it has in fact been all along, and from which, unfortunately, it is now about to be spent. In this same window, you can change the end date for your savings goal. In the gloomy scenario we are imagining, you might have to set it further in the future. Equally, a win on the National Lottery could let you bring it a lot closer. Whatever adjustments you make here, when you return to the Savings Goal window you will see that the graph has changed appropriately, and that a new monthly contribution has been worked out for you.

What if, on the other hand, you actually spend some money towards the goal? You're saving for a holiday at Disneyland, and you decide you're doing well enough that you can afford to put down a deposit with the travel agent? Or you're saving for school fees and the first term's fees are now due? I think the best way to handle that situation is like this:

- "Withdraw" the necessary amount from your Savings Goal, as just described.
- At the top of the Savings Goal window, click on Edit. Subtract the amount of the deposit from the total amount of the original goal. In the Edit Savings Goal window, fill in the new amount.
- Pay the travel agent, school bursar, or whomever.

Quicken has another psychological booster to help you achieve your savings goals. It's called the Progress bar. It's described in the next section.

3.6 Snapshots and Progress Bars

Progress bars show you graphically how near (or how far) your goal is. They work rather like the mercury in a thermometer. You can use them to monitor your progress towards your budget in any category or supercategory, or towards the achievement of any of your savings goals as described in the previous section. You can have two Progress bars visible at all times, whatever you are doing in *Quicken* – although I wouldn't advise it, for reasons that will be clear in a moment. In addition, you can have as many more Progress bars as you like on your Snapshot pages. More about that in a moment, too.

To set up your first Progress bars, click on Plan in the Menu Bar and choose Progress Bar. You will see them at once, based on the first two categories in your budget. That is quite likely not to be a particularly interesting choice. Click on Cust (for Customize) to the right of the Progress bars.

FIGURE 3.14 PROGRESS BARS

In the Customize Progress Bar window, you will want, first of all, to select something for your two bars to measure. Click on the button beside the field for the Left Gauge Type or the Right Gauge Type to specify whether you want to monitor a savings goal, or the budget for a category or for a supercategory. Needless to say, you cannot have a Progress bar monitor progress towards a budget amount until you have set up some budget amounts. See Section 3.2 earlier in the chapter.

Once you have made those two decisions, you will naturally enough want to go on to choose what budgeted category, or what savings goal, you want to follow. Click on the buttons below the fields. They are now appropriately labelled "Choose category", "Choose supercategory" or "Choose goal", according to your previous choices. Click on first one and then the other, and make the appropriate choice from the list.

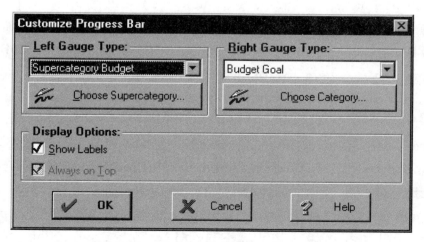

FIGURE 3.15 THE CUSTOMIZE PROGRESS BAR WINDOW

There's another choice you can make from the Choose Category or Choose Supercategory window, an important one which it's easy to overlook. That is, the date range. You can set it to Current Month, Current Quarter or Current Year. There are a great many financial hurdles in life that come at irregular intervals, and many situations, therefore, which are best viewed in a quarterly or even annual aspect.

As you look at your Progress bars, and at the Snapshots we're going to discuss in a moment, you will often notice that your cursor changes into a little magnifying glass. Whenever you see this, it means that *Quicken*'s QuickZoom feature is in operation. You can click to learn more about the figures or the graph that lie under the cursor at the moment. You'll use QuickZoom a lot – see Section 4.4. Progress bars are, in fact, a rather unfortunate place to meet QuickZoom for the first time, for here alone, I feel, this feature is not quite as useful as it might be. Double-click on a Progress bar that is monitoring your progress towards a budget goal, and you will be taken to the Budget window. But what you really want to see are the transaction details that have brought the mercury up to its present level. To do that, select your category from the category list, and click on the QuickReport icon. Don't give up on QuickZoom, though – it pulls more than its weight everywhere else in the program.

I used Progress bars recently to determine how our cost of living at our current address compared with the way things were when we lived in a different part of the country. I created a cost-of-living supercategory for all the categories that might be affected by relocation: food, electricity, gas (but not telephone), Council Tax and water bills, insurance, the costs of running the car. I got *Quicken* to create a budget based on our actual expenditure for the last full year in the old place. Then I set up a Progress bar, with a quarterly date range, for my cost-of-living supercategory.

You will notice a little mark on your Progress bar. In colour, it shows up clearly in red, but it's easy enough to see even on a monochrome monitor. That mark indicates where you ought to be on the gauge today. So you want the "mercury" to be at or below the mark for an expense category, at or above the mark for income.

There are two checkboxes in the Customize Progress Bar window. If you clear the Show Labels box the Progress bars will take up slightly less room, and the date range will no longer be shown. The name of the budget category or supercategory, the amount you have spent so far, and the budget amount you are aiming at will still be there. The other checkbox, Always On Top, keeps the Progress bars visible at the bottom of your *Quicken* screen whatever you are doing.

Caution

If you have the Progress bars always visible, or even have the Progress bar window open but hidden, Quicken will stop to do an update every time you make a relevant entry. The same thing happens if you have the Snapshot window open – for Snapshots, see below. After a time, these pauses become irritating, even with a Pentium chip in your computer. It is better to close down both Progress bars and Snapshots, therefore, when you have had a look at them.

What are Snapshots, anyway? Click on the Snapshot icon on the iconbar, or choose Snapshots from the drop-down list under Plan, and you'll see. They're wonderful.

The default Snapshot page is just a suggestion. You can choose the Snapshots most useful to your situation, and you can go on tinkering with them as long as you like. The more you work with the program, the more ideas you will have about how to arrange your Snapshots. And you can have several pages of Snapshots – although I think it's more useful to concentrate on building one or two really useful pages.

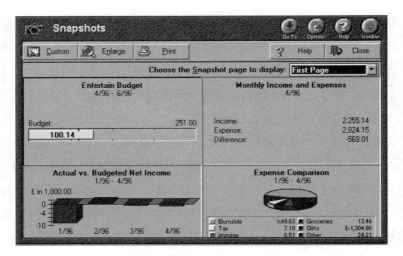

FIGURE 3.16 A SNAPSHOT PAGE

Quicken's initial suggestion consists of five different sorts of graph, and the current week's notes from your Financial Calendar. You can change it all. Click on Customize to see how.

In the Customize Snapshots window, it might be best to start with the second option: how many Snapshots do you want to see on your screen at once? *Quicken* starts you off with six. I have stuck with that number myself, but especially in the early days you may not have enough information to create six meaningful pictures. You can have two or three or four per page if you prefer. Click on the image of the page you prefer.

Now go back to the first option, Choose the Snapshot, to customise. As you select each snapshot on the map, you will see the highlight in the Snapshot Type list below move to the name of the Snapshot currently displayed in that space. To the right you will see a brief explanation of the current choice. Below the explanation you can choose whether to display this particular Snapshot as a graph or as text. And below that appears the expected Customize Snapshots window. Click on that to improve your Snapshot by filtering out any accounts or categories or classes that you think

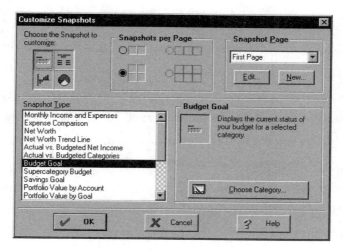

FIGURE 3.17 THE CUSTOMIZE SNAPSHOTS WINDOW

would distort the picture. Notice, as with Progress bars, that this window also offers the valuable option of choosing a date-range for the Snapshot.

As you work with *Quicken*'s graphs and reports (see Chapter 5), you will gain experience that you can put to good use by coming back to your Snapshot page and creating more sophisticated graphs. But the concept is far too good – and too much fun – to delay. You can start right from the beginning by filling your page with Snapshots of some of your budget goals, and perhaps a pie chart of current expenses. As your data builds up month by month, you can substitute more interesting graphs.

In my own page, I have chosen:

- A Progress bar for dividend income for the current month. *Quicken* created the budget for me from last year's figures. I'm glad to say that at the moment, this form of income is running slightly ahead of last year.

- Monthly income and expenses, in words and figures. This is a simple statement for the current month to date, showing how much has come in and how much has gone out, and the difference. I resisted the temptation to filter out some categories that "don't count", so that this Snapshot shows me the unvarnished truth. Things don't look so good here: the difference is negative and no more income is expected before the end of the month.

- A Net Worth graph, in which I hope to see the totals of cash-on-hand gradually increasing. I have excluded Investment accounts from this one.
- Actual versus budgeted net income, month by month – a bit of a shocker, that one.
- A Progress bar for my Food & Life category – meaning, groceries plus cash that trickles through our fingers.
- My calendar notes for the current week.

Once you get started on creating your own Snapshot page, you won't look back. And because the Snapshot page is seriously fun, you will go on looking at it and perhaps tinkering with it – and learning about your financial position as you do so. Before *Quicken 4*, there was a temptation, after an initial period of enthusiasm, to settle back and just make entries in the registers, using *Quicken* only to provide information about bank balances and to help at the various points in life where accurate records are needed, such as income-tax-time. Now the graphic capabilities of the program have a real chance to help every day. Snapshots were introduced with *Quicken 4*. I still look at mine almost every time I use the program.

In the Snapshots window itself, notice that you can select any one of the Snapshots and click on the Enlarge button at the bottom of the window to see that particular graph full-screen. And QuickZoom operates with any Snapshot.

3.7 The Financial Planning Calculators

The Financial Planning Calculators in *Quicken* are there to provide you with the longer view, and with answers to the bigger questions. I think it is best to do the detailed work first, and to work with Forecasting, before you move on to the Calculators.

They are excellent, but I approach them with a sense of caution. If there is one thing that can be predicted with certainty about the future, it is that it has some surprises up its sleeve for all of us. Life keeps moving the goal-posts. So don't take the results of your work with the Financial Planning Calculators too seriously. If *Quicken* seems to be telling you that you cannot possibly pay your mortgage, educate your children, and keep warm in old age, don't be too quick to look around for a bridge from which to hurl yourself. Something may turn up.

The idea behind all five of *Quicken*'s Financial Planning Calculators is the same: you provide the program with some data, such as how much you might be able to afford per month in mortgage payments. The program will tell you the answer to the big question: how expensive a house can you afford to buy? The Remortgage Planner answers only one question: should I switch mortgages? In each of the other four planners, *Quicken* can approach the problem in more than one way. You will see a box called Calculate in the lower left-hand corner of the Planner window. You have a choice of two or, in some cases, three things that *Quicken* can calculate from the data you give it. Depending on which one you choose, you will see the fields that you must fill in with information clearly labelled in the window above. The "answer" field is at first blocked with the word CALCULATED. When you have provided data in the other fields, the appropriate answer appears in the CALCULATED field – you don't even have to click OK. As you try out different scenarios, *Quicken* shows you instantly how each of your assumptions would work out in practice.

There are five Financial Planning Calculators in *Quicken*:

- The **Loan Planner** calculates the amount of each of your repayments, given the amount to be borrowed, the time the loan will run, and the interest rate. Alternatively, given the number of payments, the amount of each one, and the rate of interest, it can calculate the amount of money you would be able to borrow.

- The **Investment Savings Planner** calculates how your savings will grow, according to whatever assumptions you care to try out about interest rates, the amount you will be able to save each year, and the rate of inflation.

- The **College Planner** works equally well for school fees. It will calculate either the annual school or college costs you will be able to afford; or the amount you need to be saving every month; or the amount you need to have saved already – depending on which choice you make.

- The **Retirement Planner** helps you estimate how much income you will derive from each of your nest eggs, given certain assumptions about interest rates, tax, how much you can save regularly, inflation, and – honest, it's in there – how long you expect to live.

- The **Remortgage Planner** helps you decide whether it is worth switching to another mortgage to take advantage of a better rate of interest.

All of the Financial Planning Calculators are reached from the drop-down menu under Plan in the Menu Bar. Choose Financial Planners from the list, then choose the particular calculator you want to use. All are simple and straightforward. The procedure is essentially the same for each. It is described in detail below for the Loan Planner, more briefly for the others.

The **Loan Planner** will be of use principally when you are thinking of taking on a major financial obligation – buying a house, whether it's your first or a subsequent trade-up; or perhaps something slightly less financially intimidating, like a car.

Start by clicking Loan Amount under Calculate. Fill in a likely interest rate – building society advertisements quoting their current rates are never hard to find. Fill in a period of years for the mortgage – 25 years is common, if you are young enough to have that many years in hand. Most lenders will insist that the mortgage is repaid before you reach retirement age. The answer to Periods Per Year will certainly be 12 – mortgage lenders expect monthly repayments. Then comes the big one: in the Payment Per Period field, enter the amount you think you could scrape together for each monthly payment without actually going hungry. The first field, Loan Amount, now contains a figure. Add to that any savings you may have accumulated – and that's how much you can afford to pay for a house.

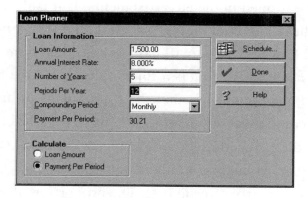

FIGURE 3.18 THE LOAN PLANNER

You will see already how the Planner lets you try out various ideas. What if interest rates go up? Go down? What if the term of the mortgage could be extended for five more years? And be careful not to estimate too much for Payment Per Period. Leave yourself some margin. Many mortgage lenders will insist that you take out life insurance; that will add to your monthly costs. What will happen if you or your partner are out of work? If you have a baby? (Even if the mother returns to her career, there will be child-care costs.) Don't be too gloomy, but don't be over-confident either. Remember the cost of moving, and of paying estate agents and solicitors. You'll probably want to do some decorating in your new house, and buy curtains, carpets and other furniture. Allow some money for that.

Of course, it could be a car you're thinking of buying, or a new kitchen. To use the Loan Planner the other way around, click Payment Per Period in the Calculate box. Then fill in the amount you want to borrow, the interest rate, and the number of years the loan is to run. If you're contemplating a bank loan, your bank manager will tell you how long you will have to pay off the loan. If you're buying a car with a loan from a finance company arranged through the garage, the length of time you have to repay the loan will probably be mentioned in the advertisements. If it isn't, ask.

When you have supplied that information, the Payment per Period field will show you how much you will have to repay every month. If you have been keeping accounts in *Quicken* for even two or three months, you will have a pretty good idea of whether that figure does or doesn't represent a sum that you could possibly incorporate into a regular budget.

If you now click Schedule in the Planner window, *Quicken* will show you a list of your loan payments. You will see how each payment is made up partly of interest, partly of principal. The proportion of interest will be very high at first, but will diminish as time goes on.

The **Investment Savings Planner** is the most upbeat of the five: it is not concerned with debt, or impossible objectives, or inevitable old age, but with your ever-increasing wealth. In the Investment Savings Planner window you can adjust interest rates, estimates of future inflation, and the amount you will regularly add to your savings, and watch your nest egg grow. *Quicken* will even express the final figure in today's money, if requested, based on the estimate of inflation you have supplied.

Even an occasional glance at the financial press will have taught you that stock market prices can go down as well as up. Maybe Aunt Emma was right and the best place for spare cash is the building society. Even so, you might want to consider a home for some of your savings more risky but potentially more profitable. Caution is needed here, but see Chapters 7 and 8 for the ways *Quicken* can help. With stock market holdings, *Quicken* will calculate your Return on Investment (ROI). This figure gives you a firm basis for comparing the success of your investments with money on deposit. You may want to come back to the Investment Savings Planner and try some different figures once you have studied *Quicken*'s portfolio management features.

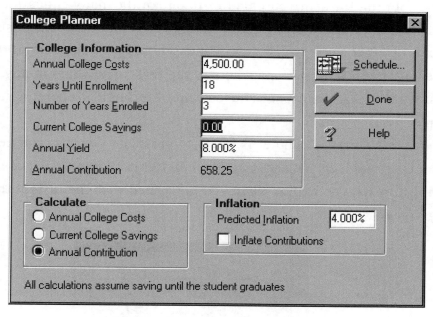

FIGURE 3.19 THE COLLEGE PLANNER

The **College Planner**, on the other hand, may prove to be the bearer of the grimmest news of all. Depending on the data you give it, *Quicken* will calculate:

- the annual school fees you can afford, or the amount of support you can give a son or daughter in higher education;
- the annual savings you will have to achieve now in order to afford a specified level of fees/support in the future;

- or else the amount you need to have saved already to achieve the fees/ support you want, given the amount you are able to save each year now.

The answers are not likely to be encouraging, especially if you are aiming at school fees as well as higher education. Remember, too, that the rise in school fees has in recent years been even steeper than the level of inflation, although there are signs that that tendency may be levelling out in the mid-90s.

The solution for many parents lies in one of the many educational savings plans on the market, where regular savings are combined with insurance policies or other savings vehicles. Some schools give substantial reductions in fees, up to 50%, to parents who pay the fees some years in advance: you might want to approach your chosen school to see if it operates such a scheme.

Quicken's College Planner is likely to persuade you that you need the help of an expert advisor. You will be much better prepared to discuss the possibilities with an expert when you are armed with the insight the Planner has given you.

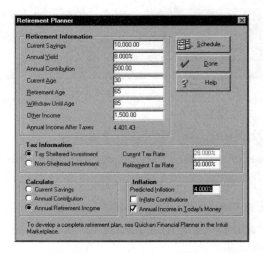

FIGURE 3.20 THE RETIREMENT PLANNER

The **Retirement Planner** aims to help you achieve a particular level of income from your savings as a supplement to your occupational pension and National Insurance retirement pension. Again, you can try out different levels of saving, rates of interest, and levels of inflation. Many pensioners who depend on building society interest to supplement their pensions saw that income fall drastically as interest rates descended from their lofty 1992 levels. Since you are contemplating a particularly long time span with this Planner, be sure to try out levels of interest and of inflation that may seem absurd at the moment.

Remember, too, that if you are in a good occupational pension scheme, and if it allows you to make Additional Voluntary Contributions (AVCs), that can be a highly effective way of saving for retirement, although it lies outside the scope of *Quicken*'s Planner. That is because you are allowed to make AVCs from your income before tax. Similarly, some self-employed people are able to take advantage of a comparable tax concession by contributing to their own Personal Pension Plan. This is another subject on which you might consider taking independent professional advice, and, again, you will be better prepared to understand your advisor's suggestions because you have explored the possibilities with the *Quicken* Retirement Planner first.

The **Remortgage Planner** is likely to prove extremely useful. With the housing market still fairly sluggish in the first half of 1996, building societies are eager to attract new borrowers. They advertise a potentially confusing variety of interest rates and deals. This planner lets you look around and then try out various possibilities. It has room for you to enter the old and the proposed new mortgage rates, of course, and also, all-importantly, the charges that both your present lender and the new one might make before you would be allowed to transfer. In particular, a new lender is likely to treat your application as a completely new mortgage, with a land registry fee

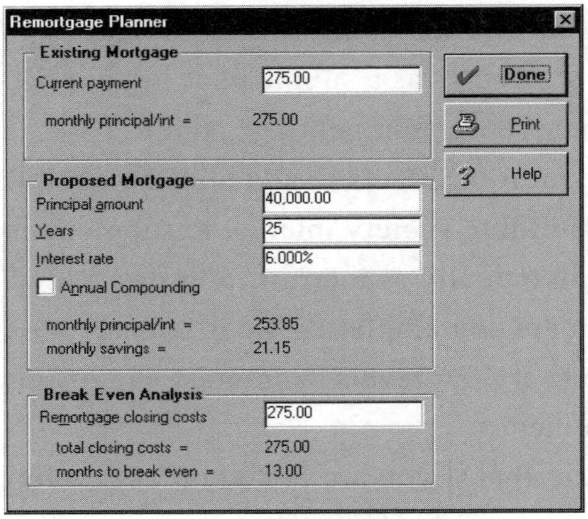

FIGURE 3.21 THE REMORTGAGE PLANNER

and solicitor's conveyancing costs to pay. You would have to ask some sharp questions about such matters, obviously, before *Quicken* could be of much assistance. When you have provided all the data, the Remortgage Planner tells you how long the new mortgage will have to continue before you will be better off than you would be if you stayed with the old one.

CHAPTER 4

Some Quicken Specialities

This chapter is something of a ragbag. Here you will find some of the unclassifiable features which make *Quicken* both fun to use (the iconbar) and a remarkably versatile financial instrument (foreign currency procedures). Skim through this chapter even if you think you know it all. You may find something here which will not only surprise you, but also make your daily use of the program smoother.

4.1 Customising the Iconbar

By now you have taken your first steps in *Quicken*, and are beginning to realise something of the program's potential. This is a good time to pause and look around, to consider how you can reconstruct *Quicken* to your own liking, for it is a wonderfully adaptable program; and to look at one or two unexpected features.

First, the iconbar. If you're using *Windows 95*, you have probably already tasted the pleasures of arranging your computer's appearance and performance to suit your own way of working. Fiddling with icons is a first-rate method of postponing the doing of any actual work. However, if you're not interested in that sort of thing, you can safely skip this section altogether. If you really hate icons, click on the Iconbar button at the top of any account register. The iconbar disappears. Click again to get it back. It may pose as a time-saver, but in fact you could accomplish everything it offers by means of a couple of clicks on the menu bar. On the other hand, if you do like this sort of thing (I love it, myself), the iconbar is a lot of fun, and makes *Quicken* feel wonderfully friendly and personal when you have got everything arranged the way you like it. Admittedly, *Quicken 5* is so easy to navigate that there isn't as much point in the iconbar as there used to be.

FIGURE 4.1 THE ICONBAR

With the iconbar turned on, you will see, immediately under the menu bar common to all *Windows* programs, a row of little pictures. They are called icons, and many *Windows* programs make use of them. You can click on one to launch a particular *Quicken* event. Better than that, you can add icons of your own choosing, delete the ones *Quicken* started off with, and rearrange them. Provision has even been made for those who are doggedly using *Quicken* from the keyboard, instead of employing a mouse. You can choose a "Speed Key" to perform the action of an icon, instead of clicking it with a mouse.

Customising the iconbar is so easy in *Quicken* that you don't need to make any big decisions before you start. As you grow familiar with the program and discover which activities you use most often, you can come back and stick in a few more icons or delete some that aren't pulling their weight. The program comes with a nice package of possible icons, offering scope for a certain amount of wit in their selection.

To start customising your iconbar, choose Options from the Edit drop-down menu or click on the round Options button at the top of any account register. In either case, you will see the Options window, itself a collection of icons. Click Iconbar, and you're at the Customize Iconbar window.

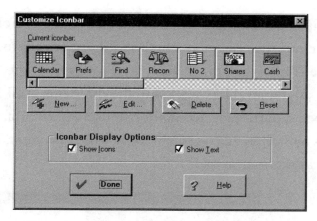

FIGURE 4.2 THE CUSTOMIZE ICONBAR WINDOW

Part of the current iconbar appears in the window. To delete an icon, select the icon you wish to eliminate by clicking on it, then click Delete. You can use the arrow buttons to scroll the iconbar along, if the one you're gunning for isn't visible. To add a new icon, click New.

When you do that, you will see the Add Action to Iconbar window, with a list of *Quicken* actions that are available for assigning to icons. Choose one of them, and you will immediately see, to the right of the list, the suggested icon for that action. If you choose Open Graphs, for example, you will see a little picture of a graph with an encouraging upward tendency. If you're satisfied with the icon on offer, and with the text *Quicken* has chosen to put under it, click OK. If not, click Change.

In the Change Iconbar Item window, you can choose a new icon for your selected action, and enter new text – up to seven letters are allowed, something of a test of ingenuity. Having icons labelled with your own text is a good touch. It makes the screen seem wonderfully homey. When you are satisfied with icon and text, click OK to add your creation to the iconbar.

In some cases, however, there are more decisions to be made. If you add the File Backup icon, for instance, *Quicken* will ask whether or not to skip the initial dialogue when you choose to do a backup. The initial dialogue for

File Backup is about disk drives and *Quicken* files – which drive do you want your backup files on? and which file do you want to back up? If you have only one floppy disk drive and one *Quicken* file, the answer will always be the same, so you might as well skip the dialogue. And if you are adding an icon to open a particular account or to use a particular memorised transaction, you still need to tell *Quicken* which account, or which memorised transaction, to use.

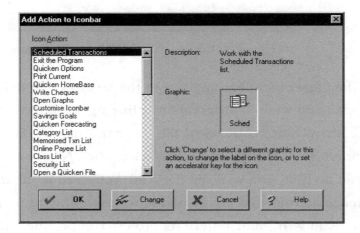

FIGURE 4.3 ADD ACTION TO ICONBAR WINDOW

That can be slightly confusing. Let's say you want to add an icon to open your Current account. From the Customize Iconbar window, click New. Choose "Use a specific account" from the Icon Action list. (You'll have to scroll right down towards the end of the list to find it.) At this point, *Quicken* has no idea which account you are going to assign to the new icon – but you do, of course. Look at the suggested icon. Is that what you want? And at the text, "UseAcct". Wouldn't you rather change that to something suggesting the name of your account, as far as that can be achieved in seven letters? And non-mouse-users will certainly want to assign a Speed Key for this action.

So click Change. Choose a nice icon for your account. Type in a better label than UseAcct. Choose a Speed Key if you like. Notice that the Speed Key you choose must be used together with the Alt key and the Shift key, all three at once. Click OK when you're ready – and only now do you get to choose the account to go with the icon, the label, and the Speed Key. *Quicken* will offer a list of your accounts. Choose the one you want, and click OK. The job is done.

In *Quicken 3* I had icons for five accounts on the iconbar. In *Quicken 4* I got it down to two. Now it's so easy to hop between accounts with the taskbar at the bottom of every account register, and the roster of open windows in the upper left hand corner of the *Quicken* window, that there really isn't any need to have accounts on the iconbar at all. That leaves lots of room for interesting icons.

Adding a memorised transaction to the iconbar is exactly the same as adding an account. And having two or three of your commonest transactions ready to hand on the iconbar is a particular convenience. For more about memorised transactions, see Section 4.3 in this chapter.

You can always change your mind. You can go to the Customise Iconbar window whenever you like, select an icon from the current iconbar, and click Edit to change the icon itself, rewrite the label, or change the Speed Key. You can rearrange the iconbar by selecting any icon, holding down the right-hand mouse button, and dragging the icon to a new position. If you put it between two others, they will slide along the bench to make room.

Which actions should you choose for your iconbar? I have "Reconcile" on my iconbar, a calendar icon to open the Financial Calendar and a little camera which takes me to the Snapshots window. There's a backup icon to encourage security backups of my precious files. I have a few icons representing particular memorised transactions that I use frequently, or fairly frequently, in exactly the same form each time – I have one set up for cash-dispenser withdrawals, for example. One click, and it's in the register. I've got the Calculator icon, too.

Notice that you can scroll the iconbar somewhat by means of the arrows at either end. You could put less commonly used icons, such as Reconcile and Budgets, perhaps, at either end where they won't be so much missed when they scroll out of sight.

Watch yourself at work in *Quicken*. You'll soon notice which are the actions you regularly perform with two or three mouse clicks and would prefer to be able to do with one. Simply add an icon.

4.2 Reminders

The whole procedure for administering timely nudges in the direction of paying your bills was rethought and rearranged in *Quicken 4*. It's essentially the same in *Quicken 5*.

When you foresee (or receive) a bill you're going to have to pay in the predictable future, you can schedule it on your Financial Calendar and tell *Quicken* to prompt you when it's due – see Section 3.3. When the time comes, you will see the Scheduled Transactions Due window as soon as you start *Quicken*. All the bills you have looming are listed there, with the due date, the payee, the account to be debited, and, of course, the amount owed all clearly shown. If you don't want to give the matter any further thought today, thank you, just click Done.

If you are ready to pay some or all of the bills listed, consider for a moment whether any changes need to be made in the details. To do that, choose a bill and click edit to see the Edit Transaction window with all the details you originally supplied. If you're about to pay by cheque, add the cheque number now. If you click on the little button beside the Num field, *Quicken* can be told to supply the next consecutive cheque number, just as if you were working in the Transaction Register. If you have been ignoring

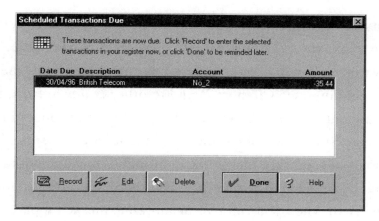

FIGURE 4.4 THE SCHEDULED TRANSACTIONS DUE WINDOW

Quicken's nudges for several days, you may have to change the date. If you scheduled a bill you were only guessing at, you can put in the precise amount now. When everything is right, click OK to go back to the Scheduled Transactions Due window, and click Record. That's it. If this is a one-off bill, it will not only be recorded in the appropriate Transaction Register, but it will also, gratifyingly, disappear from this list.

You can even pay several bills at once from this window. To select several successive bills in the list, click on the first one and then hold down the Shift key while you click on the last one. To select non-adjacent items, hold down the Ctrl key as you click on each one. (These are the same techniques you use when you are selecting files in the *Windows 3.1* File Manager or *Windows 95* Explorer.)

When you are finished working with this window (whether you paid any bills or not), click Done.

Next, unless you specifically instruct *Quicken* to the contrary, you will see the *Quicken* Reminders window. If you have no Scheduled Transactions due, this is where your *Quicken* session will normally begin. In this window you see the notes you have left for yourself on your Financial Calendar. Click on the "Show notes for" field to change the date-range for the notes displayed.

If you have a lot of notes on your calendar, you'll want to set it for "This week" or "Next week". Longer time-spans are also available.

Below that, you will see reminders relating to any investment reminders you have pending (see Chapter 7) and to other *Quicken* files, if you have any. It's a good idea, by the way, to keep all your accounts in one file if you possibly can. Since *Quicken 4,* the program handles foreign currency transactions so smoothly that you can probably manage with one file now, even though you needed two before. But there are circumstances when you must have two: when you run two or more businesses separately registered for VAT, for example.

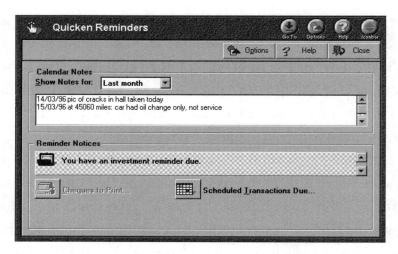

FIGURE 4.5 THE *QUICKEN* REMINDERS WINDOW

Finally, the Reminders window has two buttons, labelled Cheques to Print and Scheduled Transactions due. For printing cheques, see Section 9.1. A click on Scheduled Transactions Due will take you back to the window described earlier in this section. Perhaps you've had second thoughts and decided to pay some bills after all. If there are no cheques to print, or no transactions due, the relevant button appears to be dimmed. You can relax.

The Options button on the Reminders window (the rectangular one, not the round button in the blue field at the very top of the window) lets you make several choices:

- Do you want Billminder switched on? The Billminder is yet another reminder system, much reduced in scope from previous versions of *Quicken*. I leave it switched on, myself. For more about the Billminder, see below.

- How long in advance do you want to be reminded of things? When you enter a scheduled transaction, you choose how long in advance you want the warnings to start. For other types of reminders – post-dated cheques (Section 9.1), scheduled transaction groups (Section 4.3), and investment reminders (Chapter 7) – you make the decision here at this window.

- Do you want to start with the *Quicken* Reminder window whenever you use the program? Yes, please, is my recommended answer.

- Do you want to see calendar notes in the Reminder window? Yes, please, again.

You can add an icon to your iconbar to bring you back to this useful window at any time. See Section 4.1 for the procedure. Alternatively, reach it by choosing Reminders from the drop-down menu under Activities in the menu bar, or click on To Do in the lower left-hand corner of the *Quicken* screen.

Billminder used to be a separate program which loaded itself automatically, either when you switched your computer on or when you loaded *Windows*, depending on how it was set up to work. It scanned your *Quicken* files, even before you had loaded *Quicken* itself, looking for scheduled transactions that had become due, or for cheques due for printing. If you had more than one *Quicken* data file, Billminder scanned them all. *Windows 95* bypasses the DOS environment entirely, and so Billminder cannot function as it used to. It now appears as a "To Do" notice at the bottom left-hand corner of your screen.

If you're using *Windows 3.1*, on the other hand, the old system is available. You probably installed Billminder to load itself automatically when you first load the *Windows* environment each day. If you bypassed Express Installation and made your own decisions, you might have chosen to see the Billminder messages at the DOS prompt even before *Windows* is loaded – or perhaps you chose not to install the Billminder at all.

If you chose to have Billminder with the DOS prompt, you will see the necessary reminders whenever you turn your computer on – even if the computer is set up to load *Windows* automatically. The reminder window will appear in the middle of your screen, and stay there until you press Return. Of course, if there are no bills to be paid, there will be no reminder.

If, on the other hand, you chose to install Billminder as a *Windows* program, its behaviour will be far more discreet. It will load as an icon or perhaps, depending on how you have set up your *Windows* environment, you will simply see the words *Quicken Billminder* on the active Task List. The fact that Billminder is there as an active task means that it has some bad news for you – but you will have to make a deliberate decision to click on it before you can see its message.

My feeling is that if you think you need to be prodded by Billminder – and there's no doubt it does its unlovely task very well – you would be better to choose to see it at the DOS prompt.

It is never too late to change your mind. If you're using *Windows 3.1* and know your way around the DOS environment, you can add a line to your AUTOEXEC.BAT file later and see the reminders at the DOS prompt. The *Quicken* manual tells you how: enter the line, PATHNAME\BILLMND.EXE PATHNAME /P in your AUTOEXEC.BAT file, where PATHNAME specifies the drive and directory where your computer can find Billminder; for example, C:\QUICKENW\BILLMND.EXE C:\QUICKENW /P.

Quicken's reminding is very thorough. The Billminder will tell you about cheques to print, scheduled transactions and transaction groups to enter, and reminders you have entered in your Shares Investment account. For transaction groups, see Section 4.3 in this chapter. For Shares Investment accounts, see Chapter 7. All of that before you even load *Quicken*.

Remember that the Options button on the *Quicken* Reminders window lets you turn Billminder off altogether. You can also approach this window by clicking Prefs on the iconbar, and then choosing Reminders from the Options window.

Your reaction to these reminders will depend on both temperament and habits. I have *Quicken* in my *Windows* Start-up window, so that it is always loaded. I keep detailed accounts, and it is rare, therefore, that I sit down to the computer at all without making an entry or two in *Quicken* and having a look around the program. The *Quicken* Reminders window and Scheduled Transactions Due are all I need. I enter scheduled transactions so that the nagging starts three days before the bills are due, allowing me the luxury of ignoring the reminder for a while.

But if you are less devoted to finance than I seem to be, or use your computer more rarely, *Quicken*'s reminders can be invaluable. In the Reminder Options window, turn the Billminder on and set the figure for the number of days in advance to be warned according to your knowledge of your own computer-using (and bill-paying) practice.

4.3 Memorised Transactions

The subject of memorised transactions is a slightly confusing one in *Quicken*.

You have already met QuickFill, the feature that memorises your transactions as you enter them (unless you tell it not to) and helps you make the entry the next time that payee crops up. The QuickFill memorised transaction list can be viewed alongside the Financial Calendar.

But you can also choose to memorise frequently-used transactions "by hand". These transactions will appear on your Memorised Transactions list, available from the Lists menu in the menu bar. They will appear beside the Financial Calendar as well if you choose. Transactions you have memorised in this way can be added to the iconbar, and can be gathered together in transaction groups to make data entry even easier.

Since QuickFill is doing the donkey work by memorising your regular payees, you can keep your Memorised Transaction list short. You can confine it to transactions that are repeated identically, or nearly so, from time to time.

You probably draw cash from a cash dispenser occasionally, usually the same amount. If you memorise that transaction and put it on the iconbar, you can add a cash withdrawal to the register with a single click. When you do so, the entry point will be thoughtfully positioned in the Amount column, with the amount selected, so that if you do need to change it, all you have to do is type in the new amount. I also add a note in the Memo field to remind me where I made the withdrawal.

At the other extreme, you may have a complicated transaction involving splits, perhaps an employee to pay with deductions for PAYE and National Insurance. As soon as you have got it right the first time, you can memorise the transaction for future use. It is always possible to make alterations in a memorised transaction after you have added it to the register, of course.

To memorise a transaction, select it in the register and then click on Memorise Transaction in the Edit drop-down list. To use a particular memorised transaction if it's not on the iconbar, open the Transaction Register of the account where it is to go, then select Memorised Transactions from the drop-down Lists menu. Choose the transaction you want, and click Use. As procedures in *Quicken* go, this one is lengthy. Your most frequently-used memorised transactions, therefore, are good candidates for inclusion on the iconbar.

You can even memorise a transaction that is expressed in percentages. When you enter a split transaction, you can express the split as a percentage (Section 2.2). It is quite likely that such a split will recur, whether it represents the percentage of your telephone bill allowable against income tax, or the share of an electricity bill to be paid by each of three flatmates. If you memorise such a transaction in the way just described, when the next bill comes in all you have to do is to recall the memorised transaction and change the amount. Open the Splits window, if you like, to see how *Quicken* has done the arithmetic.

Notice that memorised transactions can be "locked". That allows you to memorise another transaction for the same payee without affecting the first one.

Transaction Groups – If you regularly write cheques at the same time for the same group of transactions, you can memorise each one of them and then memorise the group as a whole. When the individual transactions you want to include in your group have been memorised as just described, your next step is to set up the group as a scheduled transaction.

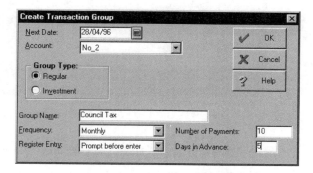

FIGURE 4.6 THE CREATE TRANSACTION GROUP WINDOW

Open the Scheduled Transaction/Standing Order list as described in Section 2.5 and click New just as if you were going to add a new Standing Order. From the Create Scheduled Transaction window, click Group. You will then arrive at the Create Transaction Group window, where you should proceed to fill in the information requested.

You must specify an account, for all the transactions in a group will be entered in the same account. Give the group a name, and tell *Quicken* the other information that is required for any Standing Order or scheduled transaction – whether to make the entry in the register without prompting, and how many days' notice you want. As always I would recommend that you tell *Quicken* to enter standing orders in your register automatically, and to prompt you to write the cheques for the bills you deal with that way.

When the necessary information has been filled in, click OK. Then you will see the Assign Transactions to Group window, with the list of your memorised transactions available. Choose the ones you want and click Done.

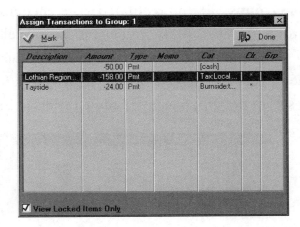

FIGURE 4.7 THE ASSIGN TRANSACTION TO GROUP WINDOW

It must be confessed at this point that I have never used this feature. I do have several bills that are paid on the first of each month, but I prefer to keep them separate so that the Scheduled Transactions Due window shows me full details, not just the name of a group. With *Quicken 4* and *5*, I can pay the bills all at once, if I want to, by selecting them as described in Section 4.2. Nor have I figured out a way to release a scheduled transaction from its membership in a group. There's nothing for it, as far as I can see, but to delete the group from the scheduled transaction list and then to add the separate transactions to the list one by one, specifying all the details.

4.4 Some of Quicken's Other Tricks

QuickZoom

One of *Quicken*'s outstanding features is called QuickZoom. You've seen it already as you explored your first Progress bars and Snapshot page (Section 3.6). As you examine a report or graph, you will often notice that the insertion point turns into a little magnifying glass. Whenever you see it, you know you can double-click for more information. You can examine unexpected results at once. How could we have spent so much on entertainment last month? Oh, yes. And you can correct mistakes. The heading Other in Summary Reports means that you have entered some transactions without assigning them to a category, perhaps inadvertently. With QuickZoom, you can go straight to the register and make the correction. If your memory goes back to *Quicken* for DOS, or to any one of a number of lesser programs, you will know that graphs, reports, and Transaction Registers used to be completely separate entities. You had to abandon the report or graph, and then toil through the transactions to find the reason for whatever had caught your attention. Now everything is linked, and you can find your answers while the questions are still fresh in your mind.

After a few weeks with QuickZoom, it will be hard for you to imagine an accounts program without it. For more about this invaluable tool, see Chapter 5, on Reports and Graphs.

Foreign Currencies

Right from the beginning of its career, *Quicken* has shown itself to be a true citizen of the world in its ability to handle multiple currencies. You can define any currency you like as the "home" currency of a *Quicken* file. Within the file, you can maintain accounts in various currencies. *Quicken 4* introduced Investment accounts in different currencies – see Chapters 7 and 8. You can enter a transaction in a foreign currency into any account and *Quicken* will translate it instantly into your home currency. You can transfer funds between accounts in different currencies and let *Quicken* do the conversion. You can prepare reports in which *Quicken* translates all figures either into the home currency or into any one of the other currencies you are using.

This feature will be of particular interest to businesses that maintain accounts abroad. But it has humbler uses. If you travel abroad with a portable computer, you can keep your *Quicken* accounts up to date, entering what you spend in francs or lire or dollars as you go along. You can bring your credit card vouchers back from a holiday in Majorca and enter them directly in *Quicken* – a valuable check on how much your credit card company charges for the exchange. If your rugby club is going to tour Belgium or your school is planning a visit to the ruins of Pompeii, *Quicken* can help immeasurably with the forward planning.

All this depends, of course, on keeping the program informed of current exchange rates. If you use *Quicken*'s foreign currency features often, you'll have to keep the exchange rate list constantly up to date. For less regular use, do the updating just before you make a foreign currency entry in a register.

From the Lists menu, choose Currency. You will see a table holding the current state of *Quicken*'s information about world currencies. You can add any currencies you like to the list. You can define any currency you choose as the home currency – although Intuit prudently recommend that once having set your home currency, you should leave it alone. You can bring the exchange rates up to date – indeed, that is an essential operation before using *Quicken*'s foreign currency facilities.

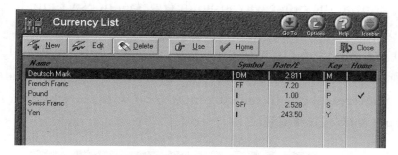

FIGURE 4.8 THE FOREIGN CURRENCY LIST

To make use of *Quicken*'s multilingual talents, start with the Currency List.

*   Make sure that the currencies you are interested in are there. If not, Click New (in *Quicken 4* it's an unlabelled plus-sign) and add them. Choose an appropriate symbol – a two or three letter code such as "SFr" for Swiss francs.

*   Make sure that the exchange rates are up to date – consult this morning's paper for information on that subject. Select the currency you're interested in and click on Edit (in *Quicken 4* it's the hand holding a pen) to see the Edit Currency window. It shows the exchange rate in both directions. The fields are labelled according to the particular currency you are editing. If you were dealing with the US dollar, for example, the labels would be "$ per £" and "£ per $" – dollars per pound, and pounds per dollar. It is the sort of thing that can make you dizzy thinking about it. If you are looking up the exchange in a British newspaper, you will find the first figure: that is, the number of foreign currency units you will get for each pound

sterling. Type that number into the upper field, the one labelled "XX per £", where "XX" is the symbol for the currency you are dealing with. *Quicken* will calculate the other field for you, "£ per XX". When you are travelling abroad, you may find it easier to perform the operation the other way around. *Quicken* doesn't mind: whichever figure you supply, it will calculate the other.

- If you are going to make foreign currency entries directly in the Transaction Register of a "home currency" account, you should assign a Shortcut Letter to the currency. You will see why in a moment.
- That's it – click OK.

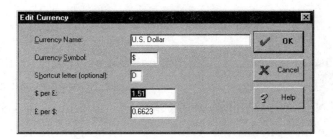

FIGURE 4.9 THE EDIT CURRENCY WINDOW

If you have a bank account in a foreign currency, just set it up in *Quicken* in the usual way. The New Account Information window has a field for currency. Choose the one you want from the drop-down list.

If you spend an occasional amount in a foreign currency, you can make the entry directly in the Transaction Register of any account. Proceed in the usual way. In the amount column, either Payment or Deposit, type the foreign currency amount. Leave the insertion point there for the moment. You can then either:

1) Select the Currency list from the Lists menu. Choose your currency. Click Use.

OR

2) Simply type the Shortcut Letter immediately after the foreign currency amount in the register – if you want to pay someone 50 American dollars and "D" is your Shortcut Letter for dollars, type "50D".

Whichever method you choose, *Quicken* will do two things:

*   It will translate the foreign amount into your home currency.
*   It will make an entry in the Memo field to remind you of the foreign amount.

25/04/96				50	00				-1,289	37
		Greenside	[cash]							
25/04/96	10642	Mr. F. van Schaik		130	00				-1,419	37
		HADM	Professional:Dental							
26/04/96	StdOrd	DHSS-J				147	58	-1,271	79
			Pension:DHSS							
26/04/96	Est.	L.L. Bean		91.87 ▣				-1,271	79
		$138.72		**Record**	Edit	Splits			▼

FIGURE 4.10 A FOREIGN TRANSACTION IN A TRANSACTION REGISTER

Remember, though, when you next receive a bank or credit card statement, that even *Quicken* can't outguess a bank. The actual amount will probably be slightly different (i.e., more), and you will have to change it in your register.

Quicken has the unpredictability of banks very much in mind in its provision for transfers between accounts in different currencies. All you have to do is enter such a transfer in the usual way, in the Transaction Register of the account from which the money is coming, or using the Transfer window. *Quicken* will translate it into the currency of the other account, and make the appropriate entry in the other register.

Note

With transfers between two accounts in the same currency, if you later change the amount in one register, Quicken automatically changes the amount in the other. With foreign currency transfers, Quicken knows that things are not so simple. When you get your bank statement, you may need to alter the amount in the receiving account, according to your bank's ideas of the exchange rate applying at the time of the transfer. Quicken lets you do this without changing the amount in the other account.

Quicken's reports take account of the built-in imprecision of this system. Normally, in a Summary Report, transfers between accounts balance each other out – the amount you have transferred from your Current account to cash equals the amount that cash has received from the Current account. Obviously. But if you have made transfers between accounts in different currencies, there is likely to have been some slippage. You could even have made a profit, although it's a lot more likely that the bank did. In either case, TOTAL TRANSFERS in a Summary Report will not be equal to zero. It will show your profit or loss on currency transactions.

You are also likely to find that bank charges in respect of the transfer have been applied to both accounts. You will understand in that moment the argument in favour of a single European currency. The *Quicken* manual suggests that you enter the charges separately, rather than trying to merge them with the transfer amounts.

Options

By now you are familiar with the Options window as a means of getting *Quicken* to do things your way. It's not a bad idea, at this stage, to have another look at the Options window, and perhaps to wander through it finding out what other things can be changed.

FIGURE 4.11 THE OPTIONS WINDOW

You can change the colours *Quicken* uses and the printing style for text. Later on, when you have started creating reports and graphs, there will be other choices you may want to make, and more still when you have an Investment account. You can change a good deal about the way transactions are entered in a register, including the order of the fields. You can have the Cheque Number field first, before the date, if you like; and you can transpose the Memo and Category fields.

Much thought has been devoted to the way *Quicken* does things at the beginning, that is, to the default settings, in computer jargon. You may like everything the way it is and never want to go near the Options window. But the chances are that you will like the program a lot more if you make a few little changes. The Options window gives you unusually wide scope for turning *Quicken* into your own personal program.

Find

Quicken's Find facility works just like the one in your word-processor. *Quicken* provides so much instant information that I don't really know why I need Find – but I do. The program has some tricks to make this feature even more useful: you can "Find All" examples of whatever it is you're searching for, whatever account they occur in; and you can "Find and Replace", again just like your word-processor.

In its simplest form, Find is used to move to a specific transaction in one of your registers. Open the register that you suspect of containing the desired transaction, and click the Find button on the register itself.

I invariably use the Find window exactly as it presents itself. I type the text I am looking for in the Find window, and leave the tick in the checkbox labelled "Search backwards". It is a good idea to use as little text as possible, especially if you suspect yourself of a touch of sloppiness in entering your transactions. "Sainsbury" will find "Sainsburys", "Sainsbury"

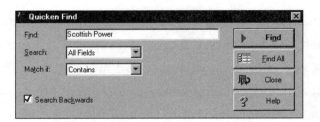

FIGURE 4.12 THE *QUICKEN* FIND WINDOW

and "Sainsbury's", but if you put either "Sainsburys" or "Sainsbury's" in the Find field, *Quicken* would be able to offer you only precise matches. If I leave the Search field of the Find window set to "All Fields", I don't even need to worry about whether the text I am looking for is a Payee, a Category, or a Memo. It suits me that way.

However, if you prefer to narrow the search, *Quicken* is ready to oblige. You can limit the scope of Find to the contents of any one of the fields in the Transaction Register: Date, Cheque Number, Payee, Amount, Cleared Status, Memo, or Category/Class. You can alter the Match If field from Contains, the choice that casts the widest net, to Exact, Starts With, Ends With, Greater, Greater or Equal, Less, or Less or Equal. You can even use "wildcards" – if you put "p?st" in the Find field, *Quicken* might come up with "past", "pest", or "post".

But since you are looking for individual transactions, not filtering a report, "Search All Fields" and "Match if Contains" will almost certainly fit the bill.

Clicking "Find All" instead of "Find" will produce exactly the result you expect – a list of all the transactions that meet your specification. For most purposes, QuickReport is the feature I use for lists of transactions, because it allows me to limit the date range, to subtotal, and to manipulate the list in various other ways – see Section 5.1. The main use of "Find All" is in conjunction with "Find and Replace".

Find and Replace is obviously an activity to be approached with some caution in an accounts program. But *Quicken* has no intention of galloping off and making wholesale changes in your records, as you will see. Note, too, that if what you want to do is specifically to change a category name for a range of transactions, the Recategorise command is the one to use – see below. Go for "Find and Replace" if (for example) you want to change the way you refer to a particular payee, or assign past transactions to a class.

It works like this. From the Edit menu on the menu bar (not the one on the register window), choose Find/Replace. In the Find and Replace window, fill in the Find, Search and Match If fields just as you would for an ordinary Find. Now click Find All – you won't be able to do any replacing until *Quicken* has listed the transactions for you. Once you see the list, you can go through it and mark the transactions you want altered. If you're absolutely sure you want to operate wholesale on all of them, just click the Mark All button. Then, in the fields above, fill in the replacement text, and tell *Quicken* which field of the transaction to put it in.

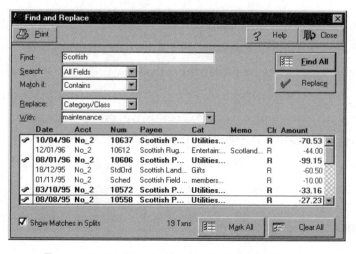

FIGURE 4.13 THE FIND AND REPLACE WINDOW

You could use this feature to tidy up your Payee list so that QuickReport can be of maximum use. Choose something minimal for the Find field, so that your list will include as many as possible of your stray lambs. I used to have monthly entries in my Cash account called "Cash:stamps and stationery", "Cash:stamps & stationery" or "Cash:stamps, stationery". An entry of "stamps" in the Find field would round them all up. Then go through the list marking each entry, and making absolutely sure that only the items you want are present. Finally, put Payee in the Replace field, and your new, definitive text in the With field. Click replace, and all your payee names are now the same.

Recategorise

Here's another good one. After you have been working in *Quicken* for a while, you are certain to want to rearrange your categories in one way or another. Since *Quicken 4* you can recategorise, making it easier than ever.

Let's say you decide you'd like to separate your Food category into two subcategories – Food:groceries and Food:eating out. Choose Recategorise from the Activities menu. In the Recategorise window, put Food in the Search Category field and then click Find All.

When you see the list of your Food transactions, go through it carefully and mark the ones that ought to be Food:eating out. When you click Replace, *Quicken* will first ask you if you are sure; and then, discovering that there is no such subcategory, the program will take you straight to the Set Up Category window. When you have set up Eating Out as a subcategory of Food, the replacement can – and will – go ahead. Repeat the process then recategorise the remaining transactions as Food:Groceries.

Account Selector

This, too, was new in *Quicken 4*. In *Quicken 5* it's become much more useful.

At the bottom of the Transaction Register of any account, you will see the Account Selector buttons, giving the names of your other accounts and allowing you to click and go directly to any one of them. When you're having a session with *Quicken*, you'll find that you are constantly hopping from one account to another. The selector buttons let you do that without constantly calling up the Accounts list, or taking up valuable space on the iconbar.

Before *Quicken 5,* the trouble was that if you had a lot of accounts, including some obsolete ones with zero balances, you didn't want to see selector buttons for all of them. *Quicken* arranges the accounts with the most-used first, except that overdrawn accounts, however much used, go to the end of the list in disgrace. In my case that means that a couple of busy accounts come first, then some relatively inactive TESSAs, then an account I closed 18 months ago, and finally, out of sight to the right, the much-used but overdrawn Current account.

Now you can hide obsolete accounts so that they don't appear at all. To do that, go to the Account List window, select the account you want to hide, and click Hide. At the account register, you can arrange the buttons in any order you like, and (unlike *Quicken 4*) they'll stay that way. Grab an account with your mouse and move it along to the required position on the bar.

The Quicken Calculator

From the Activities menu, choose Use Calculator.

FIGURE 4.14 THE *QUICKEN* CALCULATOR

This calculator is larger than the ones that can drop down at the Amount fields in a Transaction Register, and includes some of the keys, such as Memory Recall, that you would expect to find on a real-world calculator. Use it just as you would a physical calculator on your desktop. You can use it by clicking the numbers and operators with your mouse, but, for once, it is vastly easier to use the keyboard. When the calculator is operative, numbers and mathematical operators that you type at the keyboard will appear in its window, and the answer appears when you type "=". The *Quicken* calculator has a Paste button, so that answers can be entered in a register directly. Just position your cursor in the Payment or Deposit field before you summon the calculator.

CHAPTER 5

Facing Facts: Reports and Graphs

Now that you've learned how to get your data into *Quicken*, it's time to learn about getting it out again. This chapter is devoted to the subject of *Quicken*'s reports and graphs. There are a bewildering variety of them. This chapter shows you how to start with the report which becomes meaningful as soon as you have a few weeks' data on board, and proceed to the more advanced reports as time goes by. You'll learn how to use the new *Quicken 5* feature EasyAnswers to bypass some of the hard work involved in creating a report. Finally, you'll find that you can create graphs of your own financial life which look as impressive as anything you see in the newspapers, and inform you about what's actually happening to you as well.

5.1 Reports

You will find it intensely frustrating, in your early weeks of using *Quicken*, that you don't have enough data for meaningful reports and (especially) graphs. You can, of course, usefully spend the time setting up and tinkering with your budget (Section 3.2) and your Snapshot page (Section 3.6). Having a budget in place will make interesting reports and graphs possible much sooner than would otherwise be the case. You are right to be impatient: as the weeks and months go on, your reports and graphs become ever more informative. You'll soon wonder how you ever managed money without them.

Quicken 5 has a wonderful new feature called EasyAnswers which takes you straight to the reports you're likely to need most often, without any of the (slight) fuss described below. For more about EasyAnswers, see the end of this section.

Quicken offers a wide variety of reports and graphs. If you don't like the way they look at first, you can almost certainly shape them the way you want them. We'll start with reports, but graphs are more fun, and there's no reason you shouldn't put graphs first if you prefer – see Section 5.2 later in this chapter. The variety of reports offered by *Quicken* can seem bewildering at first. To make it easier, tax reports are discussed in Section 9.3 on Preparing a Tax Return. Investment reports are in Section 8.5, and *Quicken*'s many business reports are in Section 10.6.

As soon as you have accumulated a month's data, you can start exploring *Quicken*'s reports. At first, you'll probably want to stick to the predefined reports – there are lots of them. Combined with QuickReport and the EasyAnswer ones, they'll probably tell you all you want to know. Later on, you may want to throw more light on a particular corner of your finances. You may think of some interesting questions you want answered from your data. You can be virtually certain that *Quicken* will be able to answer any question you can ask.

You'll probably use QuickReport often. Select any transaction in your register and click QuickReport for a list of all your dealings with that payee. From the Category & Transfer list, select any category or subcategory and click QuickReport to find out how much you have been spending on electricity, or on running the car, or feeding the pony, or anything else on the list. Remember that accounts as well as categories appear in this list – if you have a Cash account, QuickReport can tell you how much you have drawn out in cash. For me, QuickReport has replaced several of the reports I had memorised in earlier versions of *Quicken* to monitor spending in a particular category.

From the list of classes, QuickReport will give you a detailed account of how a particular project is faring. See Using Classes in Section 2.4 . If you have any memorised transactions, QuickReport can show you, for any one of them, all the actual examples that have been entered in a register. If you have a Shares Investment account, choose any transaction involving a particular security and call up a QuickReport to see the complete history of your dealings in that security and your income from it.

QuickReports can be customised like any other report once they are on screen – click Customise at the top of the report window to change the date range and to sort and subtotal the report to your heart's content. Many QuickReports begin with the assumption that you want a report on all transactions from the dawn of history until now; others show this year's transactions only. You may want to narrow or extend that a bit.

In all your work with reports and graphs, you are likely to make use of QuickZoom (Section 4.4). Whenever you are inspecting a report or a graph on your computer screen and notice that the cursor has changed into a magnifying glass à la Sherlock Holmes, it means that you can double-click on the item under the cursor for more information. From a Transaction report (see below) you will be carried to the actual entry in the register; an item in a Summary report will be expanded into individual transactions. When you use QuickZoom to inspect part of a graph, you will see another graph showing in detail the component parts of the first one. Click again to see the actual transactions behind the charts. There is more about *Quicken*'s graphs, and about how QuickZoom can help you with them, in Section 5.2 later in this chapter.

Note (for *Quicken 4* users)

Quicken 5 has made changes in the way you select and customise your reports. Setting up exactly the report you want is now far easier. But the reports themselves are exactly the same. Call up your own Create Report window and explore its features. You will soon see how they correspond to the ones described below.

When you are ready to create a report, start by clicking on Reports in the menu bar. Choose Home, for this first example, and from the next menu choose Monthly Budget. That will take you to the Create Report screen.

If you later discover that several of *Quicken*'s standard reports suit you fine, without any tinkering, you can go to the Options window, choose Reports, and tick the box labelled Skip Create Report Prompt. That way, you will go straight from your menu bar choice to the report itself, without stopping at the Create Report window at all.

From the Create Report window, if you're stopping there, you can create any and all of *Quicken*'s reports.

FIGURE 5.1 THE CREATE REPORT WINDOW

First of all, you are asked to choose a date range for your report. *Quicken* assumes that your report should run from January 1st of this year until today. You can change that to any other date range. You can also use the now-familiar Options window to make a permanent change to *Quicken*'s starting assumption. Unfortunately, just about the only starting assumption still not available is to set *Quicken* to use the UK tax year (April 6 until the following April 5) automatically every time. I was disappointed to find that *Quicken 5* is no better than previous versions in this respect. But you can set those dates as your choice in the Create Report window, and you can memorise a report for future use with the dates in place. More on that subject later in this chapter.

With the dates set – and of course you can always go back and change them – take a look at the rest of the Create Report window. It lists the eight types of *Quicken* reports: Cash Flow, Monthly Budget, Itemised Categories, Tax Summary, Net Worth, Tax Return, Missing Cheques, and Comparison. Each label includes a brief description of what the report does. Click the Show Report Sample checkbox at the top of the window to see an actual example of the highlighted report.

You can see your report right away by clicking OK at this point. Or you can click Customise, at the bottom of the window, to go on to another window which allows you virtually unlimited freedom to arrange the report the way you want it. There is more about customising later in this chapter. We'll start with a look at some of the basic reports.

One of the first of *Quicken*'s preset reports that you'll be able to use is the Monthly Budget report – assuming you have set up a budget. (In fact, you can get a Budget report from EasyAnswers – see below; we'll do it the hard way now, for practice.) Choose that from among the home reports, if you haven't already done so, check the date range, and click OK. You will see a report with figures arranged in columns: first, your actual income and outgoings, category by category; month by month, if more than one month is called for; next, a column with your budgeted amounts; and finally, a column showing the difference. This all-important final column shows "bad" amounts in red – income categories where you received less than the budgeted amount, expense categories where you spent more. If *Quicken* has more than one month's data available, the information for the year-to-date is summarised to the right.

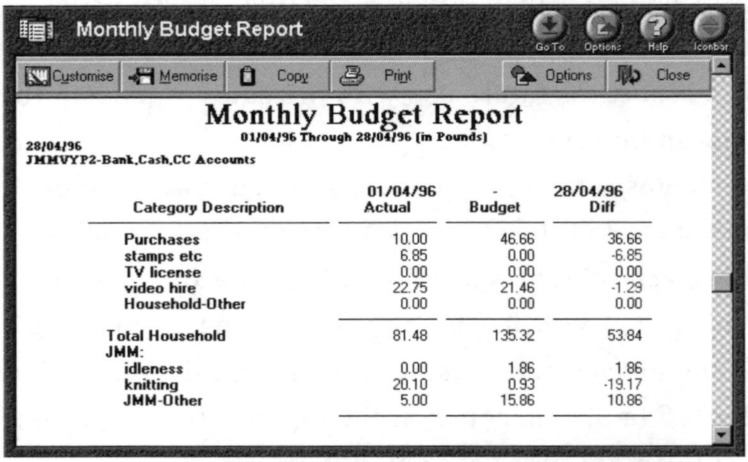

FIGURE 5.2 A MONTHLY BUDGET REPORT

The names of your categories are shown to the left. Income and expense categories are totalled separately before being considered together at the bottom of the report. There will probably be a lot of red at first. As you contemplate the report, the worst surprises are likely to be in categories such as food and motoring expenses, where the outflow is irregular. At first, your wisest course is probably to go back to the Budget screen and edge the estimates upwards. If your Budget reports go on showing too much red, you may want to find ways to adjust your spending downwards.

The bottom line of this report is particularly interesting. At the bottom of the first column you see your actual balance for the month – a negative amount there means, I'm afraid, that you spent more than you earned. That is likely to happen once or twice during a year, December being a notoriously likely example, but obviously it shouldn't be allowed to occur too often. Next comes your budgeted balance, and finally the difference between budget and actual. A negative amount here means that you spent more, or earned less (or both) than you thought you would. Positive figures in this position are rare in my experience. Your goal should be to improve your budgeting to make this figure, positive or negative, as small as possible.

When you have a lot of data available, you can include several months' data in this report, with three columns for each month, Actual, Budget, and Difference. But that adds up to a lot of columns, and *Quicken* does have a tendency to spread itself about. If you have more than the three columns of the basic Budget report, you will have to "scroll" your computer screen in order to view the figures. Note, however, that *Quicken 5* has a new trick to help you here: With your report on-screen, grab one of the small markers between the column headings and drag it to re-size the column.

I find it hard to make sense of a report that stretches too far, and therefore prefer to confine Budget reports to one time interval. Note, however, that that doesn't have to be a month – you can compare budgeted and actual amounts for a quarter, a half-year, a year, or other periods. Quarterly comparisons are particularly valuable, I think, as soon as you have enough data. When you have been keeping accounts in *Quicken* for more than a year, reports really get good: try a Comparison report for the first-quarter-this-year compared with the first-quarter-last-year.

Another report you may find interesting after your first month is the Cash Flow report. In this report, and in all reports organised on a cashflow basis, you first see your inflows, category by category; then your outflows, similarly arranged; and then the bottom line.

With two months' data in your *Quicken* accounts, you can have a Comparison report. In appearance, it is similar to a Budget report. This time, however, the comparison is between your income and expenditure for two different time periods. *Quicken* assumes, if you ask for a Comparison report, that you want to compare last year with this-year-to-date. When you have enough data, that will indeed be interesting. For now, you will have to specify the actual dates of the periods you want to compare.

From the drop-down Reports menu, choose Home, then Comparison. When you have done so, you will be asked to supply the beginning and ending dates of the two periods you want to compare. You can type in the dates, or find them on the little drop-down calendars.

Tip

The data for the time period you put in second place will form the first column in the report. Normally you would want this to be the earlier time period.

One of the things you have to sort out in creating reports is the question of how *Quicken* is to deal with transfers between accounts. This may be your first experience of actually customising a report. *Quicken* is happy to oblige with any arrangement you ask for. You can include as many or as few of your accounts as you like in a report, and you can tell *Quicken* to include or exclude transfers between accounts. Transfers between the accounts included in a particular report are called "internal" transfers; those from one of the report accounts to anywhere else are "external".

Quicken begins by assuming that you do NOT want to include internal transfers. To take the simplest example, if you have set up a Cash account to monitor the haemorrhage of actual notes and coins from wallet and pocket, and if you do a Cashflow report on your Current account and your Cash account together, you don't particularly want or need transfers between those two accounts to appear on the report. If you do, perhaps inadvertently, include internal transfers, the report will still be perfectly correct – it is just that there will be a figure for the transfer to cash from the Current account among your inflows, and a corresponding figure for transfer from the Current account to cash among your outflows. No harm in that, but not much point, either.

If you were doing a Cashflow report on your Current account alone, on the other hand, you would want to see how much had been spent as cash – i.e., transferred to your Cash account. That would count as an external transfer and *Quicken* would assume that you want it. So far so good.

It is when you start adding Asset & Liability and Savings Goal & Investment accounts that things can get complicated – and you will surely want to have such accounts, to take advantage of *Quicken*'s ability to give you a complete financial picture. In my early attempts at Budget reports, I couldn't understand why *Quicken* seemed to think we had no investment income. The answer was that *Quicken* assumed a Shares Investment account wasn't wanted as part of a Budget report, whereas all our dividend income arrives in the form of transfers from the Shares Investment account to a Savings account. The solution was to customise the report to include the Shares Investment account. So if you ever find a totally unexpected situation in one of your reports, look first to see whether you have included the right accounts, and whether internal transfers are excluded or included. It's a good idea to keep savings goals (which *Quicken* regards as accounts) out of the picture, since they're imaginary anyway.

Most of *Quicken*'s reports are variations of five standard reports: those five are Transaction, Summary, Comparison, Budget and Net Worth.

- A Transaction report lists individual transactions from the selected account(s). It is *Quicken*'s willingness to sort and subtotal transactions which makes these reports interesting.

- A Summary report lists, not individual transactions, but summaries by category, class, payee, or account. A Cash Flow report is a form of Summary report. Summary reports, including Cash Flow reports can now, in *Quicken 5*, be organised by Supercategory as well as by Category and Subcategory.
- A Comparison report compares spending by category, payee or class for two periods of time of your choice. The process of creating a Comparison report is described above.
- A Budget report compares actual with budgeted amounts for the periods of time you choose. A Budget report, too, is described above.
- A Net Worth report (*Quicken 4*: Account Balances) summarises how much money you have or don't have, and where exactly the positive balances and the overdrafts are. If you give *Quicken* enough to work on, this can become a Net Worth report. In business, it can take the form of your balance sheet.

The other three reports on the Create Report screen are in fact special cases of the Transaction report. For Tax Summary and Tax Return reports, see Section 9.3. A Missing Cheque report lists the cheques you have written on your Current account in cheque-number order, so that you can see whether any numbers have been left out or repeated.

When you click Customise for any report, you will see the appropriate Customise window for the report you have chosen. It is a dialogue screen in the popular tab format. Don't forget that you can use it to heap change upon change, restricting the report to specific accounts, for example, AND limiting the budget categories to be included, AND specifying any date range you like – and so forth.

There's a new feature in *Quicken 5* which allows you to remove any columns you like from the report. You'll find the Show Columns box under the Display tab in the Create Report window. Just click on the names of any columns you don't want to see in your report.

Remember, too, that when you actually have a report on-screen, you can click the Customise button in its border to go back to this window and make further changes. This is often the best way to fine-tune a report.

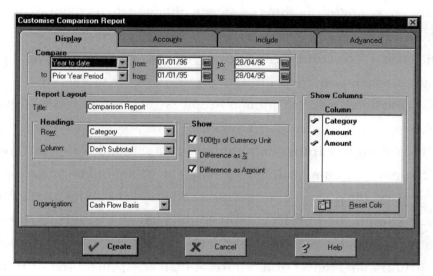

FIGURE 5.3 A CUSTOMISE REPORT WINDOW

Not every report can be customised in every respect, but the restrictions are those imposed by the nature of the report in question, not by any limitations in *Quicken*. A Summary report, for instance, can have its data summarised by category, class, payee, or account. When you are customising a Summary report, therefore, you will choose as Row Headings either categories, classes, payees, or the names of your accounts. A Transaction report, on the other hand, lists transactions. There are no row headings, and that choice is not available when you are customising a Transaction report. *Quicken* won't let you get confused. If a choice is inappropriate for the report you are creating, it will not appear in the Customise Report window.

The possible ways of customising a report simply look dizzying when you first read through the list. It might be best to come back later, when you have more data in the program and a better idea of what you want to know. For now, just remember that the program has amazing flexibility and that it is very easy indeed to take advantage of it.

Here are some of the things you can change when customising a report:

The **date range**.

The **title** – You can enter any title you choose; this is particularly useful, of course, when you are printing a report in order to keep it.

The **row headings**, in Summary reports such as the Cash Flow report – see above.

The **column headings**, in Summary, Budget, and Net Worth reports – You can have column headings for any one of a number of time periods, or for category, class, payee, or account. If you were using classes to keep track of complicated projects, you could arrange a report to show you how much income and expenditure you had for each category in each class.

Subtotals, in Transaction reports – Instead of just a list of transactions, you can subtotal by one of various time periods, or by category, class, payee, or account.

Interval, for Net Worth reports – Instead of having one column in this report showing your balances at a chosen date, you can have several columns (as many as you want, in fact) showing balances at your chosen interval of time. An interesting one, this.

You can also sort the transactions in a Transaction report by amount, smallest to largest; alphabetically by payee name; or alphabetically by category. If you don't sort a Transaction report at all, all the transactions for a particular account will appear together in date order. If you have more than one account of the same type in the report – two Current accounts, for example – they will follow one another in the report. You can also sort by

"Date/Account": transactions are sorted by date; multiple transactions on the same date are sorted by account type, then account name. It is also possible to sort by "Acct/Cnum" (Account/Cheque Number): transactions are listed by accounts in order of cheque number. Accounts of different types are, again, grouped together on this sort of Transaction report; but since you are not likely to want to sort by cheque numbers on any but Current accounts, the chances are slim that there will be different types of account in such a report.

For some reports, you can choose the organisation of your data: that is, whether the report is to be organised on an "income-and-expense" basis, a "cashflow" basis, in a "net worth" format, or a "balance sheet format". Both income-and-expense and cashflow organisation show first income, with a total; then expenditure, with a total. Income-and-expense reports then add a third section showing transfers. A Cashflow report includes transfers with inflows and outflows, as appropriate. "Net worth" format shows your net worth at the bottom of an Account Balances report. "Balance sheet" format expresses the same idea in formal accounting language: your net worth is shown (surprisingly, to non-accountants) as a liability, called "equity". See Section 10.6 on Business Reports.

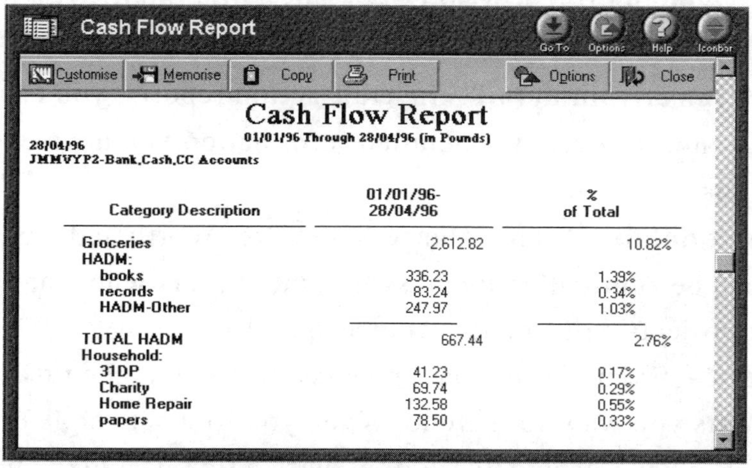

FIGURE 5.4 PART OF A CASH FLOW REPORT, SHOWING PERCENTAGES

Currency – *Quicken* can show all the figures in any report converted into a currency you select.

Currency Units – You can choose whether or not to display pence, or hundredth-parts of any other currency you are using.

Amount as a percentage – In a Summary report, you can have an additional column showing the amount as a percentage of the whole. That's very useful.

Difference as a percentage – In Comparison reports the difference between the two columns can be shown as a percentage instead of an amount if you prefer.

Totals only – In Transaction reports, you can choose to see only the totals for transactions that meet the criteria you specify. Alternatively, *Quicken* will list all the relevant transactions for you. As a (fairly useless) example, you might choose to have a Transaction report subtotalled by week, showing totals only. The result would be a week-by-week report showing for each week only the balance of income over expenditure, in black; or expenditure over income, in red; depending on what sort of week you had.

Show Memo and/or Category – Transaction reports can include columns for your memos and/or your budget categories.

Split Transaction detail – In Transaction reports, you can choose whether or not to reveal the detailed information you have entered for split transactions.

Account detail – Your Balance Sheet, Net Worth and Account Balance reports can be subtotalled by class. Business users who want to track different projects will find this choice useful.

Account – From the list that appears when you make this choice, select the accounts you want to include. When you first see the list, you will find that *Quicken* has selected every item, with a tick beside the name of each. If you want to exclude a few, find and select them in the list. Clicking on the selected item will remove the tick beside its name. If you want to include only a few accounts, first click Clear All to unmark all the accounts in the list. Then select the ones you do want to include. If you select an unmarked item by clicking on it, a tick will appear beside it.

Transactions – You can make the following choices about which transactions to include:

- **Amount** – If you click for the drop-down menu supplied with this field, you will see four choices: all, less than, equal to, greater than. The next field is waiting for you to type in an amount. In order to see all transactions for amounts of £50 or more, choose "greater than" and then type in "£49.99".

- **Include unrealised gains** – See Section 8.5 for this one. It only comes into operation if you have set up a Shares Investment account.

- **Tax-related transactions only** – See Section 9.3 on Preparing a Tax Return.

- **Transaction Types** – You can choose between Payments, Deposits, Unprinted Cheques (see Section 9.1 on Writing Cheques) or All Transactions.

- **Status** – This refers to the Clr (Cleared) column of the Transaction Register. (See Section 9.2 on Balancing Your Bank Statement.) The choices here are Blank (when the Clr column is blank, you have not yet been notified that the transaction has cleared your bank), Newly Cleared, and Reconciled. Intuit recommends that you do not clear the ticks from any one of these three checkboxes unless you are specifically creating a report to help you look for cleared or uncleared transactions.

- **Transfers** – You can include all transfers, exclude all, or exclude internal transfers. The subject of transfers is discussed earlier in this chapter. It is an important one.

- **Subcategories** – The choices (on the Advanced tab) are Show All, Hide All, or Show Reversed. If you choose to show all subcategories, you will see all your subcategories, grouped under the parent category of each. If you choose to hide them all, only the category names will appear, with all the expenditure in the subcategories reassigned to the parent. The final choice, to show the subcategories reversed, sounds surprising and can be very useful. Perhaps you have subcategories called Insurance under both Household and Motor. If you choose to show subcategories reversed, Insurance:Household and Insurance:Motor will come out like that, with the subcategory name first and the category after. They will be together in the report, allowing you to see your total insurance expenditure for a change, instead of the Household total and the Motor total separately.

- **Categories** (in Budget reports) – You can choose to include all categories, to include only categories for which you have actually entered a budget amount, or to include only categories for which either some actual expenditure or a budget amount has been entered, thus excluding Christmas, probably, from a July Budget report.

- **Categories/Classes** – This choice lets you choose which categories and/or which classes you want to include or exclude from your report. The procedure is exactly the same as for selecting which accounts to include, given above.

- **Matching** – Almost any conceivable report format which may have succeeded in slipping through the net so far will be caught by this one (on the Include tab). There are four fields under Matching: Payee Contains.., Category Contains.., Class Contains.. and Memo Contains.. You can now specify text that must be present in (or absent from) any or all of those fields. And, of course, you can have two or more "matchings" at once – you could have a report on all transactions where Marks & Spencer is the payee and Clothing:Self the category, for example.

The *Quicken* manual goes on to demonstrate how you can use ".." and "?" as "wildcards" when you are specifying matches, and "~" (the tilde) as a negative. If you are at ease with searching computerised databases for information, this sort of thing will be second nature. If not, you will have to devote some care and attention to the manual when a situation arises in which you need this sort of precision.

When you have a report in the form you want, then what? If you decide that the information is of more than temporary interest, you have three options. You can:

- memorise your report;
- export it to a spreadsheet or word-processor;
- or print a permanent copy of it.

To memorise the settings for a report, click Memorise on the button bar of the report itself while it is displayed on the screen. This can be a useful technique for any report you know you want to refer to frequently. If, for example, you have a payee for whom transactions span two or more accounts, QuickReport will not do, as a QuickReport on a payee is confined to one account only. But you could memorise a report in which all accounts are included but the payee field is restricted to the one payee you are interested in.

The Memorise Report window asks two questions: do you want to give your report a title? You may have done that earlier on, when you were customising the Report Layout. Now, you have a second chance. And, what do you want *Quicken* to do about the dates of your memorised report? You can choose Named Range, Custom, or None; Use Report Default.

Named Range is only available if you set up the report in the first place using a preset date range, such as "year to date". If you have *Quicken*

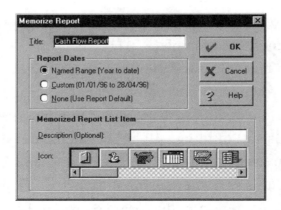

FIGURE 5.5 THE MEMORIZE REPORT WINDOW

memorise a Named Range, the next time you call up the report, the range will be used again. Obviously the actual dates for Year-to-Date, or any other named range, will be different next week from what they are today.

Custom – With this option, *Quicken* will memorise the actual dates that were used in your report. You are likely to want to memorise one or more reports using the start and end dates of the current income tax year, April 6 to the following April 5.

None; Use Report Default – With this choice, probably the most generally useful one, *Quicken* will memorise no dates at all. The next time you ask for a report using your memorised format, you will be offered the default date range just as you would for one of *Quicken*'s preset reports. *Quicken*'s default is the current calendar year. To change that, go to the Options window. You still can't set the defaults to the UK income tax year, but by choosing April-1-to-the-end-of-the-March-quarter, you can get pretty close.

It is also easy to export the report to a spreadsheet or word-processor for further manipulations. With the report on the screen, click the Copy icon on its border. Open your *Windows* spreadsheet or word-processor program and then open a new spreadsheet or document. Choose Paste, probably from the Edit menu of the spreadsheet or word-processor. It really is as easy as that.

In a spreadsheet, you may have to adjust the size of the columns to accommodate the *Quicken* information.

There's another choice in this window, a nice *Quicken 5* addition: you can add your memorised report to the iconbar right now, by choosing an icon and (if you like) a title for it.

Or you can print your report. Business users will need to do this regularly. Even domestic account keepers will probably find that there are some reports it is useful to print out occasionally and keep in a ring binder.

One of the major blessings of the *Windows* environment is that it has taken much of the stress out of dealing with computer printers. With Windows, you install your printer or printers once. All your applications, including of course *Quicken*, make use of the information about your printer that you have supplied to *Windows 3.1* or *Windows 95*.

When you want to print a report in *Quicken*, all you have to do is turn your printer on, make sure there's some paper in it, and click the Print icon on the button bar of any report. All the controls you need are right there.

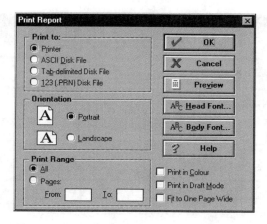

FIGURE 5.6 THE PRINT REPORT WINDOW

You will see in the Report Printer Setup window that *Quicken* knows all about your system. You can choose which printer to use, if you have more than one. You can adjust margins. *Quicken* knows already what your printer is capable of, and allows you to control it from this window. You can choose a typeface for your report from your printer's repertoire, you can have bad news printed in red if you have a colour printer. With some printers you can choose the page orientation, "portrait" or "landscape".

Quicken thoughtfully chooses a small font size for printed reports unless you tell it not to. Notice, too – another new trick in *Quicken 5* – that one of the options on the Print Report screen is "Fit to one page wide". If you choose that one, *Quicken* will do exactly what it says, no matter how wide the report.

Does all this sound a little too much like hard work? Have a look at the EasyAnswers screen – choose it from the Reports menu. You'll see that *Quicken* has anticipated the questions you're most likely to ask. Each of the little windows has a button to access a drop-down menu with which you can change the terms of the question. When you click Create at the bottom of the screen, you'll see one of the reports described above. The second

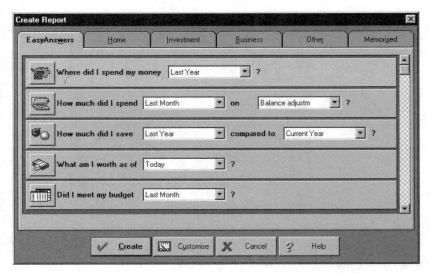

FIGURE 5.7 THE CREATE REPORT (EASYANSWER) WINDOW

question, for example, "How much did I spend last month on any-category-you-care-to-name?", produces an Itemised Category report. And if you click Customise at the bottom of the window, you'll go to the appropriate Customise Report window, again as already described.

And your EasyAnswer reports can be customised once you have them on screen, memorised, and printed, just like any other report.

5.2 Quicken's Graphs

Looking at your very own accounts in the form of a professional-looking, brightly-coloured, three-dimensional graph definitely comes under the heading of fun. It is also remarkably useful.

Quicken has four different kinds of graphs. However, as you will see, the program's graphical capabilities are much more extensive than that bold statement implies. The four types are:

- Income and Expense
- Budget Variance
- Net Worth
- Investment

Investment graphs are discussed in Section 8.6.

Quicken normally shows you two related graphs in one window. You can, if you prefer, have them in separate windows. Click the Graphs icon in the Options window, and put a tick next to "Create all graphs in separate windows". There are two other preferences for graphs which you might want to consider. You can tell *Quicken* to display patterns instead of colours in the different parts of a graph – although if your computer has a monochrome monitor, *Quicken* will do this automatically anyway. And you can specify that graphs should be drawn in two dimensions instead of three, which is somewhat faster.

Income and Expense graphs show you a bar graph and a pie chart. In the bar graph, income bars and expense bars are paired, month by month. You hope that the income bar is the taller. Below is a pie chart showing each of your expense categories as a slice of the pie. If your overall income for the period covered by the graph is (as we hope) larger than your outgoings, there will be a slice of the pie labelled "net savings" for the amount you didn't spend.

A **Budget Variance** graph shows two bar graphs. The top one compares Budget and Actual month by month for the period covered by the graph, the lower one compares Budget and Actual category by category for the same period. In the lower graph, the bars for the "good" categories are green, while those for the "bad" categories are red.

A **Net Worth** graph show two graphs superimposed. The basic graph is a bar graph again, but a double one this time, with each bar having an above-the-line and a below-the-line section to represent your assets and your liabilities, as known to *Quicken* at a particular time. A line graph connecting the bars plots the level of assets minus liabilities, that is, the change in your net worth. You hope to observe a gentle increase over time.

When a graph is on the screen, you can:

- move the cursor to a particular bar or segment of a pie and hold down the right-hand mouse button to see the actual figure that is being graphically represented.
- double-click any bar or pie slice to see another graph analysing the same data in more detail.
- double-click again on the more detailed graph to see a report on the actual transactions in words and figures.
- hide a slice of the pie or a bar by placing the cursor on it and then holding down the Shift key while you click the left-hand mouse button.

Like reports, graphs can be customised, although not nearly to the same extent. To create a graph, click on the Graphs icon in the iconbar, or choose first Graphs and then the particular graph you want from the Reports menu. By either route, you arrive at the Create Graph window.

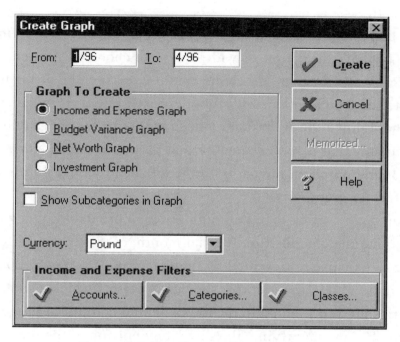

FIGURE 5.8 THE CREATE GRAPH WINDOW

As for a report, you choose a date range. Intuit recommend that you limit the date range, as graphs covering more than a year become cluttered and hard to read. It's good advice. You can then tick the box labelled "Show subcategories in graph" if you wish, and there are three further buttons allowing you to filter your graph: Accounts, Categories and Classes. If you choose any one of them, you will see a list from which you can choose the items to be included and excluded from your graph, exactly as if you were selecting them for a report. Finally, if you have accounts in more than one currency, you can specify which currency should be used as the basis for your graph.

On the window containing the graph itself, there is a Customise button. In the Customise Graph window, you can make fresh decisions about which categories, accounts and classes should be included in your graph.

Let's go back through *Quicken*'s menu of graphs and explore each in more detail.

The bars in an **Income and Expense** graph are arranged month-by-month. You do not have the option, as with reports, of choosing different time-spans for them. Remember, as you move the cursor over any one of the bars, it will turn into the QuickZoom magnifying glass. While it is in that state you can:

- hold down the right-hand mouse button to see the actual sum of money that is represented by that particular income or expense bar; or
- double-click on the bar with the left-hand mouse button to see a further graph.

If you double-click to see a graph giving more detail, you will see a pie chart giving the composition for that month, category-by-category, of the income or expense represented by that bar. Like all of *Quicken*'s pie charts, there will be a "key" in the corner showing precisely which income or expense categories are represented in the pie by which colours. Again, you can move the QuickZoom magnifying glass over any portion of the pie and hold down the right-hand mouse button to see the actual sum of money represented. You can hide any portion of the pie by moving the cursor to it and Shift-clicking the left-hand mouse button. Finally, you can double-click any portion of the pie to see a report listing the actual transactions that make it up.

If you have Qcards turned on, you will have a reminder on-screen of all these options. Perhaps you turned the Qcards off a few weeks ago, feeling you had outgrown them? You might like to have them back for a day or two while you're learning your way around graphs. Click on Help in the menu bar, and then click "Show Qcards". That will turn them all on again.

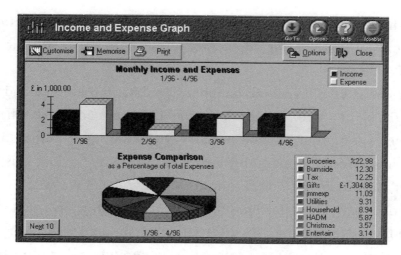

FIGURE 5.9 AN INCOME AND EXPENSE GRAPH

Go back now to the Income and Expense graph itself by closing the two additional windows you have superimposed on it by clicking QuickZoom. Below the bar graph showing income and expense month by month is your second graph, a pie chart covering the entire period. If your income was greater than your expenses, there will be a slice of the pie called Net Savings. The other slices will represent your expense categories.

In computer graphics as in real life, pies get messy if you cut them into too many pieces. *Quicken* shows your expense pie with 11 slices – 10 for your 10 largest categories, including, as we hope, Net Savings; and an 11th labelled "Other" in which all your smaller categories are lumped together. Click on the "Next 10" button to see another pie chart in which the minnows each have a slice of their own.

Tip

If you double-click any slice of the pie, you will see a month-by-month bar graph showing the level of spending in that particular category for the period covered by your Income and Expense graph.

All the previous options for clicking for additional information apply here again, except that "hiding" data only works with slices of a pie, not with the bars of a bar graph.

As soon as you have even one month's data, the Income and Expense pie chart will be of some interest. You may be surprised to see what the really big slices out of your income actually consist of. Don't draw too many conclusions from these graphs, however, until you have at least three months' accounts to go on. From there on, you can watch closely to see that the Income bars are taller than the Expense bars for most months and that the pie has a Net Savings slice (or sliver). You may want to try to cut down spending in a category that seems to be occupying a disproportionately large slice of the pie.

The **Budget Variance** graph is particularly interesting. Like a Monthly Budget report, you can't have one unless you have taken the trouble to set up a budget.

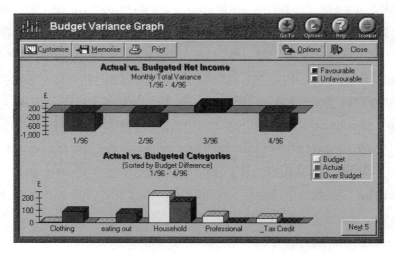

FIGURE 5.10 A BUDGET VARIANCE GRAPH

A Budget Variance graph consists of two bar graphs. The upper one shows you your Actual vs. Budgeted Net Income month-by-month for the period covered by the graph. "Net Income" is the difference between your income and your expenses. If you budgeted earnings of £1000 for last month and expenses of £950, your budgeted net income was £50. If you earned £950 last month and spent £1000, your actual net income was -£50. *Quicken* would represent that situation as an unfavourable budget variance of £100, shown by a bar below the line. "Good" months have bars above the line. They are months in which your actual net income was better than budgeted. If you click on one of the monthly bars of this graph, you get another bar graph in which budget variance is shown category-by-category for the month in question.

The lower graph of the Budget Variance graph itself shows, category-by-category, a pair of bars, one for Budget and one for Actual. The aim here is to have the bars as near as possible to the same size, although of course it is a good deal more pleasant to see an excess in an income category than in an expense category. To begin with, *Quicken* shows you the five categories that deviated the farthest from your budget, whether the deviation was "good" (you earned more than budgeted in that category, or spent less) or "bad" (you earned less than budgeted, or spent more). To see more categories, click on "Next 5". If you double-click on one of the bars of this lower graph, you will see a month-by-month pair of budget-and-actual bars for that category only.

Although bars standing up above the line in the top graph may make you feel pleased with yourself, the eventual aim of budgeting is accurate prediction. So you should do some double-clicking on any bar in the top graph that deviates too far from the middle line. Clicking on one of the monthly bars in that top graph will let you see which categories were farthest from the target that month. Clicking on one of the category bars on the lower graph will let you see which month caused the most trouble in that category. You may want to click Customise and filter out windfall income or your Extraordinary expense category to calm things down. As before, you can keep on clicking until you get to a report listing the actual transactions.

Come back to this graph often. Try to flatten as many bars as you can. There will be some that obstinately refuse to be flattened. At least you will learn which they are, and know to look out for them. Perhaps when you have enough data, you will be able to predict some of the awkward categories more accurately and flatten the bars after all.

A **Net Worth** graph lets you know if you are getting anywhere in your financial life. It is one graph, combining several elements. Bars above the line, month-by-month, represent your assets – money in the bank, and other assets. Bars below the line represent liabilities – unpaid credit card bills, the outstanding hire purchase debt on your car, and, probably worst of all, your mortgage debt. Your Net Worth at any particular moment amounts to your assets minus your liabilities. In the worst case, you will have a negative net worth, if your debts are greater than your assets. If you're in that position, you probably don't need *Quicken* to tell you.

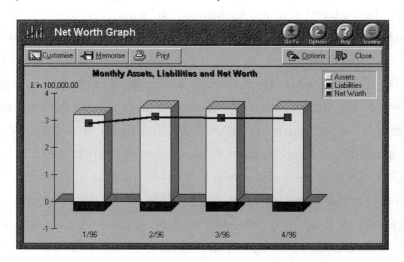

FIGURE 5.11 A NET WORTH GRAPH

For each month, *Quicken* puts a red spot on the bar at a point representing the level of your Net Worth. If you had no debts at all, the red spot would come at the very top of your asset bar, and there would be no below-the-line liability bar. *Quicken* then connects these red spots with a line. Even if, in the worst case just mentioned, your Net Worth is negative, what you are hoping for here is some sign of an upward trend from month to month. It will almost certainly be a very gentle upwards slope – never mind that, if it's going in the right direction.

It's up to you to decide how accurate you want *Quicken*'s reckoning of your Net Worth to be. So far, you have set up Bank accounts, Credit Card accounts and perhaps a Cash account in *Quicken*. In Chapter 6 you will learn about Asset and Liability accounts. Shares Investment accounts come in Chapter 7, on Starting Out in Investment. You can, if you like, include your house, your furniture, and any other valuable possessions in your Asset accounts – Chapter 6 shows you how. Your mortgage and any other debts will have to be set up as Liability accounts. If you do that, a Net Worth graph really begins to get close to showing you your net worth.

Valuing possessions is not an exact science, of course. You may prefer to leave all that aside, and let *Quicken*'s Net Worth report show you only the totals of the balances in all your Bank, Credit Card, and Shares Investment accounts, where precise amounts are a matter of record. On the other hand, you may need some sort of valuation for insurance purposes. The *Quicken* Home Inventory program (part of the *Quicken Deluxe* package) makes it easy, and posts totals back to *Quicken* itself for inclusion in an Asset account, and ultimately in reports of your Net Worth. Read Chapter 6 before you decide. Meanwhile, a Net Worth graph will show you the changes through time of the accounts you have already identified to *Quicken*. You will find that quite interesting in itself.

If you click on any of the asset or liability bars, you will see a pie chart showing the composition of your assets or liabilities for that month. Click on one of the slices to see a report on all the transactions in that account up to the end of the month represented by the original asset or liability bar.

Memorising graphs – After you've been tinkering with a graph for a while, perhaps eliminating accounts, categories or classes that seem to distort the picture, you may want to save your specifications so that you can use them to graph new data in the future. Click memorise on the button bar of the graph and, in the Memorise Graph window, give your graph an appropriate name. To recall a graph, choose Memorised Graphs from the Reports menu and then choose the one you want from the list of graphs you have memorised. You can continue to "tweak" the graph you have recalled, just as if you had created it on the spot.

Printing graphs – Domestic users won't have much reason to print graphs – they are far more useful as a running visual commentary on your financial affairs than as a permanent record. But, like much else associated with graphs, it is fun to see them in print. It is much better, but by no means essential, to print graphs on a colour printer. But if you think your old warhorse of a monochrome printer isn't up to such fancy tricks, you could be in for a pleasant surprise. You might as well try.

I find that graphs print perfectly on my own monochrome dot-matrix printer. The different slices of pie charts are easy to distinguish, with patterns replacing the on-screen colours. But the key showing which pattern is which is too small to be easily read. If I wanted to keep a pie chart in my files for any reason, I would label the slices by hand before I put it away.

Remember that you can go back to the Options window and choose to see each of your graphs in a separate window – useful if you want to print only one of them. With the graph you want to print as the active window, turn your printer on, check that the paper is properly loaded, and choose Print Graph from the File menu.

Business users who need to make a presentation to a bank manager or prospective partner will find printed graphs highly useful.

CHAPTER 6

Assets and Liabilities

You've now mastered the basics of *Quicken* – but you're still a long way from exhausting the possibilities of the program. This chapter is devoted to Asset and Liability accounts. Sounds difficult and highfalutin, but it isn't. Some of your savings, such as National Savings Certificates, haven't found their place in *Quicken* yet. Now you'll see how they can be slotted into place. And you'll learn to account for your bank loans, hire purchase debts, and, most important of all, your mortgage.

The *Quicken Deluxe* package includes an add-on program, *Home Inventory*, which sets up a special sort of Asset account, an inventory of your possessions. This chapter includes a discussion of how to make the most of *Home Inventory*.

6.1 Asset Accounts – What Are They For?

It's time to face up to some high finance. Do you want to create Asset and Liability accounts in *Quicken*?

You've probably realised already that there's a difference, budget-wise, between buying a pork chop and buying a computer. The one is soon over and done with, and tomorrow you're going to need something else to eat. Whereas the computer will (with luck) give you years of service. Moreover, there are certain things you might spend money on, such as a house or a

Rembrandt, that could even gain in value through the years. Things of permanent or semi-permanent nature (unlike pork chops) are your assets. Their total value is part of your Net Worth.

Asset and Liability accounts have special uses in business accounting – see Section 10.4. Some domestic budget-keepers may prefer to do without them altogether. For most of us, Asset accounts are invaluable for recording our National Savings Certificates and bonds. Shares, unit trusts and investment trusts whose price can be looked up every day in the newspaper belong in a Shares Investment account – see Chapter 7. Asset accounts are for assets of a real value that vary less often or not at all.

You can also use them for assets such as your house, furniture, and valuable collections. The difficulty here is to assign a fair value, one that will not fool you into thinking you are richer than you are (a dangerous delusion) but will, on the other hand, allow *Quicken* a fair stab at estimating your total net worth. Until recently, I used not to bother with this sort of thing. The *Home Inventory* program, part of the *Quicken Deluxe* package, has changed my ways. An inventory and valuation of possessions is still not an exact science, but at least it's now fun. The main purpose of *Home Inventory* is to provide a list for insurance purposes. But the program will also record the totals in a special Asset account which it creates in *Quicken* itself. See Section 6.3 later in this chapter.

To open an Asset account, click New on the Account List window. Choose Asset Account from the Create New Account window. *Quicken*'s EasyStep system will guide you through the process. The main difference between creating an Asset account and one of any other sort is that you start with a valuation of your asset as of a particular date, rather than an opening balance. If you prefer, you can start with a zero opening balance and transfer the asset itself in later, when you use money from one of your other accounts to buy a National Savings Certificate, for example, or other asset.

The Transaction Register for an Asset account looks familiar, too, except that the columns are headed Decrease and Increase rather than Payment and Deposit.

Here is how to account for various kinds of National Savings in *Quicken*:

National Savings Ordinary or Investment account – Set these up as Bank accounts in *Quicken*, since you put money in, take it out and earn interest just as you do with a bank or a building society.

"Gilts", Government Stock on the National Savings Stock Register – Keep these in a Shares Investment account, as the price varies and you will want to take advantage of *Quicken*'s ability to track the capital value of your Stock as well as the interest you receive from it.

Most other forms of National Savings are best accounted for in a *Quicken* Asset account.

Savings Certificates, ordinary or index-linked – Open a new Asset account as described above. Put the amount you paid for the certificates as the opening balance, and the date on which you bought them as the starting date. If you have held your certificates for more than a year, they will have increased in value. The next time you are in a post office, pick up one of the leaflets that tell you what the current value of your certificates is. Work out how much your certificates are now worth, and enter the amount of the increase in the Increase column of your Asset account.

When you buy more Savings Certificates in the future, you can add them to the same account, or put them in a new Asset account of their own. In either case, you will enter the purchase of the new certificates in the Transaction Register of the account from which you take the money, and designate it a transfer to your Asset account. Record the annual increase in value as just described.

First Option Bonds – As for Savings Certificates, enter the amount you paid for the bond and the date when you bought it in the New Account

Information window. At the end of a year, you will receive a statement of the interest earned on your bond. Enter the interest as an increase in the Asset account, and assign it to your normal category for interest income. It's taxable, incidentally.

Now you will have to decide whether to withdraw your capital and interest; to buy a new bond with all of the money; or to withdraw some and to buy a new bond with the remainder. If you withdraw some or all of the money, click on the Transfer button of your Asset account and transfer the money to its destination account. When you click OK and go back to the Asset account register, you will see that an entry has been made in the Decrease column. If you buy a new bond using all of the capital and interest of the first one, you do not need to make any entry in the Asset account beyond entering the interest.

Income Bonds (including Pensioners' Guaranteed Income Bonds) – Set up an Asset account by entering the amount you paid for the bond, and the date when you bought it. Income Bonds do not change in value. Instead, they pay a monthly income. Enter the income directly in the account that receives it. If you want to keep it separate from other interest income, use a class with a name such as BndInc. See Section 2.4 on Using Classes.

Premium Bonds – These are just like Income Bonds, except that you may not get any income – but if you do, it's tax free. Record your Premium Bonds in an Asset account. Enter any winnings in the Transaction Register of the account where you put the money. You will certainly want to set them apart in a special class of their own so that you can have a QuickReport on the total of your Premium Bond winnings.

Capital Bonds – These bonds have taxable interest added to their value annually, although like Savings Certificates you do not actually get to see your money until the five-year period is up. Set up the Asset account in the usual way, with the amount you paid for the bonds and the date of the purchase. Every year when you get your interest statement, add the interest to the Asset account in the Increase column.

Yearly Plan – Yearly Plan Certificates are similar to National Savings Certificates. You pay in monthly instalments over a year, and then hold the certificate for a further four years. The rate of return is guaranteed from the beginning of the plan, and is tax-free. Set up an Asset account for your Yearly Plan Certificates. Set up a Standing Order for the monthly payments – you are required to do that in real life. In *Quicken*, designate the Standing Order payments as transfers to your Yearly Plan Asset account. You will not receive an annual statement of the interest received on your Yearly Plan, but since the rate of interest is guaranteed you might like to work it out for yourself and add it to your Asset account annually.

National Savings and Yearly Plan Certificates continue to earn tax-free interest after their five-year term is up, but at a much lower rate (called the General Extension Rate). It makes better sense to cash them in right away and reinvest the money if you do not need it immediately. Now that you are using *Quicken* to keep all your financial affairs in such perfect order, you might like to make a note for yourself of the date when your certificates will mature. You can stick the note onto your Financial Calendar (see Section 3.3), or, if you have an Investment account, you can write a reminder and let *Quicken* hold it up for you to see when the time comes. See Chapter 7.

Other Assets

You may want to set up one or more Asset accounts in which you put a valuation for other property you own, so that *Quicken* can give you a fairly complete and accurate statement of your net worth. It's not an entirely easy thing to do. And remember that if you are aiming to keep *Quicken* informed about your net worth, you must set up Liability accounts for your debts, most especially your mortgage, in order to complete the picture.

As every faithful viewer of the Antiques Roadshow knows, the "insurance value" of an article is more than "what you might get for it at auction" by 20% or more. Nor is what you paid for something necessarily much of an indication of what it is worth. If you have a serious collection of anything, from stamps to race horses, you are likely to have a pretty good idea of what the individual items would fetch if you sold them. Otherwise, the most prudent course is to take the insurance value as a high estimate and not to put too much faith in any valuation.

If you want Asset accounts for your moveable possessions, your best bet is to use the Intuit *Home Inventory* program already mentioned. See Section 6.3 later in this chapter. One of the duties of that program is to open and update as required an Asset account called "Home Inventory" in your *Quicken* file.

6.2 Your Mortgage and Other Liabilities

If you're going to take your Net Worth seriously, you are going to have to include liabilities as well as assets among your *Quicken* accounts.

Some liabilities, of course, *Quicken* looks after by itself. Your overdraft and your outstanding credit card bills will figure below the line in Net Worth reports and graphs without needing any attention from you. But if you decided to include your tangible assets (as distinct from savings and investments) in Asset accounts, you must, to be fair, tell *Quicken* about the corresponding debts. Your biggest liability is almost certainly your mortgage. You may have others in the form of bank loans and hire-purchase agreements.

But always remember, if what follows seems over-complicated or otherwise daunting, that it's not essential. Your mortgage and loan payments already figure in your financial planning because the outgoings are incorporated into your budget. You almost certainly pay your big debts by Standing Order or Direct Debit, so the Financial Calendar and the forecasting features of the program know all about them. As far as cashflow is concerned, therefore, there is nothing more to do. For many people, cashflow is the really important part of budgeting and account-keeping.

Business users of *Quicken*, however, may need to draw up a Balance Sheet. And the more stout-hearted among the rest of us may want an estimate of Net Worth. *Quicken* can help – this is another important area in which the program is easier to use and more powerful than ever before.

You don't even need to worry about the abstract concept of liability. Just click Loans from the Activities menu. You'll find yourself at the Loan Setup window, ready to have EasyStep guide you through the process.

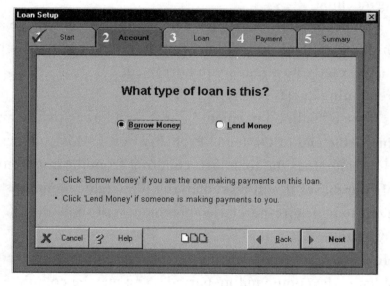

FIGURE 6.1 THE LOAN SETUP WINDOW (EASYSTEP)

Tip

Don't try to tell Quicken about the details of any loans outstanding when you start using the program – except for your mortgage. Just enter the payments into your budget and your Standing Order list.

In the future, when you take out a new loan or hire-purchase arrangement, be sure you find out what rate of interest you are going to pay. If the loan is from a bank, that should be relatively easy. For a hire-purchase agreement, watch for the letters "APR" meaning "Annual Percentage Rate". Lenders of all sorts are required by law to show this rate in their advertising – although sometimes it appears in rather small print compared to other rates that sound better. The APR is the true rate of interest you will be paying, and should include any "fees" that have been mysteriously added in.

First of all *Quicken* will want to know if you are setting up a loan you have made to someone else. Next, tell *Quicken* whether this is a new loan or a top-up of an old one. If it is a new one, you must give it a name, such as "washing machine".

Next, you need to tell *Quicken* whether any payments have already been made on this loan. *Quicken* will next want to know when you borrowed the money, and exactly how much you borrowed.

The remaining questions are:

- Is there a "balloon payment" – that is, a larger-than-usual amount – due at the end of the loan? Probably not, in this country.
- How long does the loan last, counting from the beginning? For most big purchases it will be something like eighteen months or two years. Your loan or hire-purchase agreement will show this clearly, if you've forgotten.
- How often are payments due? Probably monthly, as *Quicken* knows.
- What is the compounding period? You may be completely baffled by this one. Put "monthly". If in the future you find that your figures, as calculated by *Quicken,* don't match your lender's calculations, you'll have to ask the lender this question. It's a perfectly reasonable one, and they should be able to answer it readily.
- What is the current balance? That is, how much do you still owe? If you don't know, *Quicken* will calculate for you.
- Date for the next payment? That's easy, alas.

- Amount of the next payment? That's probably easy, too, but *Quicken* is willing to have a stab at calculating it if you really don't know.

- Interest rate? You may have forgotten, but it should be possible to find the answer to this one, too, among your papers. If the rate varies, put in the rate which applies to next month's payment.

Quicken will now show you all the information again for checking, and help you set up a Standing Order for the actual payments. It's all wonderfully easy – just like getting into debt.

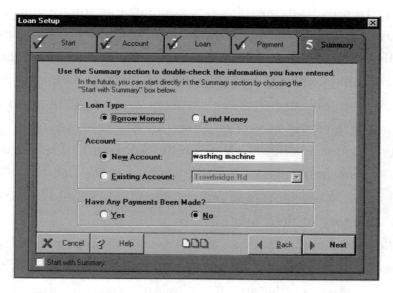

FIGURE 6.2 THE LOAN SETUP WINDOW (SUMMARY TAB)

The big one: your mortgage. If you have an outstanding mortgage when you start to use *Quicken*, you probably want to enter the details in the program. With a mortgage, you will be told at least once a year how much you still owe and what the current rate of interest is. If you have a repayment mortgage, use the information and the date on your last statement to set up the mortgage exactly as described above. If necessary, go back through your records to the beginning of the current year and recategorise your mortgage payments as transfers to your newly set up Mortgage Liability account. When the interest rate changes, click Rate Changes in the View Loans window and enter the new rate.

Click on Edit in the Set Up Loan Payment window to see a Splits window which allows you to enter any insurance or other amounts that are bundled with your mortgage payment but not, strictly speaking, part of it. You can also enter a negative amount representing the amount of MIRAS relief (Mortgage Interest Relief At Source) you are allowed. You can get the necessary figures from the annual statement sent you by your lender.

If, however, you have an endowment mortgage, you will have to proceed rather differently. For this sort of mortgage, you repay the lender interest only. You cannot, therefore, use *Quicken*'s arrangements as just described to set up the loan, because *Quicken* assumes with any loan so entered that capital is being repaid as you go along. In this case, you should set up a Liability account by clicking New on the Account List window. Put the amount of your mortgage loan as the amount of the liability. Then leave this account alone. Your mortgage interest payments should be assigned to an expense category of their own.

The "endowment" part of an endowment mortgage is represented by an insurance policy to which you are also paying premiums. At the end of the term of the mortgage, the policy will mature and repay the loan. There will probably be an additional sum for you. This policy is obviously an asset, and it therefore belongs in its own Asset account. The difficulty is to know how to value it.

Tip

Set up an Asset account in the name of your endowment policy. In the Transaction Register of your Current account, put down premium payments as transfers to the Asset account. If you have been paying premiums for some time, work out roughly (or exactly) how much you have paid so far, and credit your Asset account with that amount. But don't try to guess the current value of the policy beyond the cumulative value of your premiums. There will be some additional value, especially in the later years of the mortgage. But it might be best to let it come as a nice surprise at the end, rather than trying to build it into your calculations now.

Now that you have entered your mortgage details, and perhaps some hire-purchase debts, click Loans on the Activities menu again. This time, you'll go to the View Loans window.

The View Loans window is so interesting as to make me wish for a moment that I had more debts so that I could take better advantage of it. I could achieve the same end by becoming a moneylender, since this window records money you are owed as well as money you owe to others.

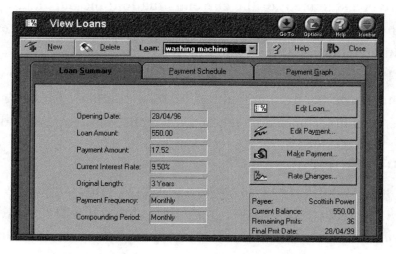

FIGURE 6.3 THE VIEW LOANS WINDOW

At the top of the window appears the name of one of your loans. Click on the button beside the field to select a different one if you like. Below, you see the details of that particular loan, and if you click on the Payment Schedule tab you will see its payment history, past and future. Each payment is divided into principal and interest. *Quicken* has calculated the amounts from the information you provided about the duration of the loan and the rate of interest. You can look down the list and see how, with each payment, the amount of principal repaid becomes a little greater and the amount of interest a little less. In the early years of some mortgages you may see, depressingly, the reverse. New borrowers are sometimes allowed to pay less than the going interest rate as they find their feet – but *Quicken* will demonstrate clearly how they are adding to their indebtedness by doing so.

If you put a tick in the Show Running Totals checkbox, you can see, instead of the individual future payments and how they are made up of principal and interest, the cumulative amount of principal you have paid back and interest you have paid out after each future payment is made.

In the lower right-hand corner of the window under the Loan Summary tab there is a statement of the current situation: the outstanding balance, the number of payments remaining, and the happy date somewhere in the next millennium when the last payment will have been made.

The Payment Graph tab lets you see how the amount you owe declines over time while the total amount of interest you have paid increases. It's obvious, of course, but seeing it helps you realise how expensive debt really is.

6.3 Home Inventory

If you have Intuit's *Home Inventory* program, either on its own or as part of the *Quicken Deluxe* CD-ROM, you will find that it will install itself in the *Quicken* group on your *Windows* desktop, and the next time you open *Quicken* there will be the Inventry icon on your iconbar. The program can be opened either on its own or from *Quicken*. Approach it on its own first.

Note (for *Quicken 4* users)

Like much else, the Home Inventory *program has been changed to make it even easier to navigate and to use. You'll find, however, that the function of your program is substantially the same as the Quicken 5 version described below.*

The main window has a cheerful, *Quicken*-like look to it. You are invited to survey your (so far non-existent) *Home Inventory* room by room, although you can approach things differently if you prefer. Click on the button by the View by Location field near the top of the window to see the list of possible locations where you might keep things. Choose one, and its inventory will appear in the space below. Even before you have made any entries, you can see how each item will be listed; assigned to a category such as Furnishings, Electronics, Clothing, or whatever; and shown with its replacement cost and resale value.

The quickest way to get to know the program is to start to use it, as the *Home Inventory* manual suggests. (This manual, like the one for the main program, is on the CD-ROM. It certainly saves shelf space.) Pick a location. Click on the first line in the empty list below, and then click on the button beside the Item Category field to see the list of categories and choose an appropriate one to start with. For this first session with the program, you will certainly find categories on the list that you can use. But note that you can edit the category names just as you did with budget categories in *Quicken* itself, deleting unnecessary ones, changing names, adding others. Just click on the Categories button on the *Home Inventory* iconbar above. If you click on the Locations button on the iconbar, you can edit the Locations list in the same way.

As you are making your first quick inventory of your possessions, you will notice that a box to the right of the window contains a suggested list of items appropriate to whatever category is selected. Select an item, click on Add Selected Item, and you will find the next line of your inventory filled in for you, complete with the program's suggestion for a purchase price and a resale value. You can, of course, change these.

You cannot edit the item list directly. But when you come to something in your possession that doesn't appear on the list, just type it in yourself, in the space for Item Description.

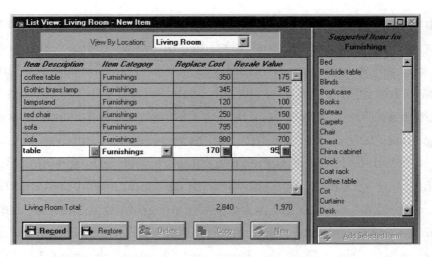

FIGURE 6.4 THE *HOME INVENTORY* PROGRAM (LIST VIEW)

Once you have made a first, off-the-cuff inventory, click on Policies on the iconbar to inform the program about the details of your insurance policies. I would suggest that you do this thoroughly from the beginning – locate the policies and enter all the details. In the space kindly provided for notes, I would suggest putting something to remind yourself where you normally keep the policy documents. There is nothing like a crisis for making it difficult to remember quite straightforward things like that.

Before you go further, it might be a good idea to have a look at the Options window to see what aspects of the program you can change. Choose Options from the drop-down menu under Edit in the menu bar. The most important item here is the figure *Home Inventory* is to use for the resale value of items. The program starts off by suggesting 50% of the purchase price – a sensible and realistic suggestion. If you buy jewels, works of art or antiques, you might want to put the figure higher. But even in those cases, the resale value is never likely to be more than 80% of the purchase price to begin with (because of the seller's profit), although such items may well gain in value through the years.

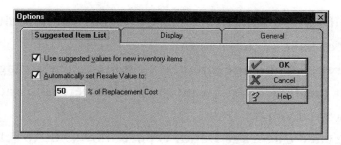

FIGURE 6.5 THE *HOME INVENTORY* OPTIONS WINDOW

When you are ready to add more detail about a particular item, select it in the list and click on the button beside the Item Description field. You will see the Detail View window in which you can enter more information, as much or as little as you like. The purchase price can now be included. You can click on Receipts & Records to keep track of your paper work connected with the item. You can record which of your insurance policies covers the item, and even where you bought it. In future years you can come back to this window and change the figure for the resale value. When you do that, *Home Inventory* does not forget the earlier figure but adds it to the Resale Value History for the item in question.

When you have entered even a sketchy inventory, you will be able to choose Reports from the menu bar and begin to explore the usefulness of the program.

Inventory Value report – this report lists the information you have supplied, with grand totals at the end for the replacement value and resale value of all your items.

An **Inventory Detail report** can be arranged by location, category, or (insurance) policy. You'll probably want to print one out by location to begin with, so that you can go around the house and look for the things you have missed. You'll be surprised how many there are.

The **Inventory Checklist report** is for use if you are letting furnished property. It provides a list which can be gone over with your tenants, and signed by all parties, before the tenancy begins. There is plenty of space on this report for handwritten notes.

An **Insurance Coverage Summary report** can be arranged by policy, category, or location. You'll want to have a careful look at this one to see how well insured you are.

An **Insurance Coverage Detail report** allows you to select an insurance policy, and then select from the items covered the ones you are interested in, perhaps because you need to make a claim.

When the sad day comes when you do need to make an insurance claim, click on Claims in the iconbar. You'll be able to select a particular insurance policy, and then select the items which have been lost, damaged, or destroyed. If items have been damaged rather than destroyed, you can specify the damage in the Notes field in the Item Description window, and the notes you write will be printed in the Insurance Claim Detail report. An Insurance Claim Summary report lists all the items in the claim with their . replacement values.

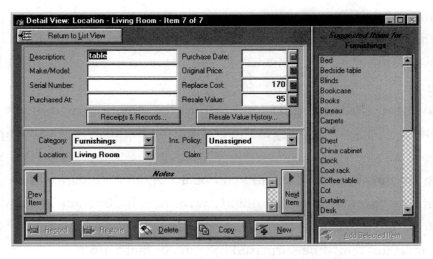

FIGURE 6.6 THE *HOME INVENTORY* DETAIL VIEW WINDOW

You will find *Home Inventory* simple and straightforward to use, and a powerful aid to getting your act together as far as your possessions are concerned. The way the program interacts with *Quicken* itself is one of its neatest features.

If you click on the Update Quicken button near the top of the main window of the *Home Inventory* program, the resale values of your possessions will be used to open and keep up to date an Asset account in *Quicken* called Home Inventory. This account cannot be edited from within *Quicken*. You will find it on your account list all right, but when you select it and click Use, you will be returned to the *Home Inventory* program itself.

Traffic in the opposite direction is even more interesting. As you use *Quicken*, you will often find yourself recording the purchase of an item that belongs in your inventory. Enter the transaction in the usual way and put a description of the item in the Memo field. Then click on the Inventry icon in the iconbar, or select *Home Inventory* from the Activities drop-down menu. You will be asked "Add toothbrush holder (or whatever your purchase was) to inventory?" Click yes, and you will find yourself at the Item Details window. All the details from your *Quicken* transaction – the price, where you bought the item, the date – have been filled in already. You need only assign the item to a location and a category.

There is one respect in which *Home Inventory* interacts with *Quicken* in a less than perfect way. When you use the program in the way I have just described, the purchase of (say) a grandfather clock will be recorded in your *Quicken* records in your usual way – my category for such things is called Household:Purchases For. When you click on the Inventry icon and add your new clock to your inventory, your original choice of category is unaffected.

But in strict accounting principles, the purchase of the clock ought to be entered as a transfer of funds to your Asset account, which is called Home Inventory. The difference between the purchase price and the immediate resale value would have to be entered as a decrease to the Asset account, attributed to an expense category such as Depreciation. You may think that only an accountant would fuss about such things. If so, just carry on with *Home Inventory*. Perhaps, however, you have a valuable collection and would like to keep your accounts more precise. In that case, set up "proper" Asset accounts in *Quicken*, with income and expense categories for gains and losses in the value of your possessions, as described earlier in this chapter. You'll still find *Home Inventory* very useful, but you'll have to keep its records separate from your *Quicken* files.

CHAPTER 7

Starting Out in Investment

Portfolio management software before the days of *Quicken* was available only in the form of a separate program, often costing several hundred pounds. With *Quicken* you can consider your investments where they belong – as part of your financial life, whether you have one or two holdings or a collection large enough to deserve the title "portfolio". There are now other programs on the UK market that combine these functions, but *Quicken* remains far and away the most versatile and useful. *Quicken 4* added a much-needed feature, the ability to include Tax Credits. The way Tax Credits are handled in *Quicken 5* is still short of perfection, but their presence is a great stride forward.

If you set up a Shares Investment account in *Quicken*, it becomes part of your Net Worth reports. Your dividend income can be part of your budget. You can use the Investment Savings Planner to plan the savings with which you will add to your investments.

This chapter tells you how to classify your investments, how to set up your first Investment accounts, and how to make entries in the Transaction Register of an Investment account – including the vexed question of how to deal with Tax Credits.

The fancy stuff is reserved for the next chapter – how to draw graphs of the price history of your shares and set up Investment Performance reports to tell you what return you are getting on your investment, considering capital growth and dividends together – a valuable benchmark.

Investments are one area where *Quicken*'s American origins tend to peep through. This chapter contains some suggestions about how to make the program work for UK investors.

7.1 Investment Accounts

Quicken's investment features are good. But there are problems. And the improvements in *Quicken 5* don't really help. The program is now easier to use – for Americans. Over here, it's actually slightly harder.

If you're upgrading from *Quicken 4*, don't worry. The program works the way it used to, and there's a nice new feature for you, the ability to transfer shares from one account to another.

If you have only a few investments, half a dozen or so, again, don't worry. *Quicken*'s American accent won't trouble you much.

But if you have a substantial portfolio, you're going to have to stop and think how to make the program work for you.

The difficulty is that in the US, all the shares on the stock exchange are simply listed in alphabetical order, from beginning to end. In this country, investment "sectors" – Alcoholic Beverages, Banks, Breweries, Building and Construction, etc. – are listed alphabetically, with the shares themselves alphabetically within each sector. For various reasons, especially your own convenience when you're updating share prices, you're going to want to arrange the shares in your portfolio by sector. The problem is, how to persuade *Quicken* to let you do it?

Quicken lets you assign a "type" to each of your shares. One approach to the problem, therefore, is to change the program's list of types into the investment sector names your newspaper uses. When you are updating share prices, *Quicken* will present your holdings alphabetically by type, with the shares themselves listed alphabetically within each type. Fine, but *Quicken* allows a maximum of only 15 types – that's still true in *Quicken 5*, alas. If you have a large portfolio, it may well extend over more than 15 sectors. Here is another way around this problem, which you may want to consider:

Tip

For each of your shares, determine the sector under which it is listed in your newspaper. Put the first two or three letters of the sector name in front of the name of the security itself. By that system, your shares in Abbey National would appear as "BanAbbey", because Abbey shares are listed with Banks; British Telecom would be "TelBT", because BT comes under Telecommunications. You can now use types as Quicken intended, to keep shares, Gilts, unit trusts and other types of investments separate.

More about this later. It's time to start from the beginning.

Everybody knows that share prices can go down as well as up. Recent history illustrates the point. Throughout most of 1994, stock market returns were dismal. Many investors showed a loss for the year, and of those who came out ahead, most would still have done better to put their money in a good building society account for that year. Things improved greatly in 1995. By the early months of 1996, the stock markets on both sides of the Atlantic were booming and commentators were beginning to fear that a collapse must be imminent.

That sort of thing is hard on an investor's nerves. One thing is certain: stock-market investments are most emphatically not for money that you are likely to need soon – to pay this year's school fees, the down payment on a house or an income tax bill; or to provide the cushion we all, ideally, like to have against whatever is waiting around life's next corner.

But excessive caution can be as dangerous to your wealth, in the long run, as over-optimism. Over the decades the stock market has proved a reliable bastion against inflation. Capital soberly invested in good shares has done as well as money invested in property or pictures, and far better than money deposited in interest-bearing accounts. My advice is, forget the tipsters and the experts. Think long-term.

Quicken's Shares Investment accounts are designed precisely for investors. If you lead a more exciting life, trading in options, perhaps, you can still make *Quicken* work for you. But the advice in this chapter is not really meant for you.

First of all, it might be as well to consider just what it is you might want to put in a Shares Investment account. We know already that money goes in a Bank account, many forms of National Savings in an Asset account. What are shares, exactly? The answer is, pretty well any financial entity whose price you can look up in your daily paper:

- Shares in any of the companies listed on the Stock Exchange. Most newspapers print at least a partial list of these shares with their current price and dividend yield every day. You will find a complete list in the Financial Times. You buy and sell them by giving an order to a stockbroker, who will make a charge for his services.

- Unit trusts – You usually buy these directly from the bank, building society, insurance company or other institution that manages them. Each unit trust makes investments in a variety of shares, not just on the London Stock Exchange but anywhere in the world. The price of each unit reflects the current value of the stocks and shares in the unit trust. A management charge is usually built into the cost in that the "offer" price of the units – that is, the price you pay when you buy them – is slightly higher than the "bid" price, the price you get when you sell your units back to the company. In addition, the managers will take a small percentage of the value of the trust every year as their fee. Unit trusts are very popular, as they offer a relatively safe way for small investors to take their first steps in the stock market.

You can choose a unit trust for a particular purpose – High Income, Capital Growth, Far Eastern Markets, and so on virtually ad infinitum.

- Investment trusts are similar to unit trusts, but the price, for technical reasons, may be somewhat higher or lower than the price of the underlying securities. If so, the investment trust is said to be trading at a "premium" or a "discount" to its asset value. You normally purchase shares in an investment trust through your stockbroker.

- "Gilts" – British Government securities. Each Gilt pays a fixed rate of interest guaranteed by the Government. Some Gilts, those on the National Savings Register, can be bought for a small fee by using a form available in post offices. Gilts on the National Savings Register pay gross interest, although it is taxable. Other Gilts must be purchased through your stockbroker; that sort will have Basic Rate income tax deducted from the interest before you receive it, as do dividends from shares, unit trusts, and investment trusts.

- Other fixed-interest securities – for example, the preference shares issued by some companies; Permanent Income-Bearing Bonds from building societies; bonds issued by municipalities.

There are two types of Investment account in *Quicken*. Most of us most of the time will use normal Shares Investment accounts. These accounts can hold both shares and cash. That makes them ideal for PEPs (Personal Equity Plans), where dividends are paid into the PEP account that holds your shares or unit trusts. But they are also perfectly suitable for any share portfolio. This may sound a bit surprising, if you are in the habit of keeping your share certificates under a floorboard and paying your dividend cheques straight into the building society. How does cash figure in your Investment account?

In *Quicken* you enter the dividend in the Shares Investment account, as a transfer to the account where the money really went. That way, the Shares

Investment account "knows" about the dividend and can use the information to keep track of the return you are getting for your investments.

In the US, it is much more common than it is here for investors to have an account with a stockbroker. The stockbroking company holds the shares in its own name, collects dividends, and sends the shareholder a monthly statement listing the shares and also showing the total of accumulated dividends. You can even have a cheque book and credit card so that you can draw on your funds directly, without transferring them from the stockbroker's account to another bank account. Many American investors never see a share certificate. This system, similar to what already happens with PEPs, will become much more common in the UK as the new automated system called Crest comes into effect. *Quicken* is ready. The Shares Investment account is perfect for such an arrangement.

Quicken also offers Unit/Investment Trust accounts. These accounts show not a cash balance but a share balance. Each account of this sort will hold the shares of only one unit or investment trust. This sort of account is the better choice if you have an arrangement with your unit trust managers whereby your dividends are automatically reinvested in more units. In that case, you will receive a periodic statement from the company telling you how many units and fractions of units you have been credited with.

You can change a Unit/Investment Trust account into a normal Shares Investment account at any time, but you cannot make the change in the opposite direction.

With other *Quicken* accounts, you were able to plunge in and learn what to do by doing it. With shares investment you are going to have to think things through to some extent before you start.

First of all, what shares in which accounts? You have probably already decided whether or not you want a Unit/Investment Trust account. Now you need to think about whether to have more than one Shares Investment account, and, if so, how to divide your holdings among them. And don't worry if you wind up with the family holdings of GEC or British Telecom divided among five different accounts – you can still view the family holdings in one list, and update the price in one go. The purpose of the complications suggested below is to enable *Quicken* to help you with the Rich Man's Curse – the list of dividends and Tax Credits received during the year which you must provide with your income tax return.

- If you have any PEPs, set up each one as a separate Shares Investment account. No tax is payable on the dividends you receive in your PEP, of course.

- Shares that you and your partner own jointly should be together in one account. Each of you is liable for tax on half the dividends received.

- Shares that either of you owns in your sole name should be in separate accounts – one account for you, one for your partner. Each of you is responsible for your own income tax in this case. Watch out particularly for privatisation shares. In many cases, husbands and wives applied separately for privatisation issues in order to qualify for more shares. You may think of it as a joint holding of 200 shares, but perhaps BAA has you down for 100 shares each. Check with the voucher that came with your last dividend if you are not sure.

- Your tax inspector will want dividends from unit trusts to be listed separately from other dividends, and the interest on Gilts separately again. I would advise putting them in separate accounts, again remembering to separate them by ownership as well. But *Quicken* is happy to accommodate them together with ordinary shares in one account. If you prefer, you can do it that way and produce the necessary tax lists by filtering the report.

Once these decisions have been made, you're ready to open your first Shares Investment account.

From the Account List window click New; or choose Create New Account from the Activities menu. In the Create New Account window, click on Investment. As always, EasyStep is ready to help. You should certainly let *Quicken* walk you through the process this first time. Don't worry – you're not going to enter any actual share dealings for the moment. This is just to get an account set up ready for them. If you're keen to get cracking, click on Investments in the HomeBase screen, and then choose the Set Up Investment button on the Portfolio window. That way, you can set up your first account and investments to go in it, all in one go.

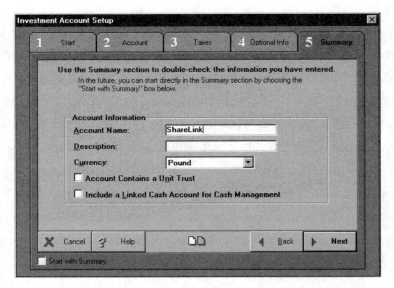

FIGURE 7.1 THE INVESTMENT ACCOUNT SETUP WINDOW (SUMMARY TAB)

With EasyStep, the whole procedure is utterly simple. Help screens guide you every step of the way.

You will have the opportunity to assign transfers of funds in or out of your Investment account to particular headings of the income tax return, just as you did when you were setting up categories (Section 2.1). It is not likely at the moment (1996-7) that transfers into the account will have any relevance to income tax, but things could change – incentives for savers, for example, could involve the opportunity to invest money tax-free. Transfers out of the account will normally be either dividends (certainly of concern to the tax man) or the proceeds of your share sales (potentially a capital gain). My own feeling is that *Quicken* is still not entirely ready to help an investor with income tax, so I don't bother to assign even transfers out to a tax category. More on this subject below.

When you have finished, you have a chance to survey all the answers you have provided. When you're satisfied, click Done and you have an Investment account – with no shares in it.

Now reread the beginning of this chapter, and decide what you're going to do about investment sectors.

If you're going to use my suggestion about naming your shares "BanAbbey" and "TelBT", etc., you can now proceed *Quicken*'s way. Click Set Up Investment on the Portfolio View window and let *Quicken* guide you through the process.

But if you're going to change *Quicken*'s investment types into British investment sectors, that's your next job. Click on Lists in the menu bar, and choose Security Type. Edit the list in a way appropriate for your own portfolio. If you have shares in more than 15 sectors, you'll have to make judicious use of "Miscellaneous". Then open your Investment account (as you would any other account), click on Action, and choose "ShrsIn" for "Shares In".

Either way, you're going to have to identify the security to *Quicken* – that is, tell the program the names of the securities you own or are interested in. This system ensures that you are protected in the future from the danger of causing confusion to *Quicken* and to yourself by mistyping a share name. Don't worry – when *Quicken* wants the information, it'll ask for it.

Whichever way you do it, there is certain information the program will need:

- You must give your share a name. On the whole, that's easy, but remember the discussion of investment sectors at the start of this chapter.

- You will have to enter a "type" for your share. If you're using the Set Up Investment button on the Portfolio View window, the "type" will *have* to be "Share", "Unit Trust" or "Bond". But if you're entering shares directly in an account, you can use your own "types" which you may have transformed into investment sectors as just described.

- You may also enter a symbol. The purpose of the symbol is to make it possible for you to update share prices automatically. If you have a modem that connects your computer to the telephone system, you might subscribe to a data service that provides up-to-the-minute share prices in a form that can be read into your *Quicken* files. Or you may consider installing a Teletext card in your computer, so that the share prices listed on the stock market pages of Teletext can be read in automatically. Share prices are increasingly available on the Internet – if you're already on-line, have a look around. Whatever system you use, the symbol you enter in the Set Up Security window will have to be identical to the one used by your data supplier. You probably don't know what that symbol is yet. Leave it blank for now, and fill it in later.

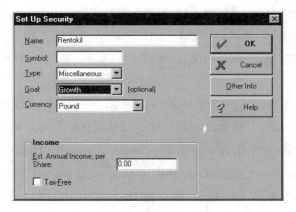

FIGURE 7.2 THE SET UP SECURITY WINDOW

If you like, enter a goal for your security. The main purpose of doing so is to allow you an additional way of sorting and subtotalling securities in an Investment report. *Quicken* has in mind goals such as Income, Growth, High Risk, Low Risk – but you can change those or add others of your own, just as for types. You might like to associate some of your shareholdings with a particular long-term savings goal dear to your heart.

- You can specify the currency for your share – a very valuable feature in *Quicken*. A security must be assigned to an Investment account that has been defined in the same currency when you were setting up the account.

- You can add a figure for Estimated Annual Income if you like. The most recent shareholders' report from your company will tell you how much was paid out in dividends per share last year. In addition to the dividend you receive from the company, you will also receive a Tax Credit towards the tax due on your investment income. Currently (1996-7) the Tax Credit is equal to 20% of the total dividend. That works out at 25%, or one quarter, of the amount you actually receive from the company. If your O-Level maths is a bit rusty, you'll have to trust me on that one. Your income from your shareholding consists both of the cash dividend and of the Tax Credit. Therefore, you will probably want to take the figure your company provides and add 25% to find the amount that should be entered here as the Estimated Annual Income.

Whether you boldly started by choosing the "Shares In" option, or are letting *Quicken* help by asking all the questions, you're soon going to come up against an important decision: how much historical detail are you going to supply to *Quicken* concerning the shares you already own?

- If your records are in perfect order, you will be able to enter each share with information about the date when you bought it, the price per share at the time, and the amount of commission and stamp duty you paid on the transaction. This is the course Intuit recommends, and if you have the information readily available, by all means use it. *Quicken*'s Investment reports will be much more meaningful right from the beginning.

- At the other extreme, you can just use today's date and today's share price. You can always dig out the old papers and fill in the historical data later. It will be a year before an Investment report will be of much use to you, but time soon passes. In fact, you can set up your Investment account without entering a price for your shares at all (I did).

- There may be a middle course. Perhaps you have an old valuation of your portfolio with a date on it. Use that as the starting date and price.

- If your papers are in a bit of a muddle, remember that you can take advantage of *Quicken*'s easy-going ways by entering full details for some shares, and today's price or an old valuation for others. Again, any less-than-perfect entry can be revised later.

The Add Shares to Account window is prominently labelled "SHRSIN" (for Shares In"). That is the "action" that will appear in the Transaction Register when you have finished filling in the blank fields in the window.

- Date – What you put here depends on what you decided to do about providing *Quicken* with historical information. According to the state of your paper files and your inclination for hard work this afternoon, you will enter:
  1) The date you bought or otherwise acquired the shares – this is the ideal solution.
  2) The date of an old valuation of your portfolio.
  3) Today's date.

- Account – This field has already been filled in with the name of the Shares Investment account you were just using. If you now realise

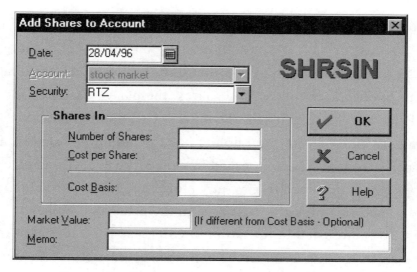

FIGURE 7.3 THE ADD SHARES TO ACCOUNT WINDOW

that the shares you are starting to enter belong in a different account, it's not too late – you can make the change here in this window.

- Security – Put the name of the company in which you have shares, or of the unit or investment trust or Government security. *Quicken* will ensure that you enter the name exactly as you did when you were adding it to the Security list. If you put a name that is not yet on your Security list, *Quicken* will give you a chance to add the name to the list.

- Number of Shares – This one is relatively easy, except in the case of Gilts. The price of shares in the UK, including unit trusts and investment trusts, is normally quoted in pence, although there are a few exceptions. But for Gilts, a price is given which represents the cost of £100 "par value" of the Government security. (Most Gilts change hands for more than their par value, a few for less.)

Now, the last thing you want to think about when you are updating share prices is, where does the decimal point go? That's how mistakes happen. Here's what to do, using an actual example as the simplest way to explain a not-altogether-simple matter. If you bought £1000 par value of Treasury 8½% 2007 last Friday, it would have cost you £1030 (plus charges), because Treasury 8½% 2007 stood at 103 that day. You should enter that transaction in your *Quicken* account as 1000 shares: the par value. Then for the next field, Price per Share, put 103. To enter a Gilt you already own, therefore, put the par value of your total holding as the number of shares, and the price as the price, as if it were expressed in pence like everything else. If you do it this way, you don't need to give any more thought to par values when you're updating the price of a gilt. Just type in the price as it comes.

(If you're interested in investing in Gilts, ask for a leaflet at the post office called "Buying Gilts on the National Savings Stock Register". The price of Gilts, like the price of any share, can vary. Generally speaking, Gilt prices go down as interest rates go up, and vice versa.)

- Cost per Share – This field is an either/or with the one beneath it. If you have all the paperwork handy and are entering the details of your original purchase of the share, it is probably easiest to leave this field blank and put the total of your stockbroker's bill in the next field, Cost Basis. *Quicken* will work out the cost per share, including the charges you paid. If, on the other hand, you are using an old valuation or the value of the share as of today's date, the only information you will have available is the cost per share. For Gilts, this price regularly includes a fraction. Type the fraction just as it appears, "13/32" for example, and *Quicken* will convert it to a decimal for you.
- Memo – You can add a note to yourself if you like.

Click OK, and you have made an entry in your Shares Investment account.

7.2 Investment Transactions

Once you have entered your shares in the appropriate accounts, you are ready to start entering investment transactions. If you have chosen to supply

Quicken with historical details of your share dealings, however, there may be more work to do. After the initial purchase of a share, you may have bought more shares at some point, or sold a few, or reinvested a dividend, or benefited from a scrip issue or rights issue. If your shares are held in a nominee account with a stockbroker, you may even have to enter past dividends received in order to bring things properly up to date. You will have to decide from the state of your own records and the time-span covered how much of this is feasible. The important thing is to concentrate on the transactions that affect the total number of shares held, so that when you are finished *Quicken*'s total corresponds with reality.

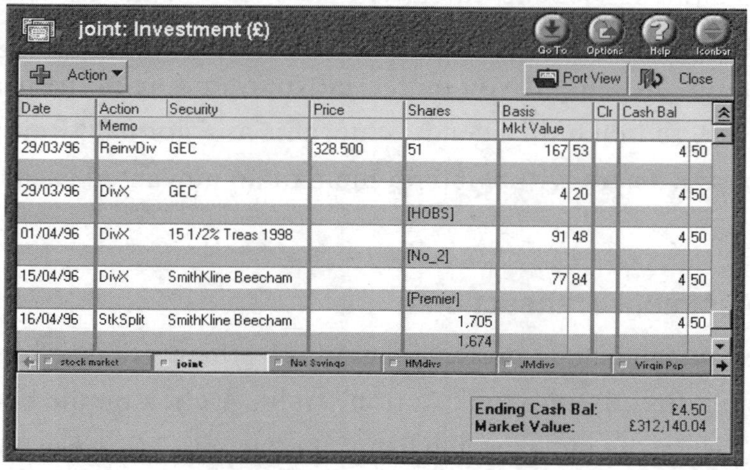
joint: Investment (£)
Go To
Options
Help
Iconbar
Action
Port View
Close
Date
Action
Memo
Security
Price
Shares
Basis
Mkt Value
Clr
Cash Bal
29/03/96 ReinvDiv GEC 328.500 51 167 53 4 50
29/03/96 DivX GEC 4 20 4 50
[HOBS]
01/04/96 DivX 15 1/2% Treas 1998 91 48 4 50
[No_2]
15/04/96 DivX SmithKline Beecham 77 84 4 50
[Premier]
16/04/96 StkSplit SmithKline Beecham 1,705 4 50
1,674
stock market
joint
Nat Savings
HMdivs
JMdivs
Virgin Pep
Ending Cash Bal: £4.50
Market Value: £312,140.04

FIGURE 7.4 THE TRANSACTION REGISTER OF A SHARES INVESTMENT ACCOUNT

For all transactions you can follow the procedures described below, although the description is worded in terms of the new events that you will record in the future, now that your Shares Investment account is operational. While you are still catching up on ancient history, however, there are a couple of points to notice:

- Share purchases – You can record additional share purchases as SHRSIN, like the first one. In that case, *Quicken* doesn't worry about where you got the money. Alternatively, you can record the purchase as a "Buy" transaction. In that case, you will notice that the amount involved appears, in negative form of course, as the cash balance of the Shares Investment account itself. When you have finished supplying *Quicken* with all your historical information, you will have to create a Balance Adjustment to get rid of this cash balance.

- Share sales – You will have to record these as ordinary "Sell" transactions, not as SHRSOUT, because the amount you received for the sale is an important part of the historical information you are recording. Again, this will give rise to a cash balance in your Investment account which will have to be removed by a Balance Adjustment in the end.

- Shares-in-lieu – If you increased your holding in the past by accepting shares in lieu of dividends, enter this as a normal "Reinvestment" (see below). There will be no problem of an unwanted cash balance in this case.

Entering Investment Transactions

Old *Quicken* hands may prefer to enter investment transactions the quick way, typing directly into the "Action" field. A click on the button by the field produces, as you would expect, a list of the "actions" *Quicken* understands, with a brief definition of each. While you're getting used to the program, it's probably easier to fill out a form. Just click on the Action button at the top of the register window, and make your selection from that list.

And there's one transaction for which the use of a form is obligatory:

Caution

When you receive a dividend and want to enter it in Quicken with its associated Tax Credit, you must use the Record Income form. If you just type "Div" in the Action field, you will not be able to record the Tax Credit.

Take a look at the Transaction Register of your Investment account. Notice that there is an account selection bar to enable you to hop gracefully from one of your Investment accounts to another. As with the selection bar at the bottom of your Current account, you can rearrange the account names by dragging them about with your mouse button. If you have separated investments into "his", "hers" and "theirs", as I suggested, you'll be using the selection bar a lot. Take a moment to arrange it conveniently.

The buttons on the currently-selected entry are Record, Edit, and Form. Record behaves just as it does for any other account – it makes the entry official, and instructs *Quicken* to record it on the hard disk of your computer. Edit offers a range of possibilities, similar to the Edit button on other account registers. And Form takes you to the form you filled out when you made the entry in the first place, so that you can make changes the easy way.

The choices on the Action button at the top of the window are: Buy, Sell, Income, Reinvst (for Reinvest), ShrsIn, ShrsOut, MargInt, MiscExp, Reminder, RtrnCap, ScrIssue, Xin, Xout – and, if that doesn't seem like enough, Advanced, which produces a further menu.

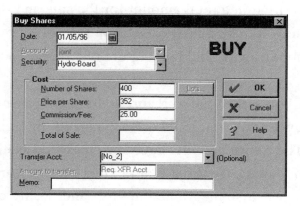

FIGURE 7.5 THE BUY SHARES WINDOW

Buy – Use this one when you buy shares through a stockbroker, or Gilts through the Post Office, or a privatisation or other new issue directly from source. You will need to supply the name of the security, the number of shares you bought, the price per share, the charges you paid, and the account from which you took the money, unless you used cash that was already in your Shares Investment account. Enter the price in pence, as it is listed in the newspapers. There's room for a memo, too. *Quicken* will work out the remaining field for you, the Total of Sale. Check that it matches the total on the invoice from your stockbroker. In privatisation issues and other shares that are sold directly to the public when the company first comes to the Stock Exchange, there are no charges.

Sell – Use this one whenever you sell shares. It is virtually identical to the Buy window. You will notice a greyed-out button called Lots. It activates itself if you sell shares in a security that you bought in more than one lot, that is, on different occasions. You can use it to indicate which lot, or part-lot, you are selling now. This facility relates to the way capital gains tax is calculated in some countries. UK users normally have no need for it, but maybe you can think of one. You will also notice a greyed-out field towards the bottom of the window labelled "Amount to transfer". It becomes active once you have filled in a total amount for the sale and the name of account where the money is to be put. It offers you the option of transferring only some of the money away, and leaving the rest in the Shares Investment account itself.

Income – Choose this one to record a dividend payment you receive. The Income window allows you to record a dividend, interest, or a capital gains distribution. The return on Gilts could be classified as either dividend or interest income – the only thing that matters is to be consistent. Capital gains distributions, also mentioned in this window, are considerably rarer. A capital gain, of course, is the profit you make by selling a share or other investment for more than you paid for it. Each UK taxpayer is currently (1996/7) allowed to make £5,800 in capital gains each tax year completely tax-free. Some investment schemes take advantage of this fact to make capital gains distributions instead of normal (taxable) dividend payments. If you're in such a scheme, you will know about it.

There is also a field, as you see, for the Tax Credit associated with your dividend. The voucher you receive from your company at dividend time will show you clearly both the dividend payment and the associated Tax Credit. These figures are always shown separately, so all you have to do is copy them into the *Quicken* form. The amount shown as "Dividend payable" on the voucher – which is also the amount on the cheque – goes into the first field in the *Quicken* form, Net Dividend. The amount of Tax Credit shown on the voucher goes into the third field on the form, Tax Credit. Keep the vouchers in a safe place, by the way – you'll need them at tax time.

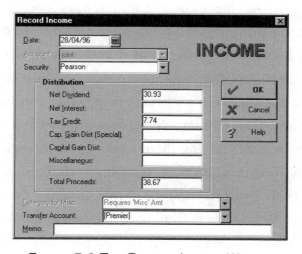

FIGURE 7.6 THE RECORD INCOME WINDOW

Towards the bottom of the window is a field in which you can enter the Bank or Building Society account in which your dividend income is actually received, assuming the amount is not to remain in the Investment account itself.

When you click OK after entering a dividend and Tax Credit, you could hear no fewer than three of the little beeps *Quicken* uses to tell you that a transaction has been recorded. Take a look at the register to see what has happened.

- First, *Quicken* has entered the total dividend you received, that is, the actual dividend and the Tax Credit added together. The action in the action field is "Div" – the dividend has been recorded as an increase in the cash balance of the Investment account.

- Second, the amount of the Tax Credit has been transferred out of the Investment account to a special category called Tax Credit, set up by *Quicken*. The action this time was MiscExp, meaning Miscellaneous Expense, of course.

- Third, if you did in fact deposit the dividend money in a Bank or Building Society account, the transfer is recorded. The action is given as Xout, meaning that cash has been transferred out of the account.

It shouldn't happen very often, but if you ever do need to delete a dividend you have recorded, you must delete all three of these transactions.

If you hold your shares in a PEP account, your dividends and capital gains are tax-free. The company that administers your PEP will reclaim the Tax Credits on your behalf and add them to the cash balance in the account. In this case, the easiest thing to do is to enter both the dividend and, later, the Tax Credit as (net) dividend income. You can make the entry directly in the register, putting Div as the action, or you can use the form.

Reinvst (Reinvest) – Many companies these days offer their shareholders the opportunity to take dividend payments in the form of additional shares. There are tax advantages for the company, and the shareholder benefits by building up an investment without paying any charges. If you take dividends in this way, click Reinvst to make the entry. Your company will tell you all the information you need to enter in this window, including the notional price-per-share. Shares taken in lieu of dividends are taxable just as if you had received cash, and there is a field for Tax Credit just as in the Record Income window.

Some unit trusts allow unit-holders to reinvest dividends automatically. If you have such an arrangement, you may have put the unit trust in its own Unit/Investment Trust account. When you receive notification of a new dividend, fill in the Reinvst window. The voucher you receive from the unit trust company will tell you both how many new shares you have received, including fractional shares, and how much each one was deemed to have cost.

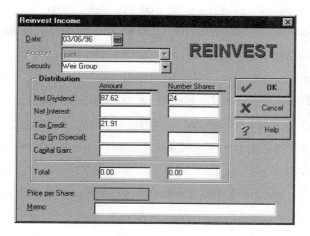

FIGURE 7.7 THE REINVEST INCOME WINDOW

ShrsIn (Shares In) and **ShrsOut** (Shares Out) – These are the ones to use for all transactions that don't involve money – if you are given or inherit some shares, or, alternatively, if you give some away.

MargInt (Margin Interest) – This one is a reference to the possibility that you might buy shares with money which, in effect, you borrow from your stockbroker. The idea is that you will sell the shares fairly soon, and make enough profit to pay the interest on the loan and have something left for yourself. This is a form of speculation which is not common in the UK – here, the same speculative purposes are achieved by buying and selling put or call options, a subject beyond the scope of this book.

MiscExp (Miscellaneous Expense) – This one has just come in handy for recording Tax Credits. You might also want to use it for the charges levied on your PEP account.

A **Reminder** transaction is a note to yourself that will appear in the Transaction Register of your Investment account until you double-click in its Clr (Cleared) field. If you are using Billminder (see Section 4.2), you will be reminded every time you turn your computer on, and you will also see a note in the *Quicken* Reminders window telling you that you have an investment reminder due – although you will not see the reminder itself. If you are reminding yourself of something well in the future, like a National Savings Certificate that will mature in 18 months' time, it would probably be better to stick a note on your Financial Calendar. That way, the actual words of the reminder will show up in the Reminders window when you start the program.

RtrnCap (Return of Capital) – This rather recondite concept will be your choice when a Gilt matures and the Government repays your bond at its "par value". You will also use this one if, in a rights issue, you sell your rights rather than take up the offer. For rights issues, see below. Return of Capital also has a special use in the case of privatisation issues. For that, too, see below.

ScrIssue (Scrip Issues) are happy occasions on which your company issues you with some free shares. Companies sometimes do this when the share price has become very high. The scrip issue has the effect, as you might imagine, of lowering the share price, since there are now more shares about. It is believed that the lower price can encourage investors.

When you choose ScrIssue, you will see the Scrip Issue window. There's a small but useful improvement here in the way things are explained in the instructions.

The Scrip Issue window now asks you to enter the ratio of new shares to old, instead of the number of "old shares" and "new shares". It comes to the

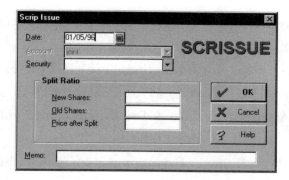

FIGURE 7.8 THE SCRIP ISSUE WINDOW

same thing, in fact, and it sounds complicated, but it isn't. The information you receive from your company will tell you this ratio. It may be an "easy" one, like 2 to 1, or something more complicated like 7 to 5, or worse. Just type in the ratio, and *Quicken* will do the work, figuring out how many shares in the company you now own.

Xin and **Xout** are for transferring money into and out of an Investment account. If you're making your own entries directly in the register, instead of using the Action list, you'll need these to account for where money comes from and goes to when you buy and sell shares.

And what about the "Advanced" menu?

Transfer Shares Between Accounts – This is a new feature in *Quicken 5*. You may never need it, if you start out in the way I suggested above. I certainly could have used it in the days when I was struggling to separate one Investment account into "his", "hers", and "theirs" – the way I should have set them up from the beginning, but didn't.

Corporate Name Change – Another new feature. Use this when your company suddenly writes to tell you that henceforth it's going under a new name – Bowater plc changed its name to REXAM recently, for example.

Corporate Securities Spin-Off is for use in situations such as the one which arose in 1993 when Imperial Chemicals Industries (ICI) gave birth to the Zeneca Corporation. ICI shareholders found that they now owned Zeneca shares as well as ICI shares, and that the "new" ICI shares (understandably) were worth less than "old" ICI shares had been. *Quicken*'s Corp Spinoff window makes it easy to deal with all this.

Corporate Acquisition (Stock for Stock). Once you start reading the financial pages, you'll see that "take-overs" are a matter of constant concern in the world of high finance. If you own a company which is taken over, you may simply be paid cash for your shares – enter that as a "Sell" transaction. But you may be given shares in the other company in exchange for your former shares. That's when you'll use this window.

Finally, **Stock Dividend** is for the rare cases when your company gives you more shares instead of giving you a dividend. This is not a common situation – don't confuse it with shares offered in lieu of a dividend (your choice), which often happens; see above. Don't confuse it, either, with a "Scrip Issue", also discussed above, when the shares you own are effectively split into smaller units.

You won't find any of these "advanced" situations arising often. When they do, you'll be glad that *Quicken* has made such careful provision for them.

There are a vast number of special situations in the world of investment, and more keep coming as clever people think of ways to adapt to new tax laws. As you become familiar with *Quicken* and its facilities, you will not have much trouble figuring out how to classify most of the investment transactions that come your way. There are two special cases, however, which deserve mention here:

Rights Issues – Companies often raise money by offering shareholders the right to buy new shares at less than the current market price.

If you take up a rights issue, enter it as a Buy transaction in the usual way. Then, if you're at the Transaction Register window, click Port (for Portfolio) View. (For more about Portfolio View, see Chapter 8.) Find the share that made the rights issue in the Portfolio list. Move the highlight to it, and click Prices, one of the buttons immediately below the window. You will see a list of dates and share prices – at least, you will if you have been updating the prices of your shares from time to time as described in the following chapter. The rights-issue price at which you just bought your new shares will be at the top of the list. That price is not really part of the price history of your company – you don't want it to appear on your graphs as an unexpected dip in the share value. So move the highlight to it, and click Delete.

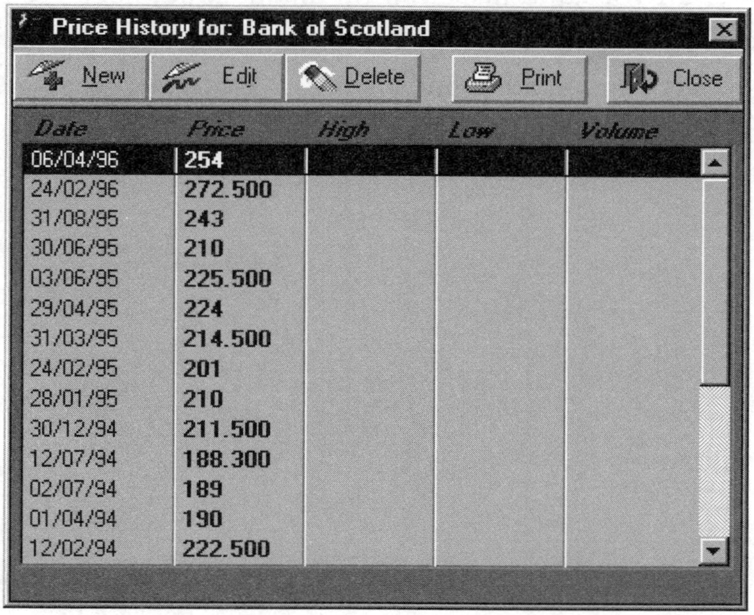

Date	Price	High	Low	Volume
06/04/96	254			
24/02/96	272.500			
31/08/95	243			
30/06/95	210			
03/06/95	225.500			
29/04/95	224			
31/03/95	214.500			
24/02/95	201			
28/01/95	210			
30/12/94	211.500			
12/07/94	188.300			
02/07/94	189			
01/04/94	190			
12/02/94	222.500			

Price History for: Bank of Scotland — New · Edit · Delete · Print · Close

FIGURE 7.9 THE PRICE HISTORY WINDOW

If you sell your rights (or let them lapse and the company sells them for you), enter the cash you receive as a Return of Capital. You now own a slightly smaller fraction of the company than you did before.

Privatisation Issues and other shares sold on the instalment plan – Many people have had their first experience of share-owning in recent years through the highly-publicised Government sell-offs of companies such as British Telecom and the regional electricity boards. Payment for privatisation issues is always made in instalments. The Government has not got very much left to sell off, but if you ever do buy shares by instalments, here's how to account for them in *Quicken*:

- Make the initial purchase in the usual way.
- When it is time to pay the next instalment, transfer the necessary amount of cash into your Shares Investment account as an Xin.
- Enter a RtrnCap transaction for an equal but negative amount. In the Security field, you will of course name the share involved.

This sounds complicated, but it works – *Quicken* has an accurate "cost basis" for your shares.

CHAPTER 8

Monitoring Investment Performance

This is the chapter where investments start to be fun.

You'll learn how to use the Portfolio View window to update share prices and to monitor the performance of your investments. If none of *Quicken*'s preset views suit you, you'll find that you can devise your own. And you'll see how to conjure up reports and graphs to provide an ongoing record of investment events.

8.1 The Portfolio View Window

Now that you have a Shares Investment account up and running, what can you do with it? I think you'll agree that this is an area in which *Quicken* is very good indeed.

From the Activities menu, choose Portfolio View, or click the Port View icon in the iconbar or on the Transaction Register of your Investment account. Alternatively, click Investments from the Homebase screen. The Portfolio View is the engine room of portfolio management.

Let's look at it from the top down.

First of all, there is the **Action** button which produces the menu for investment transactions, exactly as we met it on the account register of your first Investment account. You can make any entry here at the Portfolio View window, if you prefer.

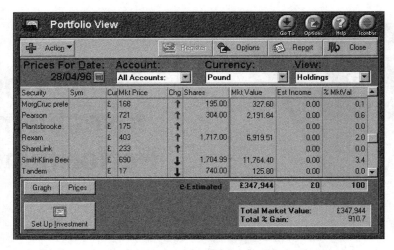

FIGURE 8.1 THE PORTFOLIO VIEW WINDOW

The **Register** button takes you to the account register of the Investment account named in the window on the next line.

The **Options** button lets you make a lot of interesting changes to the Portfolio View window. More about that later.

Select any share in the list and click the next button, **Report**, to see all the action involving that share – purchases, sales, dividends received, and anything more exotic that may have occurred.

The Portfolio View window starts with the assumption that you're here to update your share prices. That explains the starting position of the four fields which come next:

The words "Prices For Date" are followed by today's date. Change the date if you like – perhaps copies of the Financial Times have been piling up while you were on holiday, and you want to type in some old prices. Or you want to remind yourself how things stood this time last year – if you change to a date in the past, *Quicken* will change the price and value information displayed in the window below to correspond.

The next field shows the name of the particular Investment account currently displayed, if you have more than one. You can choose All Accounts for this field, or select some accounts and not others. You will notice at this point a most important characteristic of *Quicken*. Whichever account or accounts you have selected to display in the Portfolio View window, you can have *Quicken* list all the securities you own in any of your accounts (or not, as you prefer). If a share doesn't figure in the account currently displayed, however, the only information about it you will see in the Portfolio View window is the current price. To see not just one account but your total holdings in the Portfolio View window, click on the button beside the Account field and choose All Accounts from the end of the list.

The Currency field comes next, and lets you decide what currency *Quicken* should use to display share prices. If you have different Investment accounts scattered around the world – a happy thought – you may want to see all your shares listed together, or you may want to restrict each list to a particular currency. If you do have them all listed together, shares will be converted into the currency named at the top of the window, giving you a bird's eye view of your total investment wealth. Very useful.

The fourth field is called View. The point here is that there is not just one Portfolio View, but a variety of options. As you choose different Views, *Quicken* will display different columns, giving you different information about your portfolio. The Portfolio View starts off with *Quicken*'s preset "Holdings" view:

In the first column is the **Security** list – all the securities known to *Quicken*, arranged alphabetically according to the type you assigned to each, and again alphabetically within each type. If you would prefer to see only the names of the shares in the account currently displayed, that can be arranged when you customise this window. See Section 8.3 later in this chapter. If the order in which your shares appear seems unsatisfactory, reread Chapter 7 on the subject of types and make any necessary changes. To change the types themselves, choose the Security Types list from the Lists menu and edit any of them you have had second thoughts about. To assign the securities to different types, open the Securities list from the Lists menu and edit any of them.

The next column is headed **Sym**, for Symbol. If you assigned a symbol to any of your securities, in order to import share prices into *Quicken*, it appears here.

The next column, **Cur** for Currency, shows the currency in which each security has been defined.

Next is the **Mkt Price**, the most recent Market Price *Quicken* knows about for each of your shares. If you have chosen "United Kingdom" in the International Options window, the price is expressed in pence, as is normal in this country. If for any reason you want to change that, go back to International Options and clear the checkbox labelled "Share price in 100's of currency unit".

The next column, **Chg** for Change, doesn't come into play until you start typing in new share prices. Then you'll find that it contains, for each share, a little arrow pointing upwards or downwards according to how well that share has behaved since the last time its price was updated.

Next comes **Shares**, showing how many shares of that security there are in the account on display. If you have made several sales and purchases, or taken shares in lieu of dividends, *Quicken* draws it all together here and shows you the total. If you have chosen to view All Accounts, this field shows the total family holdings of each security. If the account named at the top of the Portfolio View window does not hold shares of a particular security, this and the following columns will be empty or contain zero values.

Then, the big one – **Mkt Value** for the Market Value of your holding.

Est Income, in the next column, gives you an Estimated (annual) Income for your holding of each share, as long as you provided an estimated income-per-share when you were setting up the security. Even when there is more than a year's data available, *Quicken* will not work out an Estimated Income for itself. But you can always go back to the Security list and put in a figure for income-per-share. A good time to do it is in the spring when you get your company's annual report.

The final column, **% Mkt Value**, shows you what percentage of the total market value of your portfolio is made up by each holding.

Below, you will see another important figure, the total market value of your holdings, along with the "Total % Gain". It is important to note that the meaning of the figure for percentage gain depends on the information you provided when you set up your Investment account and recorded your portfolio in it. If you provided the full history of each share, the "Total % Gain" shows the percentage by which your total investment has grown. Otherwise, it shows the gain since the date of the valuation you used for the initial ShrsIn transactions. It is also worth noting that even if this figure is completely accurate, you must make a mental adjustment according to the time span covered. A 26% "Total % Gain" over one year is good news; over ten years, rather less so.

8.2 Updating Share Prices

Before we go on to click the buttons below the Portfolio View window, it might be a good idea to update share prices – a delightful activity, especially when the market is rising; and one that you will often want to perform in the early days. If enthusiasm cools later, and you enter new prices less often, it won't worry *Quicken*. Your graphs will still show the time-axis accurately, even though there are fewer points on it. I try to update share prices once a month, at the end of the month.

Updating share prices couldn't be easier. Arm yourself with a newspaper and check that the date at the top of the Portfolio View window is the date of the newspaper. In the View field, click the drop-down button and change Holdings to Price Update. That move is optional – you can update share prices from any view of the portfolio. Using the Price Update view makes things more fun, though.

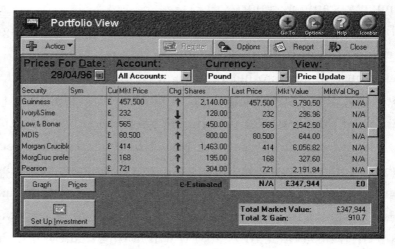

FIGURE 8.2 THE PRICE UPDATE VIEW

In the Price Update view, the columns are:

Security, Sym, Cur, Market Price, Chg, and Shares, as before; and three more:

Last Price – When you start work, Last Price is identical to Mkt Price. You are about to proceed down the column changing the Market Price, and it is often interesting to look back at the Last Price column to see how great was the change.

Mkt Value – As before, but now it is going to change before your eyes as you work.

Mkt Value Change – This column is empty before you start work. As you enter each price, it will show the change, in pounds, to the market value of each holding. I find this column particularly interesting. It is easy to forget the proportional size of different holdings. A 5p change in the price of a major investment is more exciting than the same movement in a share on which we only staked £50. The figures in the Mkt Value Change column make it instantly clear which are the price movements, in either direction, that have seriously affected our wealth.

Now you're ready to start. Move the highlight to the security name at the top of the list, and away you go. There is only one column in the Portfolio View window that you are able to change directly, and that is Mkt Price. Type in the new price, replacing the old one. Move the highlight down to the next share. That's all there is to it – no clicking, no Tab key, no pressing Enter. As the highlight moves down,

- A little arrow appears in the Chg column, pointing up or down, depending on the new price you have just typed in;

- the columns headed Mkt Value and Mkt Value Change now reflect the new situation;

- the figures at the end, Total Market Value and Total % Gain, have also been altered.

Caution

If a price is unchanged, type an asterisk, *, over the old price. The "e" for estimated will disappear and Quicken will understand that the old price is repeated for the new date. I find this feature irritating – there always seem to be a couple of shares that are the same price as last time, and I always forget about the asterisk and try to inform Quicken about the unchanged price by typing it in again, or pressing Return to confirm it. It doesn't work. Eventually I'll learn.

You don't need to do anything else to record the prices, but you might like to choose Print Summary from the File menu on the menu bar when you have finished. Too much paper can be less informative than none at all, but I find it very helpful to print out the Price Update view once a month and keep the results in a ring binder.

You may have decided by now that you want to track the prices of one or more stock market indices, such as the FT-SE-100 Share Index, known familiarly as the "Footsie"; or the All-Share Index. Or perhaps there is a share you are thinking of buying in the future, and you'd like to track its price while you wait for the right moment to pounce.

You can achieve this by simply adding an index or any security you don't own to your Security list, as described in the last chapter. Then click Options at the top of the Portfolio View window, choose the Securities tab, select the index or security in question from the list, and click "Show Always".

On the other hand, you could also set up a separate Shares Investment account. Call it "Watching" or something like that. Start things off with a ShrsIn transaction, just as you did for your real portfolio. For a date, use the date on which you started monitoring the index or share. For Number of Shares, put "1". For Price Per Share put the current price, or the level of the index. Then *Quicken* will be able to calculate the return-on-investment (for which, see below) of the indices and of the shares you don't own, so that you can compare it with the return you are getting on your real portfolio. You will have to remember to exclude this account from Net Worth reports.

8.3 Customising Portfolio View

Switching from the Holdings to the Price Update View has given you a taste of what *Quicken* can accomplish by changing the columns in the Portfolio View window. It's worth looking at the other possibilities. This is a subject that will become much more meaningful and interesting as you build up data on your portfolio over the months and years. Take a little time each week or month, after you have entered the new prices, to take other views from this window and see what you can learn about your investments.

In most of the views, the first six columns remain the same – Security, Symbol, Currency, Market Price, Change, and (number of) Shares. Later, as we explore the Customise options, you can drop some of those permanent columns from view if you want to. When you change to a different view, it is usually only the final three columns which change. Here are the choices:

In the Performance View, the final three columns are headed Amount Invested, Amount Return, and ROI. We're in deep water right away.

Before we tackle the meaning of those column headings, click the Options button at the top of the Portfolio View window. We'll come back to Portfolio View Options soon and explore all the possibilities. For now, click the Miscellaneous tab to see what dates have been set for your return calculations. When you're just starting, the only possible choice is the first one, Entire History. Later on you might be interested in the alternatives: This Year (meaning, this calendar year, 1996 or whatever it may be); Last 365 Days; or From a-date-of-your-selection. I usually have it set to "Last 365 days".

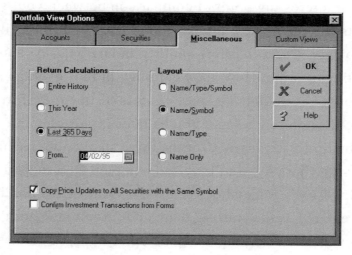

FIGURE 8.3 THE PORTFOLIO VIEW OPTIONS WINDOW, WITH MISCELLANEOUS SELECTED

Now, click OK to go back to the Portfolio View window, with Performance View showing. The Amount Invested column shows you what each holding was worth at the beginning of the time-span you have chosen, plus the cost of any investments you have made since that date. Reinvestments such as shares-in-lieu of dividends, however, are not included in the Amount Invested.

The Amount Return column combines two elements: the amount by which the value of your holding has gone up, or down, since the date you chose for calculating your return; and the amount the holding has yielded during that time in actual income, such as dividends.

ROI, in the final column, means Return on Investment. It is expressed as a percentage. *Quicken* works it out by dividing the Amount Return, in the previous column, by the Amount Invested. So if a holding was worth £200 at the beginning of the current tax year, and is now worth £300, but paid no dividends, the Amount Return would be £100 and the ROI would be 50%. These figures can be seductive and, to an extent, deceptive. A rise in a share price is not quite the same thing as money in the bank. Nevertheless, ROI gives you an interesting point of comparison between your stock-market investments and the money you have kept more cautiously in your bank or building society. *Quicken* offers another and perhaps even more interesting answer to the question, How are we doing? in the "average annual total return", which is calculated as part of an Investment Performance report. See the sections on reports and graphs later in this chapter.

The Valuation View shows, for the three final columns, headings which are by now familiar: Amount Invested, Amount Return, and Market Value. "Amount Invested", remember, means the value of the holding on the date you have selected as the starting date, and "Amount Return" means the amount by which the holding has gone up or down in value since then, plus the dividend return.

Quotes is a new view in *Quicken 5*. It's a bit different from the others. The columns here are called Security, Sym(bol), Cur(rency) – and then, Last Price, Chg (for Change), High, Low, Volume. This is high-flying stuff. By the time you're ready for it, you'll probably also be ready to move your investments on from *Quicken* to a portfolio-management program which will also provide exciting graphs and better help with income tax. Here's what it means:

Last Price and **Change** are familiar, except that now, until you update the price, you will see an "e" for "estimated" in the Change column, as well as the actual change represented by the most recent update.

High, **Low**. The stock market prices you read in your morning newspaper are the *closing* prices, at the end of the previous day's trading. During the day, your share may have gone substantially higher or lower. The difficulty is that this information, easy to come by in America, is not normally published in British newspapers, even the Financial Times.

Volume refers to the number of shares in a particular company which changed hands during a particular day's trading. Some analysts like to watch these figures. An unusually large number of dealings in a share may mean that something is going on. Most newspapers with a serious business page print the previous day's volume figures for a small, selected list of major companies.

If none of the Portfolio Views is quite what you want, two Custom Views are available for you to define – and to keep changing, if you like. You can include any of the column headings that appear in *Quicken*'s own views, or choose from a considerable selection of other possibilities. When you've discovered an arrangement which seems particularly useful, you can give it a name and save it for future use.

To approach this wealth of choice, click the Options button at the top of the Portfolio View, and choose the Custom Views tab. You are already familiar with the Portfolio View Options window, as you used it to set the starting date for *Quicken*'s calculations of your Return on Investment. Before you go on to select the columns for your own Custom Views, pause to consider the other aspects of the Portfolio View window that can be customised to suit your preferences.

Select Accounts – In the Account field at the top of the Portfolio View window, you already know that you can choose any one of your Investment accounts, or "All Accounts". There is another option as well, Selected Accounts. Here in the Portfolio View Options window, you can choose what those selected accounts are to be. From the Portfolio View window itself, you can still pick and choose from all your Investment accounts. This option simply allows you to form a preset group. If you have several PEPs, for example, you might want to define them as the "selected accounts" group.

Securities – Click on the Securities tab in this window to see a list of all the securities known to *Quicken*. Here, you can select any security in the list and mark it to be listed always or hidden always, whichever accounts are on display. There is also a choice available here about foreign currency securities. On that subject, see Section 8.4.

Click the **Miscellaneous** tab to instruct *Quicken* how to calculate your Return on Investment. You are already familiar with that. Here under Miscellaneous you will also find:

Layout – This is where you can include or remove the columns that show the Type and Symbol for each security. There are two checkboxes below:

- "Copy Price Updates to All Securities with the Same Symbol" – This allows for the possibility that you want to have two different lots of the same share in the same account. The manual suggests that you give them slightly different names but the same symbol. If you do that, a tick in this box will ensure that all shares with the same symbol are updated together. I think it would be better, as suggested earlier in this chapter, to put his and her shares in separate Investment accounts.
- "Confirm Investment Transactions from Forms" – A tick means that when you are using one of *Quicken*'s forms to enter an investment

transaction – entering a dividend and Tax Credit would be a common example – the program should ask for confirmation before making the entry in the register.

Still in the Portfolio View Options window, click on the Custom Views tab to set up your own Portfolio Views alongside the ones *Quicken* has already defined for you. In the future, you can recall your views by choosing them in the View box, just as you recall *Quicken*'s preset views.

If you decide to set up a Custom view, click on the buttons beside the three fields representing the three final columns in a Portfolio View. You will see a list of possible column headings. Any one of them can be used in any position. Some of them you have already met, some are new. Whenever "cost" is mentioned in one of the explanations below, remember that *Quicken* can do nothing unless you have provided information about the original cost (or perhaps later price) of your shares. Here are the possibilities:

Mkt Val. – the market value of your holding.

Last Price – the price before the most recent price known to *Quicken*

MktVal Chg – the change in the market value between the last two prices known to *Quicken*.

Est Income – Your estimated income reflects the income-per-share you provided when you identified the security to *Quicken* in the first place.

% Yield – The estimated income per share divided by the current market price per share. The accuracy of this one depends on your keeping *Quicken* informed of changes in the dividend payment. Whenever one of your companies announces a changed dividend, go back to the Securities List, choose the company in question and click Edit. Then type in a new figure for the Estimated Income per Share. Remember that your company announcement covers the net dividend only, not the Tax Credit. While the Tax Credit remains at 20% (as it is in the 1996-7 tax year), divide the dividend by four and add the answer to the dividend to get a figure for the estimated income.

Newspapers commonly list a figure for yield, expressed as a percentage. They are taking Tax Credits into account, so you had better see that *Quicken* can too.

Average Cost – The average cost to you of a share of the security. This would be particularly interesting if you have been accumulating small parcels of shares over the years by taking shares in lieu of dividends. The average which *Quicken* works out, however, is only as good as the cost basis you provided at the start.

Amt. Return – The total return, or profit, on a security. This one takes everything into account, including profits you have made on any shares of the security already sold. It will be of particular interest to active traders.

ROI means Return on Investment. You met this one in the Performance View, above.

Gain/Loss – The market value minus the cost basis. In your early days as an investor, the Gain/Loss column will be virtually identical to the Amount Return column in the preset Performance View. They diverge later on, as reinvestments complicate the picture and you reset the starting date for Return on Investment calculations.

% Gain/Loss – The gain or loss on a security, expressed as a percentage of the original cost: namely, the market value minus the cost basis divided by the cost basis. That sounds a bit complicated. In practice, the information that you are showing a 25% gain or a 10% loss, overall, on a particular holding is easy to understand and of considerable interest.

Amt. Income – Total income received, including reinvested dividends. If you want to use this column, it is probably most useful to set the time-span as "Last 365 Days".

% Income – Total income received from a security, divided by the cost basis. This one leaves out reinvested income, so don't use it if you ever take shares in lieu of dividends. And since it goes back to the cost basis, it is also potentially misleading in the case of a share you have held for many years:

the "% Income" might sound good in cases where recent performance had been poor.

% Market Value – You've met this one in the Holdings View, above.

% Cost – The cost basis of a particular security expressed as a percentage of the cost basis of all securities displayed. Comparison of this figure with the "% Mkt Value" column (which you have already met, as part of *Quicken*'s Holdings view) can show you whether or not a share is pulling its weight. If % Mkt Value is higher than % Cost, your share is outperforming others in the portfolio.

% Invested – The amount invested in a particular security, as a percentage of the amount invested in all securities. As with "% Cost", the interesting thing is to compare this figure with "% Mkt Value".

Inv. (for Investment) Yield – The estimated annual income divided by the amount invested. The estimated annual income depends on the amount you specified when you set up the security. To keep the yield correct, you must update the figure whenever your company changes its dividend payout. Remember, again, *Quicken* defines the "amount invested" according to the starting date you have set for calculating returns.

Amt. Invested – You met this one in the Performance View. It means the amount invested at the starting date you told *Quicken* to use for calculating your Return on Investment, plus any subsequent purchases, but excluding reinvestment of dividends.

Cost basis – The total cost to you of all the shares in a holding. Again, this will be of interest mostly to investors who have accumulated shares over a period of time. If you are in the habit of taking shares in lieu of dividends, it is easy to underestimate how much money you are putting into the holding. This column will make things clear. Note, however, especially in relation to a share you have held for a long time, that *Quicken* makes no allowance for inflation. The cost basis is simply the total amount you have spent in buying a particular set of shares, whether or not that was in "yesterday's money".

8.4 Foreign Currency Investment Accounts

Perhaps one day all our investments will be priced in Euros. For now, we can only be glad that *Quicken* allows us to have Investment accounts in any foreign currency.

The procedure is perfectly straightforward. If you have already set up even one Investment account in pounds sterling, you will find nothing here to cause surprise. Proceed in the usual way (see Chapter 7). Fill out the details as usual, specifying whatever currency you require in the Currency field. There is one possible difficulty here, although a remote one: you cannot specify a currency that is not already on *Quicken*'s currency list. If you don't find the one you want on the drop-down list beside the Currency field in this window, you'll have to click on Lists in the menu bar, choose Currency, and then add your desired currency to *Quicken*'s list.

When you come to add shares to your foreign Investment account, the procedure is precisely the same as for any other shares. There is only one difficulty – prices.

Caution

In this country, share prices are normally expressed in pence, even though the vast majority of UK shares are worth more than £1 and some more than £10. UK investors therefore normally put a tick in the checkbox labelled "Share Price in 100s of Currency Unit". (That checkbox is found by clicking the International button in the Options window – you'll find Options in the drop-down menu under Edit.) But if Quicken expresses UK share prices in "100s of Currency Unit" – that means, in pence – the program will do the same for all other share prices. For a currency like US dollars, that would mean you would have to leave out the decimal point when prices were being typed in. For some other currencies, you would actually have to add two zeros on the end of the price.

There's no easy answer to this problem. As long as you are aware of it, you'll be able to work out the solution that is the best and most convenient for your own circumstances. If you have a substantial number of foreign holdings, you may find it easiest to clear the "Share Price in 100s of Currency Unit" checkbox and put a decimal point in UK prices. If you only have one or two foreign holdings, you'd probably be better off adding the zeros to their prices. Or you could make the appropriate change every time you update prices.

However you get around that one, you will find that *Quicken* will convert foreign currency values into your home currency in all the circumstances when you want to view your holdings together, such as for a Net Worth report.

In the Portfolio View window, you may not want to see your Italian holdings mixed in with your British ones. When you have set up your foreign Investment account, click on Options at the top of the Portfolio View window. Click on the Securities tab, and put a tick in the checkbox labelled "Show Only Securities Matching Portfolio View's Currency". You can keep the checkbox clear if you like, but you will probably only confuse things if you do. To view your foreign account in the Portfolio View window, select it in the Account field and then select its currency in the Currency field. You will then see only the shares belonging to the foreign account. Needless to say, you can have as many different foreign accounts in as many different currencies as you like.

8.5 Investment Reports

Once you get your Investment account going, you will certainly want to look at *Quicken*'s Investment reports. As always, QuickReport is at hand to tell you everything you want to know about a particular security in your portfolio. From the Portfolio View (not the Transaction Register), highlight the share you are interested in and click QuickReport. I have already suggested printing out the Price Update view once a month or so, after you have finished updating prices. Other views, including your customised ones, can be printed whenever you like by choosing the Print option from the File menu.

And there is more. If you choose Investment from the drop-down menu under Reports, there are no fewer than five choices: Portfolio Value, Investment Performance, Capital Gains, Investment Income, and Investment Transactions. Of those, I find Investment Performance of the greatest value. I would recommend returning to it regularly.

Portfolio Value – This report is similar to a Portfolio View, but of course allows you to subtotal the results in various interesting ways. See Section 5.1 for a discussion of what it is possible to do in a *Quicken* report. The column headings in a Portfolio Value report are Security, Shares (meaning, number of shares held), Current Price, Cost Basis, Gain/Loss, and Balance (meaning market value of the holding). The Gain/Loss column expresses a simple monetary gain or loss by comparing the current value of the holding to the cost basis. The longer you have held a share, the less you should be impressed by large "paper" gains. If you have any foreign holdings, you can set the currency for this report either to your home currency or to the foreign currency.

Investment Performance is a corker. It shows the average total return over a specified time period, taking both dividends and changes in the market value into account. It gives best value, I think, if set to show the performance over the past year. This way of looking at investments is probably more common in the US than in Britain. The European tendency has been to keep capital and income in watertight mental compartments. Neither approach is "right" or "wrong". *Quicken*'s Investment Performance report is an extremely interesting way to view your investments, but it's not the only way. If you held shares in 1987, the year of the "crash", your Investment Performance report would almost certainly have shown a negative return. And yet you are quite likely to have enjoyed a steady or a rising income from your investments over that year.

Capital Gains – this one is not for use in the UK, where capital gains are calculated rather differently from the U.S. and also from Australia. In fact, since each investor is allowed a generous threshold of capital gains in each tax year before any tax at all is payable, you may never have to worry about the tax.

Investment Income – This report summarises your investment income and expenses by category. Tax Credits are summarised as an expense here, and subtracted from the total – appropriately enough, since they represent money you haven't got. The "bottom line" of this report, therefore, shows the income you have actually received, rather like the bottom line of a pay slip after all the deductions have been made.

Investment Transactions – This one lists investment transactions. It can be subtotalled in various ways, by time periods, by security, or by accounts, for example. This report is the one you are going to have to use to produce the dividend and Tax Credit list for your income tax return. It's not ideal for the purpose. See Section 9.3.

8.6 Investment Graphs

If you have been imagining yourself in shirtsleeves shouting down the telephone to your broker with a *Quicken* Investment graph on the screen in front of you, you might be slightly disappointed when you see what is actually on offer. The Investment graphs in *Quicken 4* and *Quicken 5* are a considerable advance on those in *Quicken 3*, but still not as interesting as those in *Quicken* for DOS, because graphs for different shares cannot be viewed together. Portfolio management software takes this a good deal further than *Quicken* has attempted.

While Portfolio View is displayed, you can select any security and click on the Graphs icon below the list of shares to see a graph of the Price and Value History of the share. When you first view the graph, you will see a line representing changes in the price of the share over time. You can change the starting and ending dates in fields available near the top of the window. For a share or index that you are monitoring but do not own, this is the only graph available. But for one in which you actually hold shares, you should put a tick in the checkbox labelled "Show Mkt. Value" and wait while *Quicken* redraws the graph. The value graph, in almost every case, will show much more movement and give you a more accurate idea of how your share is performing. (The reason for this is a technical one: *Quicken* plots the changes in actual share price; most portfolio programs plot the percentage change, which is much more revealing.)

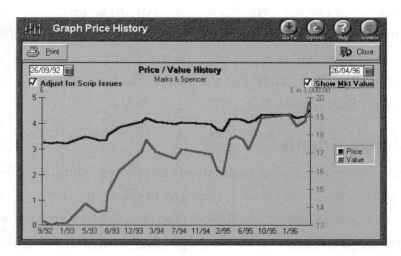

FIGURE 8.4 *QUICKEN*'S GRAPH OF A SHARE'S PRICE AND VALUE HISTORY

For graphs involving your whole portfolio, or selected parts of it, choose Graphs, and then Investment Graphs, from the drop-down Reports menu.

There are two graphs on offer by this route, normally viewed together: the top one, Monthly Portfolio Value, is a stacked bar graph, in which the heights of the bars and the size of their different segments are both significant. The lower one is called Average Annual Total Return. Despite the word "annual", it covers the same time-span you select for the upper graph.

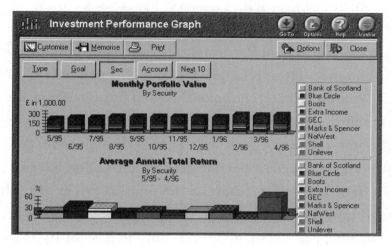

FIGURE 8.5 INVESTMENT PERFORMANCE GRAPH FROM THE REPORTS MENU

In the upper graph, Monthly Portfolio Value, you will see one bar for each month of the time-span you choose. *Quicken* recommends, as with other graphs, that you set a time-span of not longer than a year. The height of the bar represents the value of your portfolio, and the segments originally represent individual securities, but you can change that by clicking on Types, Goals, or (if you have several Investment accounts) Accounts at the top of the window. It is pleasant to see the bars becoming gradually higher, and interesting to see the size of the segments change as one security (or type, or goal, or account) does better and another worse.

The lower graph focuses more sharply on that question of relative performance. The bars here represent the average annual total return – a concept we met in the Investment Performance report. When you first see this graph it is arranged by security, and thus shows with startling clarity which of your shares have been pulling their weight lately, and which haven't. This graph, too, can be changed with a single click to show the return by Type, or Goal, or Account. Notice the line extending across the lower graph to represent "Total IRR" – the total Internal Rate of Return on the entire portfolio. It provides a useful benchmark for all the others – do their bars reach and extend beyond this line, or not?

As with the Investment Performance report, this graph is interesting, but needs caution in its interpretation. Especially if you have held shares for a long time, you should neither be too excited nor too depressed by what you see in a graph showing performance over the last year only. Go back to Portfolio View and take a look with a longer perspective. And never forget that a "paper gain" doesn't pay the grocery bills. You haven't really made that profit until you sell the share. Stock-market prices can fall so suddenly that a small investor may not have time to get out and save profits. It doesn't often happen, thank goodness, but the possibility should never be entirely forgotten.

8.7 Importing Share Price Data

It is not possible, in the UK version of *Quicken*, to import share prices automatically. This section, therefore, is only for those who enjoy messing about with computers the way some people like to mess about with cars.

Although it can't be done automatically, *Quicken* can read an external data file of share prices in ASCII form. The formatting essentials are clearly set out in the manual: only one symbol and one share price per line. There can also be a date, in the form DD/MM/YY. If your data has inverted commas around the separate data items, you can use either commas or double spaces as delimiters, but not both in the same line. If you do not have inverted commas, you must use double spaces as the delimiter.

Where to get the share data? It is not as easy to come by in the UK as in the US, because the London Stock Exchange owns and jealously protects the copyright to its share prices. If you have a modem, you can go on-line with British Telecom's CitiService. That is an excellent option, but a seriously expensive one. There are also small firms which offer subscriptions to daily share price data very much more cheaply. Look for advertisements in publications like the Investors' Chronicle. Shop around, comparing both prices and the data "packages" on offer. Explain *Quicken*'s formatting requirements and insist on a guarantee that the data you receive will be in an acceptable format. There should, in fact, be no difficulty about that. Your data supplier will give you a list of share symbols that you can enter in *Quicken*. If you're on-line to the Internet, there are subscription services available there at very reasonable rates.

Alternatively, you could consider installing a Teletext card in your computer. The software provided with the card will allow you to download share prices from Ceefax and Oracle in ASCII format. The names of the shares will be in the format used by Ceefax and Oracle. You will have to replace them with symbols yourself before importing the file into *Quicken*.

Most modern word-processors nowadays have a facility for recording macros. You could do the necessary conversion this way:

- Load your Teletext data file into your word-processor.
- Turn macro recording on.
- Go down the list, replacing each share name with an appropriate three-letter symbol.
- Turn macro recording off.

In future, you can use the macro to do the job, as long as your share list remains the same. Then save the file in ASCII format.

To import share data into *Quicken*, however you have acquired it, open Portfolio View and change the date in its window, if necessary, to the appropriate date for your data. Then choose Import Prices from the File menu and enter the name and full pathname of the DOS file containing your share data.

CHAPTER 9

Hard Graft

This chapter is about things that are no fun to do in any system, but essential to financial health: namely writing cheques, balancing bank and credit card statements, and preparing tax returns. *Quicken* has done a lot to make the whole thing as painless as possible (like modern dentistry). But you've still got to face up to it.

9.1 Writing Cheques

In the United States, home-accounting programs that can print out your cheques on a computer printer have been part of the scene for a number of years. *Quicken* was the first program to bring this feature to Britain.

When I first met *Quicken* in 1992, I didn't expect that cheque-printing would be of much interest to ordinary users over here. Americans on average write more cheques than we do – gas, telephone, and electricity bills are paid monthly; Standing Orders and Direct Debits are virtually unknown; Americans are much more prone to run multiple credit cards. Add to all that the fact that the necessary stationery for printing cheques is relatively expensive and that, depending on what sort of printer you have, you may need to fiddle around replacing your normal paper with the cheque forms. I thought only business users would be interested. I was wrong. Computerised cheque-writing is popular, and growing more so. *Quicken* certainly comes as close as any system could to making it pleasant to part with your money.

If you're interested in having *Quicken* write your cheques, you will need to order stationery from Intuit. It is not yet possible just to tear a cheque out of your chequebook and feed it through your printer. Some sample cheques and an order form were included with your package when you bought the program. Intuit guarantees that the cheques will print on your printer, and that your bank, and everyone else, will accept them. You can have a company logo printed on your cheques if you like.

The physical process of getting the cheque forms to work with your printer is carefully and lucidly described in the *Quicken* manual. *Quicken* includes some elegant ways to help you line up the cheques with absolute precision. Intuit will help by telephone if you get stuck.

You don't need to wait to write a cheque in *Quicken* until the day you want to send it off. In fact, one of the chief merits of the system is that it allows you to deal with the chore of cheque-writing and the business of forward-planning in one go. Write cheques when the bills arrive. Let *Quicken* remind you when they're due – on that subject, see Section 4.2. When you're good and ready, tell *Quicken* to print some cheques. You can even have the payee's address printed on the cheque and send them off in Intuit's special window envelopes if you choose.

To write cheques in *Quicken*, choose Write Cheques from the Activities drop-down menu or the HomeBase window. If you decide to go in for computerised cheque-writing, you'll probably want to add a write-cheques icon to your iconbar. On that, see Section 4.1.

The Write Cheques window offers you a realistic if slightly American-looking cheque to fill in. Look at the title bar: has *Quicken* chosen the right account for you? The program picks the Bank account you were using most recently, but if that's not right, use the selection bar at the bottom of the

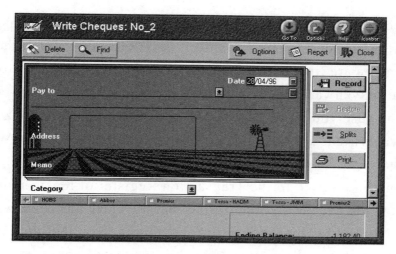

FIGURE 9.1 THE WRITE CHEQUES WINDOW (WITH ARTWORK)

window to select another. Then all you do is write the cheque, exactly as you would make an entry in the Transaction Register. As in the register, *Quicken* starts you off by filling in today's date. In many cases, you will want to change that to a date in the future which is the last moment, according to your careful calculations, for the dispatch of that particular cheque. Whatever date you put now, *Quicken* can be instructed, if you choose, to change automatically to the current date when you print the cheque.

As you fill in the payee, QuickFill will finish the job for you as usual if it has ever seen that name before. When you have put the amount in figures and moved away from the space by pressing the Tab key, *Quicken* writes the amount out in words: you'll never have to do that again. If you're planning to use Intuit's window envelopes, you will now want to fill in the complete address of the payee. QuickFill will memorise it for future dealings with this payee.

Note

There is room for a memo – but notice that it will print on the cheque, so don't put anything too embarrassing.

You can, and should, assign the cheque to a category just as you would any other transaction. You can split it between categories in the usual way.

When you are finished, click Record. The cheque you have just written will rise heavenwards in a most satisfactory fashion, revealing another blank cheque in case you want to pay another bill. For a second look at cheques you have written, use the vertical scroll bar at the side of the Write Cheques window.

When you go back to the Transaction Register of the account on which you wrote the cheques, you will find that the entry has been made for you. In the Chq No field is the word "Print", reminding you that the cheque, although written, still exists only in the memory of your computer. If you summon up the Financial Calendar, you will see that your cheques have been entered on that, too.

When the day comes when you can no longer postpone the actual printing, signing and posting of your cheques, choose Printer Setup from the File menu, and then choose Cheque Printer Setup. Here you can choose which printer to use, if more than one is installed. Click the Font to change the style of writing for the body of your cheques, or for your company name and address. Switch on your printer, line up the Intuit cheques according to the instructions in the manual, open the account the cheques are drawn on, and choose Print Cheques from the File drop-down menu, or from the Write Cheques window if that's where you happen to be.

The Select Cheques to Print window tells you how many cheques there are waiting in the wings, and how much they add up to altogether. First of all, look at the number on the cheque that will be the first through your printer. If necessary, change the number shown in the Select Cheques to Print window to the number of that cheque.

Next, decide what you're going to do. There are three choices: you could print all outstanding cheques; you could print all cheques up to a certain date – *Quicken* suggests today's date, but you can change that; or you can select individually which cheques to print. If you choose that third option, you will see all the cheques on the waiting list. You can scroll through the list clicking Mark for the ones you want to print today. Then click OK, and finally click Print from the Select Cheques to Print window.

When you next go back to the Transaction Register, you will see that the word "Print" in the Chq No field has been replaced with the actual cheque number.

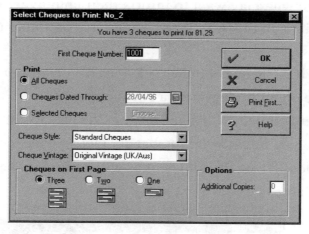

FIGURE 9.2 THE SELECT CHEQUES TO PRINT WINDOW

What happens, you may wonder, if you need to write a cheque by hand away from home? No problem. You can either use an ordinary cheque as supplied by your bank, or use one of your computer cheques from Intuit. If you use an ordinary one, the sequence of numbers will be different from the sequence on your printed cheques – but that won't worry either *Quicken* or your bank.

You have already used the Options window to change the way QuickFill works and to customise the iconbar. You won't be surprised to learn that you can set your own preferences for the way cheques are written. Click

Options in the Write Cheques window, or click on Cheques in the Options window. First, you can choose a style of date to be printed on your cheques. Next there are four checkboxes to be ticked or cleared.

- "Print Categories on Voucher Cheques" – If you have split a cheque among several budget categories and if you are using cheques with perforated vouchers attached, a tick in this one means that the names of the budget categories and the amounts assigned to each will print on the voucher. This choice is chiefly of interest to business users of *Quicken* who may want to inform their employees about payroll deductions in this way. See Chapter 10, on Using *Quicken* in Your Business.

- "Warn if a Cheque Number is Re-used" – *Quicken* will warn you if you are about to duplicate a cheque number.

- The third choice, "Change Date of Cheques to Date When Printed", is the one you might want to change. *Quicken* has not ticked that checkbox. If you do, all cheques will be printed bearing the current day's date.

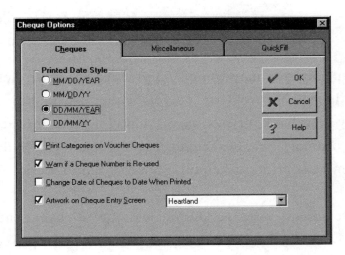

FIGURE 9.3 THE CHEQUE OPTIONS WINDOW

- "Artwork on Cheque Entry Screen" – The last one is just for fun. If you like, put a tick here and select something from the drop-down list. Your on-screen cheques – but not your printed ones – will be wonderfully transformed.

As well as saving a certain amount of time and trouble, writing cheques in *Quicken* offers a very convenient way to plan future cashflow. If you make a practice, as suggested, of writing your *Quicken* cheques as soon as your bills come in and dating the cheque as far in the future as you dare, your Financial Calendar and Forecasting Graph will show you what is happening to your cash. Business users, in fact, can "write cheques" as a simple and efficient method of tracking Accounts Payable.

9.2 Balancing Your Bank Statement

Balancing bank statements is one of the chores in life that we sometimes find it easier not to think about. I lived like that, for years. One horrified glance to see how low the level had sunk, and trust the bank for the rest. It is not a good idea. Banks make mistakes, and so do you and I. The only way to catch them is to face up to a reconciliation once a month, or however often a statement arrives. These days, reconciling an account is probably an even more important activity than it used to be. Most of the high street banks have cut back on staff in the last few years. My impression is that the overworked survivors are making more mistakes than they used to. We read in the newspapers about "phantom withdrawals" from cash machines. Are there any on your statement? Were your Standing Orders and Direct Debits paid at the right time to the right people for the right amount? Does Switch really work? There is a lot that can go wrong.

Nor is it only banks and you and I who make mistakes. Occasionally you will get a dunning letter from a creditor referring to a bill that has already been paid. If you can check back in your *Quicken* records and see that the amount has been duly entered in the register and marked as cleared, you know for sure that the debt has been paid. It won't happen often, but when it does, that little mark in the Cleared column can spare you uncertainty and anxiety. Save your bank statements, too: they don't take up much space. *Quicken* can reassure you that your creditor was paid, but in extreme cases, it may take the bank to persuade the creditor.

Your first reconciliation is going to be the worst. Later on it gets to be almost fun.

For the first as for all subsequent reconciliations, start by gathering the current bank statement, the previous bank statement, and your cheque book before you sit down at the computer. Open the account that is about to be reconciled, and then click the Reconcile icon on the iconbar, or choose Reconcile from the Activities window.

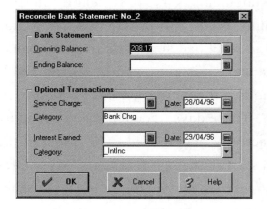

FIGURE 9.4 THE FIRST RECONCILE BANK STATEMENT WINDOW

The process begins with the first Reconcile Bank Statement window. The first field here is the Bank Statement Opening Balance. The amount shown should be identical to the amount called "Balance Brought Forward" at the top of your bank statement, which in turn should equal the final figure in the Balance column of your previous bank statement. If this is your first reconciliation, it will also be the amount that you entered as the opening balance when you set the account up in *Quicken*. Make sure it's right before you go any further. Change it, if it's not.

Next comes Bank Statement Ending Balance. Enter the last amount in the Balance column on the bank statement – the one you always took a quick look at even in the bad old days, to see how much money you had left. Be careful to enter this amount correctly. Tracking down mistakes when you are trying to balance a bank statement can be incredibly difficult. Be sure you don't make it harder for yourself by getting this important item wrong at the start.

Then there is provision for you to enter any charges that have been deducted from your account, or interest you have earned. Dates and categories can be assigned. *Quicken* will remember the categories you used for the first reconciliation (such as Bank Charge and Int Inc). Next time, you will find that they have been entered automatically. When all that is out of the way, click OK.

You will then move on to the second Reconcile Bank Statement window. Take a look at the window itself before you start work.

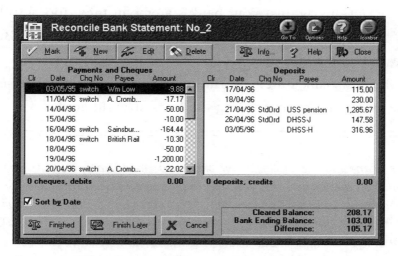

FIGURE 9.5 THE SECOND RECONCILE BANK STATEMENT WINDOW

On the left, you see a list of Payments and Cheques. They appear in date order, just as they do in the Transaction Register and on your bank statement. The transactions won't be in exactly the same order on the bank statement, because some of your creditors carry cheques around in their pockets for a while before depositing them, while other transactions go through like greased lightning. But it will be pretty close. If you would rather separate out the actual cheques and have them arranged by cheque number, clear the checkbox at the bottom of the window marked Sort by Date. Your decision here will probably depend on how many electronic transactions you have. Cheques make up only about a third of my bank statements these days, and I much prefer to have the transactions sorted by date.

On the right of the window appears the list – almost certainly shorter, alas! – of the money you have received during the month.

If you entered any bank charges or interest earned in the previous window, you will see that they have already been entered in the appropriate list. They are highlighted and are marked with a substantial tick. As you check other transactions against your bank statement, they, too, will look like that.

You're ready to start. The other buttons on the Reconcile Bank Account window will come into play soon.

Lay the new bank statement flat on your desk and consider using a ruler to make sure that you're reading the lines straight across.

Tip

Take the transactions in the order they appear in the bank statement, not the order Quicken shows you. As you find each one on the screen, simply click it, or use the cursor keys to move the highlight to it and then press Return. Before you go on, tick it off on the bank statement, too. Be very careful not to unmark anything on the screen with an injudicious click. The emphatic way that Quicken distinguishes between marked and unmarked entries is a great help in this respect.

If you find something on the bank statement that does not appear in your records, click Edit to go to the Transaction Register. Click Insert to add an entry, or go to the end of the register and add it there. Click Record before returning to the Reconcile window. Never neglect the possibility that the bank is wrong, not you. If you find a transaction that you believe shouldn't be there, add it to the register anyway, because the bank has certainly added it to your account. Put a circle around it on the bank statement. If you win your subsequent argument with the bank, you can then create a balancing entry in your Transaction Register, just as the bank will have to do in its records.

The first time you reconcile a bank statement in *Quicken*, you are almost certain to have some transactions to add, representing cheques which you wrote before you started using the program but which hadn't cleared your bank at the time of the preceding statement. Add them to your Transaction Register as just described.

You are also likely to find entries that need to be altered. Again, consider the possibility that the mistake was made by somebody else, not you. One of *Quicken*'s first triumphs for me was the day a reconciliation revealed that my bank had paid out £78 on a cheque I had written for £48. I paused very briefly to look at the cheque stub on my way from the computer to the telephone – that's why it can be handy to have the chequebook present.

Most of the time, unfortunately, the mistake will be yours, a digit wrongly entered, perhaps. Move the highlight to that entry and click Edit to go directly to the entry in the register. Make the necessary changes and click Record, then go back to your reconciling.

When you have worked your way to the end of the bank statement, take a look at the lower right-hand corner of the Reconcile Bank Account window. You will see three, or possibly four, crucial figures.

Cleared Balance – This is the balance in your *Quicken* account taking into account all the transactions you have marked as cleared and omitting all the others.

Bank Ending Balance – This is the balance you typed in when you embarked on the reconciliation process, the ending balance of your most recent bank statement.

Difference – This figure should be £0.00. If the Difference is not zero, the question is, why not? This is where the fun starts.

The fourth possible figure is **Opening Balance Difference**. It will appear above Cleared Balance if it is there at all, and it refers to any change you may have made in the Bank Statement Opening Balance figure at the very beginning of the reconciliation process. More about that in a moment.

You may decide that the Difference is so small that you do not want to be bothered with it. Just click Done, in that case. *Quicken* will offer to create an adjustment transaction. Accept the suggestion, and your job is finished.

You may prefer to stick with the task and see it through. Or the figure for the Difference may be too large to be ignored.

To check the information you provided at the beginning, about opening and closing balances, click the Info button at the bottom of the window.

Quicken keeps you informed of the totals of the debits and of the credits that you have marked in your reconciliation session. Your bank statement may give you the equivalent information in the form of "Total Withdrawals" and "Total Pay-ins". The totals on the screen when you finish reconciling should be equal to the bank's totals. If your bank statements run to more than one page, you will have to add together the figures for Withdrawals and Pay-ins at the bottom of each page to see whether they equal the ones in *Quicken*. A comparison of this sort will tell you whether the mistake lies in a deposit or a pay-in or, in the worst case, both.

Quicken will also tell you how many withdrawals (debits) and how many pay-ins (credits) have been marked as cleared. The bank statement is unlikely to provide that information directly, but you can count the items. Bear in mind, however, that you may have paid several cheques into your account on one pay-in slip. That will probably appear as one transaction on your bank statement, although you will have listed each cheque separately in *Quicken*.

If the Difference figure remains intractably large, you may have to go back through the bank statement. Check again that you entered the opening balance and ending balance correctly, exactly as they appear on your bank statement. This time, examine the amount of each transaction with even more care than before. Look out for transposed digits.

My own experience is that the one-off payments to interesting payees are easy. The most frequent source of trouble lies with payees who appear frequently (the supermarket, the garage, British Rail), and especially when they are paid by Switch rather than by cheque. Switch payments appear on the bank statement as the name of the payee and the amount – creating a temptation to look no further than the name of the payee before triumphantly ticking them off. Cheque payments, which are listed by cheque number and amount, demand and receive more scrutiny.

So if there are several payments to the same payee to choose from, be sure that the one you mark off in *Quicken* corresponds to the one you tick on the bank statement. Cash dispenser withdrawals are especially tricky. There are likely to be quite a few of them on your statement. Carefully check the date of each against the date in your *Quicken* accounts before marking it as cleared. When you make a cash machine withdrawal at the weekend, your account will be debited on the next working day, but the bank statement should also show the exact date and time of the withdrawal. Are you sure you recorded all of your cash withdrawals? It is easy, when life gets frantic, to forget to tell *Quicken* about one, and then to mark the wrong one during reconciliation.

Eventually you will either succeed in sorting out the difficulties or you will give up. If you do surrender, you can always go back and put things right if you later figure out what was wrong. It is also possible to knock off for a while and later return refreshed to the fray – click Finish Later at the bottom of the Reconcile window, and *Quicken* will save the work you have done so far. Or you can wipe the slate clean and start again – I have done that, with success, when all else had failed. Click Cancel and choose Don't Save. If you're that desperate, consider changing the status of the "Sort by Date" checkbox. Clear it, to see all your cheques listed together after the electronic transactions. Tick it, to have the cheques distributed among the other transactions by date. A change of view, in whichever direction, might be just what you need.

When you decide that you are going to reconcile no more, click Done at the bottom of the window. If there is still a discrepancy, let *Quicken* enter an adjustment transaction in the register. *Quicken* will offer to print a Reconciliation report, a useful summary of cleared and uncleared debits and credits. This can be especially useful in your early weeks as a *Quicken* user, when reconciling a bank statement may still be a novel experience for you. And note that "print" can mean "print to the screen", if you choose. You can also go back later and ask for the Reconciliation Report. It's listed with the other options in the drop-down menu under Reports.

What about the Opening Balance Difference, if there was one? This problem arises when the figure *Quicken* shows for the opening balance is not the figure that appeared as the closing balance on your previous bank statement – although when things are going smoothly, it will be. *Quicken*'s opening balance is the balance of all reconciled transactions in the account. So if, for any reason, you delete a reconciled transaction, or click in the

Cleared column of a transaction yourself to mark a transaction with an "R" for "Reconciled", instead of letting *Quicken* do it as part of the reconciliation process, you will affect the opening balance. Problems can also arise (although they shouldn't) if in a burst of enthusiasm you go back and enter transactions from old bank statements in order to get *Quicken*'s reports and graphs up and running faster.

Quicken will offer to create a balancing transaction to cover this discrepancy, too, just as it did if the Difference figure was not zero at the end of the reconciliation process. If this problem arises the first time you reconcile the account, Intuit suggest that you go ahead and let the program enter the balancing transaction. It is almost inevitable that a balancing transaction, quite likely a substantial one, will be needed in each account at the very beginning of record-keeping. In a Cash account, it takes the form of an initial "dump" of money which was simply not there when you counted. After that, though, it is much better to roll up your sleeves when things don't add up, and figure out what went wrong.

Think how proud you will be the day you get a bank statement and reconcile it first go, with no changes necessary to the Transaction Register because your account-keeping was perfect. It doesn't happen often, but it's a great feeling when it does.

Reconciling a credit card statement is essentially the same – usually easier because there are fewer transactions. If there are gaps in your records because you didn't enter every transaction as life unfolded, and if you are satisfied that the credit card company has got it right, you can let *Quicken* enter all the missing transactions in a lump by creating a balance adjustment at the end. That doesn't let you assign transactions to their individual categories, however – for that, you should copy them in one by one from your statement.

FIGURE 9.6 THE MAKE CREDIT CARD PAYMENT WINDOW

When you finish a credit card reconciliation, *Quicken* will ask you on the credit card company's behalf whether you want to pay some or all of the bill. In the Make Credit Card Payment window, you select the account from which the payment is to be made, and decide whether *Quicken* is to write the cheque for you. You can reject that option and click the box for handwritten cheques. When you have made the choice, *Quicken* writes the cheque or makes the entry in the appropriate Transaction Register and, a thoughtful touch, takes you directly to the cheque or entry with the insertion point poised on the date. If you're writing the cheque by hand, you can change the date in the Transaction Register to the one on which you intend to pay. If *Quicken* has written the cheque, you can date it when you print it. In either case you can take the opportunity to reduce the amount and pay only part of the bill.

You may have other accounts such as Deposit accounts and Building Society accounts that are so rarely used that you don't think it worthwhile to toil through the reconciliation process. With only one or two transactions a month, you can see at a glance that everything is all right.

The trouble with that approach is that months soon add up into years, one or two transactions a month into a long, grey list. If there are only a couple of transactions each month, reconciliation will only take you a moment or two. And then if anything ever does go wrong, you will be able to pinpoint the difficulty quickly because your reconciliations will show you the latest point at which everything was known to be all right.

9.3 Preparing a Tax Return

Quicken will be of considerable help when you are preparing your income tax return.

First of all, having your accounts in order will make an almost unbelievable difference to the anguish of this annual chore. But *Quicken*'s help is more specific:

See Section 2.1 for details of how to set up your income and expense categories to take full advantage of *Quicken*'s tax facilities. Briefly, the procedure is:

- Choose Options from the Edit drop-down menu, and in the Options window click on International. Make sure there is a tick in the checkbox labelled "Use Tax Return with Categories".

- Look down the Category and Transfer list and pick out the income and expense categories that need to be reported on your tax return. Look to see if the word "Tax" appears after the name of that category. If not, select it and click on Edit. Put a tick in the box labelled Tax-related.

- Select each tax-related category one-by-one, click on Edit, and make sure that you have selected a "Line" in the field at the bottom of the window. That field relates the category to particular sections of the income tax form. Your building society interest, for example, goes down as "Income from other UK banks, building societies and deposit takers".

You can take these steps at any time. Once everything is in order, call for a Tax Return report, which is one of the choices in the Create Report window. Remember that the dates for the report have to be reset to the UK income tax year, April 6 to April 5. You will see all the transactions in all the categories that have been assigned to a tax return "line", grouped and subtotalled by "line". (In some cases, different categories contribute to the same "line".) All you have to do is copy the totals from the *Quicken* Tax Return report to the proper box on the tax return form.

A Tax Summary report, on the other hand, shows you the transactions and totals for all the categories that you have marked as tax-related, whether or not you have assigned them to "lines". In this case, the transactions are subtotalled by category.

This works well with some sorts of income. It is particularly useful for National Insurance pensions and benefits which are paid by the week and which do not provide an annual statement of the total you received.

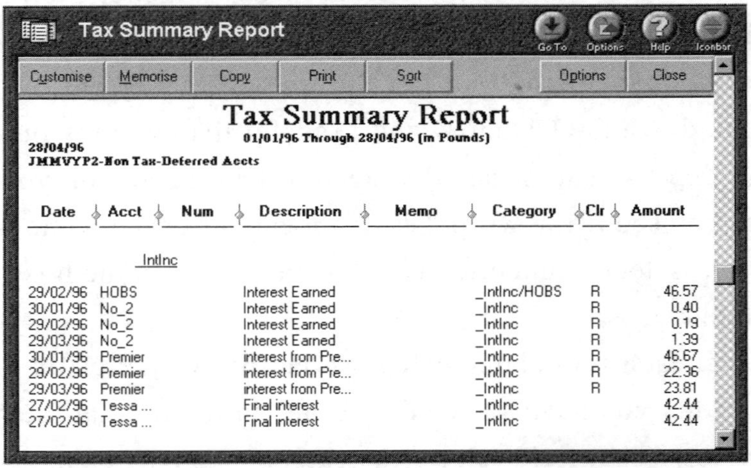

FIGURE 9.7 PART OF A TAX SUMMARY REPORT

With other forms of income, there can be problems, some of them considerable.

- Husband and wife are taxed separately. If you have any joint bank accounts, building society accounts, or shareholdings, each of you is liable for only half the tax. If you have separately-named bank accounts, each is liable for the tax on all interest received in his or her own name. Therefore you must set your *Quicken* accounts up carefully under the name or names of the account-holders, and remember to enter only half the interest, dividend, Tax Credit, etc., on the tax return in cases where the account or asset is jointly held.

- People on low income, including married women regardless of how much their husbands earn, can claim back some or all of the tax that has been deducted from their bank and building society accounts, and of the Tax Credits that have been added to their dividends. The form they use to do this requires income to be set out rather differently from the longer, standard income tax form, so if you set up *Quicken* properly for one it won't be quite right for the other.

- *Quicken* does not make automatic provision for tax deducted from bank and building society interest. However, your bank or building society will provide you with a statement at the end of the tax year showing how much interest you earned in all, and how much tax was deducted. On the tax form, you will be asked to fill in the net interest amount, the amount of tax deducted, and the gross amount, which is simply the first two amounts added together. Your *Quicken* records probably contain only the net interest figure, the amount you actually received. Use the bank or building society statement to fill in the other figures.

My own feeling is that the best course is a careful combination of *Quicken*'s Tax Return report and your accumulated documents. It is probably easiest, for example, to rely on the P60 form which your employer will supply for the details of "earnings in employment" required on the tax return; and on the statement from your bank or building society, as just described, for interest earned and the tax deducted from it. Mortgage companies provide annual statements of a borrower's position.

You will need each of these documents to back up your tax return if any questions arise. My feeling is that you might as well use them to provide the figures in the first place – double-check, of course, with your *Quicken* records.

If you have dividend income, you will need to submit not just totals but a list of the dividends you have received, and the associated Tax Credit for each. If you only have a few shares, it might be easiest to copy the figures from the vouchers your company sent you when you received your dividend payment. But for shares in even as few as half a dozen companies or unit trusts, that process soon becomes tiresome. And *Quicken* doesn't offer a dividend-and-Tax-Credit report yet.

There are two possibilities here:

- Use *Quicken*'s Investment Transaction report. Set the dates to the income tax year in question, and click Customise. Under Report Layout, choose to have your report subtotalled by security. Under the mysterious heading Show Rows, exclude all transfers. The resulting report is eccentric from a Tax Inspector's point of view, because it shows Tax Credits as a Miscellaneous Expense, whereas for income tax purposes, they're income. But all the necessary information is there. You could copy the report into your word-processor and tidy it up a bit, including the elimination of a lot of white space. The easy process of copying a report to a word-processor is described in Section 5.1.

- Alternatively, you could create an Investment Transaction report, subtotalled by security again but limited to the category _DivInc. Copy the report to a spreadsheet, as above, and add a column for Tax Credits yourself, remembering that with Tax Credits at 20% as at present (1996-7), each Tax Credit will be 25%, or one quarter, of the associated dividend. This is the way I do it; it works pretty well.

There are other parts of the tax form, however, where *Quicken* comes into its own. I find it most useful for keeping track of the expenses that can be set against income and earnings. This is a difficult subject, and one on which you may want to consult an accountant. Broadly speaking, your Tax Inspector will be much more generous in allowing you to set necessary expenses against self-employed and freelance earnings and rental income than against earnings in employment, but even for the employed there are some allowances.

You can either set up appropriate categories for these expenses, or lump them in with the income category itself. I use both of these systems. My husband is able to set the (considerable) expense of the books he buys against his earnings from scholarly writing. We have a separate expense category for books. On the tax return, only the total needs to be entered. But I know that *Quicken* is waiting with a complete, itemised list of the year's book purchases if it is required. Before the days of *Quicken*, I used to have to add up all the receipts by hand.

On the other hand, we have a small amount of rental income from three fields upon which some sheep reside. In that case any expenses by way of fence-mending and the like are just put straight into the income category. *Quicken* understands that when an item of expenditure goes into an income category, it is to be subtracted from the total. A QuickReport on the category provides all I need to know for that part of the tax return. If it were more complicated, I could keep income and expense in separate categories and, indeed, use *Quicken*'s system to group them together as one line of the tax return.

If you go in for charitable covenants, keep them all together in one expense category. You can print out the list of them you will need for your tax return by highlighting the category in the Category & Transfer list and clicking QuickReport.

When you first come to grips with an income tax return with a whole year of *Quicken* accounts behind you, you will certainly think of other ways in which *Quicken* does, or could, help your particular situation. When you have completed that first return, take stock and see if there are some adjustments you could make to the *Quicken* set-up so that the job will be even easier next year.

CHAPTER 10

Using Quicken in Your Business

By now you have a pretty good idea of *Quicken*'s power and flexibility. If you have even a nodding acquaintance with traditional accounting methods, computerised or not, you will have seen a lot to surprise you. In *Quicken*, there is no terminology to learn. You don't have to draw up your "Chart of Accounts" or "Nominal Ledger" before you start – you don't even have to know what those terms mean. Can so easy and pleasant a program really look after your business accounts?

The answer, almost certainly, is yes.

This chapter shows how *Quicken*'s methods relate to traditional bookkeeping systems. It has suggestions about how small businesses can use the program. It goes on from there to more difficult matters such as VAT (including the question of whether or not to use an accrual accounting system) and payroll. You will find descriptions of *Quicken*'s business accounts, and also of the add-on program, *QuickInvoice*, which is part of the *Quicken Deluxe* package.

10.1 An Introduction to Bookkeeping

Quicken is the ideal answer for sole traders and small businesses where the proprietor is also the bookkeeper. It is the perfect solution for anyone at all who has been relying on the traditional shoebox method. (Under that system, you throw all your financial paper into a shoebox and deliver it to an accountant every so often.) A great deal of thought and expertise has been devoted to the subject of VAT – *Quicken* is ready to handle anything you can throw at it in that line, and to make your quarterly return to HM Customs & Excise a much less soul-searing experience.

There are things it can't do. There is no provision for stock control. You will have to work out for yourself how much to deduct from your employees' pay for tax and National Insurance. If you pay wages by cheque, *Quicken* can print the cheques with itemised vouchers attached showing the different deductions. But if you pay directly into your employees' bank accounts, *Quicken* cannot print a pay slip for them. *Quicken* is not suitable for larger and more complicated businesses with more than (say) 10 employees, although it is not easy to define a cut-off line with a program as good as this one. Intuit say that many big corporations in its native America use *Quicken* for their cash accounting.

If your business involves much invoicing, you should seriously consider adding *QuickInvoice* to *Quicken* itself. *QuickInvoice* is available separately, and also comes with *Quicken 5* as part of *Quicken Deluxe*. See Section 10.7, later in this chapter, for more about how *QuickInvoice* can help.

Traditional double-entry bookkeeping developed, at least in part, as a system of checks and balances. Every transaction was entered twice, as a debit and as a credit. When you paid an electricity bill, for example, you would credit your bank account (yes, that's right, credit it) with the amount, and debit your expense account "Electricity". A trial balance was drawn up periodically to test whether the total of debits equalled the total of credits – if it didn't, there was a mistake somewhere. If it did, there could still be a mistake, or deliberate fraud. A transaction could have been entered for the wrong amount, or left out of the books altogether. But the trial balance provided a basic check.

Computers have, to a considerable extent, made the traditional methods obsolete. Neither *Quicken* nor any other accounting software is going to get its debits and its credits confused, or make an entry in the wrong ledger. But the old terminology and methods were carried over to computerised accounting, partly out of habit, just as early motor cars were shaped like horse-drawn carriages; partly to provide comfort for those used to the old system.

The traditional system is particularly strong in providing a structure to deal with the credit transactions which feature so importantly in most businesses. When a customer makes a purchase, a double-entry is made. The customer's account is debited: the amount he owes you is increased. The sales ledger is credited: the value of the widgets you have sold this quarter is increased. When the same customer eventually pays you some money, again a double-entry is made: the customer's account is credited with the amount, reducing the sum he owes you; and your bank account is debited with the same amount. It's a tight and efficient system, but it's difficult and creates plenty of room for mistakes to be made.

Quicken, as you will have suspected already, does not work like that. You do not have to master the double-entry system at all to use *Quicken*, although the program is in fact entering each transaction under two headings. When you pay an electricity bill, you have less money in the bank and the total of your Electricity expense category is higher. Simple, when you put it like that. *Quicken* can also handle credit accounting – "accrual accounting", as it is usually called. The program would not be of much use in business if it couldn't. The system *Quicken* uses for accrual accounting is easy to understand and to use, as you will see as this chapter unfolds. If you are not registered for VAT, in fact, you will have no problems at all.

If VAT does figure in your business accounts, things are not quite so easy. You don't need *Quicken* to tell you that. You're going to have to work out clearly in your own mind which system applies to you – accrual accounting, cash accounting, or a mixture; and then concentrate single-mindedly on how to use *Quicken* in your situation. Even so, it's not nearly as bad as it sounds.

This chapter is devoted to *Quicken* as a business program, with particular emphasis on the two areas of particular difficulty, accrual accounting and VAT. It does not attempt to replace the excellent *Quicken* manual. Any user would be foolish indeed to entrust valuable business records to this (or any) program without studying the manual. As a registered user, you also have access to Intuit's expert telephone help. You'll probably never need it, but it's nice to know it's there.

Caution

Two essential precautions: if you have an accountant, consult him or her about the forthcoming transition from your present accounting system, whatever it is, to Quicken. Secondly, set yourself a rigorous backup and security routine and stick to it. Your records are valuable. Back them up every time you use Quicken. Make a backup at least once a week. Keep it in a different room from the computer. If others have access to your computer, consider protecting your files with a password. Last, and by no means least, think about the physical security of the computer itself. It is almost as attractive as a video to a casual thief.

10.2 Basic Business Accounts

This section is about getting started in business accounting, but let's not make heavy weather of it. Perhaps you don't need to "get started" at all, in any formal sense.

I keep my earnings from writing in an income category among the rest of our domestic income categories. Relevant expenses, both tangible things like printer supplies and more abstract notions like a proportion of telephone and heating bills, are lumped together in a "writing" expense category. Having these categories in the same *Quicken* file as domestic ones means that I can use the Splits window to calculate a percentage of telephone bills for domestic purposes, another percentage to set against my earnings.

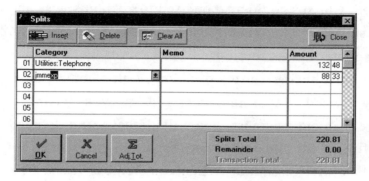

FIGURE 10.1 SPLITTING A TELEPHONE BILL

At income tax time, a Tax Summary report limited to those two categories provides all the information I need for an income tax return. Limiting the report to the expense category only provides an itemised list of expenses which can be attached to the tax return as it stands.

Tip

Remember that you can enter percentages as well as actual amounts in the Splits window – very useful if you are going to claim, say, 10% of your heating bills as a business expense in relation to your home office.

I have a friend who owns a house and a caravan which she rents to holidaymakers. If I could persuade her to give up manual bookkeeping, I would suggest the same approach to her. She could have one income category and one expense category for the accounts related to her letting business, and use classes to distinguish between the properties.

A bed-and-breakfast business is another in which there will be many expenses shared between the business and the household, including food, heat, light, cleaning, laundry, repairs and decoration. There is every advantage in such a case in keeping all accounts in one *Quicken* file, perhaps with one income category and one expense category for the bed-and-breakfast business. The expense category could have as many subcategories as required. Classes could also be used to keep business and domestic accounts separate. There is more about the use of classes in business accounting later in this section.

But for most business users of *Quicken*, this homespun approach won't do. You will need a separate *Quicken* file for your business accounts. If you have more than one business, you will almost certainly need more than one *Quicken* file. If your businesses are separately registered for VAT, separate files are absolutely essential. When you create a *Quicken* file, you can choose to load business categories rather than domestic ones. Or you can create your own categories.

If you have been using a system, either manual or computerised, which includes the traditional Chart of Accounts with numbers for each income and expense category, there is no reason you shouldn't retain the numbers in *Quicken*, using them as category names. Add a description (such as "Sales", "Returns", "Purchases") for each category in the Set Up Category window. Then go to the Options window and click the Reports icon. Under Category Display, select Both, meaning that both the name and the description of your categories will appear in reports.

But if you aren't involved already with a Chart of Accounts of this sort, my advice would be to avoid it. The point of the numbering system is to keep related categories together. In *Quicken*, you can achieve that by using subcategories. The drop-down list at the category field in the Transaction Register shows only the name of each category and its type, Income or Expense. If all you see on that list is a series of numbers, you will have to keep referring to a printed list, at least in the early days, to see which number means what. It's tedious, and mistakes can creep in.

Two other points to note as you set *Quicken* up for business use:

1) In business accounts, every transaction must be assigned to a category. A traditional accounts package would force this practice on you by refusing to accept a transaction without a category. *Quicken*, as you know, doesn't go in for force. But in this case, you can tell the program that (gentle) force may be required. Click the Options icon at the top of any Transaction Register window, or choose the Register icon in the Options window itself. Then select the Miscellaneous tab, and make sure there is a tick in the box labelled Warn Before Recording Uncategorised Transactions. And if you ever notice any sums called "Other" in one of your Business reports, it means that some transactions have slipped through the net. Use QuickZoom to identify them and correct the problem.

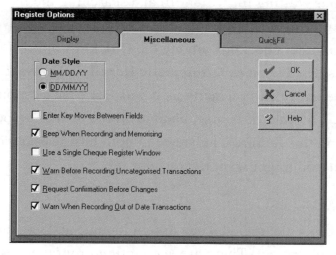

FIGURE 10.2 THE REGISTER OPTIONS WINDOW, WITH MISCELLANEOUS SELECTED

2) It does not really matter whether domestic users are consistent in the spelling of payees' names, although consistency is a good idea, as it enables *Quicken* to be far more informative. In business, it is

important that both your customers' and your suppliers' names are spelled in exactly the same way every time they appear in the register. In a traditional program, you would enter full details for all customers and suppliers before you started entering transactions. After that, the program would enforce consistency. In *Quicken*, you can and should use QuickFill to achieve the same end. See also Section 10.7, on *QuickInvoice*.

From the same Register Options window, click the QuickFill tab. Be sure that there is a tick in the checkbox labelled Automatic Completion of Fields. After that, whenever you start to type a name in the Payee field that has appeared there before, QuickFill will take over from you and finish the typing. If it ever fails to do so with a name you know should be on its list, click the drop-down button on the Payee field and scroll through the list to find the name. Waiting for QuickFill and searching the list can make the process of entering a transaction take a little longer. It's worth the trouble.

There is another checkbox among the QuickFill options which you might want to consider. If you tick Automatic Recall of Transactions, *Quicken* will complete the entire entry exactly as it was last time as soon as you leave the Payee field. You can, of course, change all the details before you click Record. I find this feature a nuisance in both business and domestic account-keeping, but you might want to consider it.

Classes

Using *Quicken*'s classes, you can assign income and expenses to a particular client or job or project. There are accounting programs costing many times more which would not allow you to do that.

Classes are discussed in Section 2.4. They provide another way, beyond categories, to classify income and expense transactions. There are no preset classes in *Quicken*. You define your own, either "on the wing", as you type in transactions; or by choosing Classes from the Lists menu, and then clicking New. A class, like a category, can have a brief description.

As an example of how classes might be put to work, imagine you own a number of holiday cottages. Each one could be defined as a separate class in your accounting system. Items of income and expense could be assigned to the proper category, and in addition assigned to the particular house involved. Your rental income will always derive from one house or another, and you can easily use the classes you have set up to distinguish the source: "Rent/Dunroamin" or "Rent/Seaview".

But there will frequently be occasions when you have to pay a bill that relates to work done on more than one of the houses. Enter the date and the total amount of the bill, and then use the Splits window to separate the total into appropriate amounts for each house. Don't forget that the Splits window can work out percentages. All you have to do is decide that, say, 35% of the bill relates to one house, 45% to another, 20% to another. Fill in the first line of the Splits window with "Decoration/Heather_Cot" in the Category field and "35%" in the Amount field. *Quicken* will replace "35%" with the actual amount, and fill in the remainder in the Amount field on the second line. You should then put "Decoration/Loch_Cot" in the Category field on the second line, and replace the figure in the Amount column with "45%". Again *Quicken* will calculate the amount, and enter the balance in the Amount column on the following line. All you then have to do is fill in "Decoration/Burnside" in the Category field of the third line. *Quicken* has already calculated the value of the remaining 20%. Click OK and then, back at the Transaction Register, click Record.

This system has obvious uses in a wide variety of businesses. If you own more than one shop, you can keep your accounts in one *Quicken* file (as long as the shops are not registered separately for VAT, in which case the accounts must be in separate files) and assign both income and expenses appropriately. If your business provides a service, you can divide income and expense amounts as they relate to particular clients or jobs. If the same percentages will apply to another bill in the future, memorise the transaction for reuse – see Section 4.3.

Remember, too, that transfers between accounts can be assigned to classes, although they cannot be assigned to categories. So you can keep particular sums of money logically separate when they relate to different aspects of your business.

If you use classes in this way, you will want to use QuickReport frequently to see a report of all transactions in a particular class. Choose Classes from the Lists menu, select the one you are interested in, and click on the QuickReport icon.

Depreciation

If your business is a limited company (or perhaps even if it isn't) you will want to draw up a balance sheet from time to time. To do that, you need to include in your accounts the assets owned by your company, and to make allowance for their depreciation. But accounting for depreciation can be of use to many small enterprises even if a balance sheet is not in question. If you have part-time, free-lance earnings, for example, you will probably be able to set the depreciation of the tools and even the furniture you use for your craft or trade against your earnings for tax purposes. You should consult an accountant about the tax rules. *Quicken* will make light work of the accounting.

Set up an Asset account. The *Quicken* manual suggests calling it something like Cap Equip, for Capital Equipment. Start with an opening balance of £0.00. List in the account each of the assets your company owns, putting the current value of the asset in the Increase column. Roughly speaking, an asset is something that lasts, something you don't use up the way you use up computer paper. And some things last longer than others – that's where depreciation comes in.

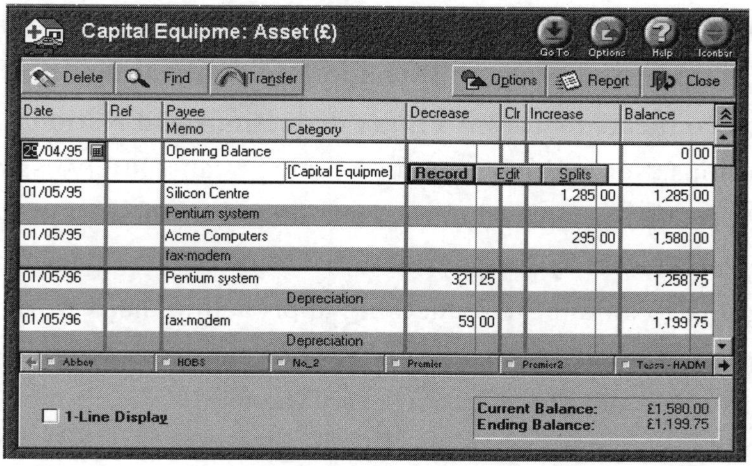

FIGURE 10.3 A CAPITAL EQUIPMENT ACCOUNT, WITH ENTRIES FOR DEPRECIATION

In the future, whenever you purchase an asset, record the purchase in the Transaction Register of your Current account in the usual way, but instead of putting the name of a category in the category field, put the name of your Capital Equipment account. That means, of course, that you are entering the transaction as a transfer of funds from your Current account to your Asset account. Put the name of the asset you have just bought (computer, filing cabinet, van, or whatever) in the Memo field. Then click on Edit just below the entry you have made, and choose Go to Transfer from the drop-down menu. In your Capital Equipment account, replace the Payee name with the name of the asset.

You will probably want to record depreciation once a year. You may need an accountant's advice about what proportion of the cost of each asset can be depreciated each year. To record depreciation, open the Asset account and enter a transaction with the name of the asset in the Payee field, and the amount of depreciation you are claiming in the Decrease field. You will need to create an expense category called Depreciation and assign such transactions to it.

10.3 Doing Your Payroll

All it takes is one employee for you to find yourself involved with all the problems connected with PAYE tax deductions and National Insurance contributions. Scrupulous account-keeping is absolutely essential in this area of business life. Compared to the ease-of-use of the rest of the program, getting *Quicken* ready for payroll accounting and then doing your first pay-day is going to amount to something approaching hard work. But you only have to do it once. After that, even if your employees are paid different amounts each time, *Quicken* will carry the load.

You may pay your employees by cheques that you write in *Quicken*. It is somewhat more likely that you will pay them either in cash or with direct transfers from your bank account to theirs. The way you set *Quicken* up for payroll accounting is the same in each case, and the actual procedure on pay-day not much different.

As far as your own accounts are concerned, you want to know your total outlay on wages, including amounts such as Employer's National Insurance contributions that you pay in addition to wages, not to the employee but to the Government. To achieve this, set up an expense category called Payroll. Set up subcategories of Payroll that will add up to your total wages bill. Use "Payroll:Gross" as the subcategory for your employee's total wages. That total will include PAYE tax which you will deduct from gross wages and pay directly to the Inland Revenue, and there will be other deductions that you must make from your employee's gross wages. Never mind that for the moment – this subcategory, Payroll:Gross, is for the employee's total, the amount that will appear on his or her P60 at the end of the tax year. The other subcategories of Payroll are for your additional obligations. They will certainly include Employer's National Insurance. For each of these, use a subcategory name that starts with "Comp" for "Company". Thus you will have a subcategory called "Comp_NI", and there may be others such as

"Comp_Pension" and "Comp_Medical". All of these subcategories added together amount to your gross wages bill.

When you actually pay an employee, you will withhold some PAYE tax and National Insurance contributions. You will become liable for Employer's National Insurance and any other employer's obligations that you have set up as a "Comp" subcategory. Until you pass these amounts on to the appropriate authorities, they are, of course, amounts that you continue to owe, and therefore liabilities. Whenever you draw up a balance sheet, those amounts must be shown as a liability, even though the actual money may temporarily reside in one of your Bank accounts.

So the next thing you must do is set up a separate *Quicken* Liability account for each one of them. Go to the Accounts list and click New. Choose Liability Account from the Create New Account window. Give each of these Liability accounts a name beginning with the word Payroll: Payroll-NI, Payroll-PAYE, Payroll-Pension, and any others you need. There should be a Liability account to match each of your "Comp" subcategories, and additional ones for the deductions you must make from your employee's gross wages.

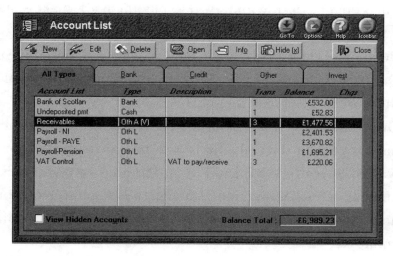

FIGURE 10.4 ACCOUNT LIST SHOWING PAYROLL LIABILITY ACCOUNTS

You're now ready to roll.

Remember that *Quicken* cannot help calculate the amounts you must deduct from wages nor the additional amounts you must pay in respect to each employee. The chances are you know all about these deductions from past experience. If you are just starting out in business, talk it over with your accountant and be sure you understand the calculations you must make.

The procedure for actually paying your staff is almost identical for any one of the four possibilities:

1)   *Quicken* writes the cheques.

2)   You write cheques by hand.

3)   You pay wages in cash.

4)   Your bank transfers the money to your employees' banks.

Open the Transaction Register of the account from which the wages will be paid. If *Quicken* is going to write the cheques, choose Write Cheques from the Activities menu. Otherwise, make the entry directly in the Transaction Register. In either case, you should read all of what follows carefully.

Fill in the employee's name as Payee. Even if you have several employees and are making one cash withdrawal to pay them all, make separate entries in the register for each one.

• Before you enter any figure in the Amount field, open the Splits window.

• On the first line, put your Payroll:Gross category. For the amount, put the employee's gross wages.

• On the next few lines, enter the names of the Liability accounts you have set up for the deductions you must make from your employee's wages: Payroll-PAYE and Payroll-NI are two certainties. Enter the amount of each deduction as a negative amount. Notice that you have not, so far, entered anything for your own additional obligations as employer.

- Leave a few lines blank. If you are tracking VAT, make your next entry on line 9. If not, go right on down to line 17. In either case, put a hyphen ("-") in the Memo field of each of the lines you skip, so that *Quicken* will not close up the gaps. For VAT-tracking, see Section 10.5 later in this chapter.

- Now you are going to add lines for your additional obligations as employer. Each of these obligations must appear as a double entry, one positive and one negative, so that the total amount of your employee's pay is not affected. For the category Payroll:Comp_NI enter a positive amount. On the following line, put the Liability account Payroll-NI and enter an otherwise identical negative amount. Proceed to make other double entries in the same way for your other obligations.

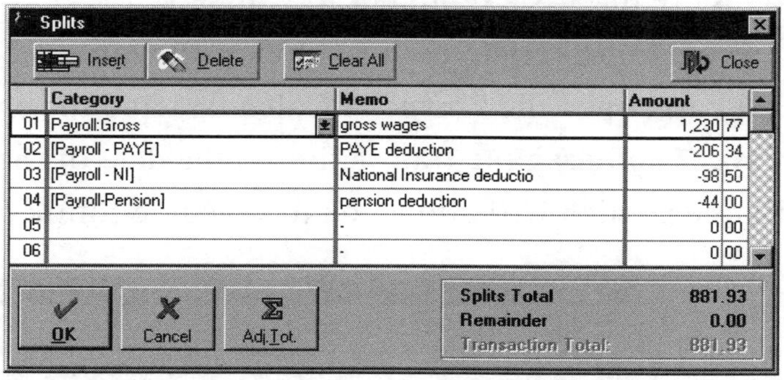

FIGURE 10.5 THE SPLITS WINDOW SHOWING PART OF A PAYROLL TRANSACTION

And that's it. Click OK in the Splits window. Take a final look at the transaction to make sure that the total showing is the amount you will actually pay your employee. Then click Record.

If you have other employees, proceed to make similar entries in the register for them as well. As soon as you have finished with the last one, memorise each of the transactions. See Section 4.3 for details of that procedure. From the Scheduled Transaction list, click New. In the Create Scheduled Transaction window click Group. Give the group a name – why not "Payroll"? – and then choose the date of the next payment and the time interval (it will probably be weekly or monthly). You can put 999 for the number of payments so that the group payments will continue indefinitely. Click OK to see the list of your memorised transactions, from which you can select each of your payroll transactions for inclusion in the group.

In the section of the Create Transaction Group window headed Register Entry, your procedure will depend on how you pay wages. If you go to the bank yourself and draw out cash for your employees, or if you write cheques by hand, choose Prompt Before Enter. If the bank makes the payments automatically, choose Automatically Enter. In either case, you will probably want the prompting to start or the entry to be made a week or so before monthly wages are due, as a reminder to yourself.

If you have only one employee, you obviously won't need a transaction group. In that case, open the Financial Calendar, find the employee's name in the list of Payees and drag the transaction to the date of the next payment. A window will open which will allow you to schedule future payments.

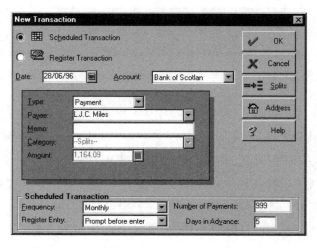

FIGURE 10.6 SCHEDULING FUTURE PAY-DAYS

If your employees receive the same amount of money on each pay-day, you can now sit back and let *Quicken* take over until the Chancellor of the Exchequer changes the tax rules or you give everyone a raise. If overtime and bonuses affect your wage bills, you will have to make the appropriate changes before each pay-day. If you have only one employee, you will find the transaction on the Scheduled Transaction list. Click Edit, and then in the Edit Scheduled Transaction window, click Splits. You'll find all your careful work from last time.

If you have more than one employee, you will find that the Scheduled Transaction list shows only the name of your pay-day group. To edit an individual's pay in that case, go to the Memorised Transaction list; click Edit; and then, at the Edit Memorised Transaction window, click Splits. Again, you will see the Splits window just as you carefully prepared it last time. All you have to do is make any necessary changes in the amounts. Click Adj Tot to tell *Quicken* to adjust the total of the transaction.

Finally, if *Quicken* is going to write the cheques for you, enter the date and the employee's name on the screen cheque. Then click Splits and proceed exactly as above. The procedure remains the same when you have

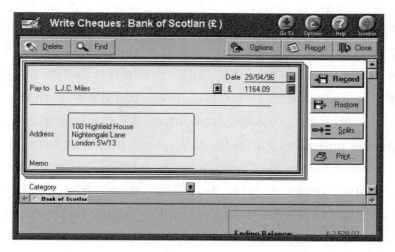

FIGURE 10.7 WRITING A PAY-CHEQUE IN *QUICKEN*

finished entering all the Splits: for several employees, memorise each transaction and set them up as a group. For one, schedule the next pay-day on your Financial Calendar.

10.4 Accrual Accounting

It's time to face up to accrual accounting. If your business, like many, operates largely on credit, one of the most important duties of your accounting software will be to tell you exactly how you stand. How much do you owe? How much do other people owe you? How long do your invoices go unpaid? Which of your customers owe you the most?

Using *Quicken*'s Asset and Liability accounts, you can keep close tabs on all of these questions. Don't worry about that phrase "accrual accounting" if it sounds like the sort of thing that makes you run a mile from the whole business of keeping books. There's no difficulty about the idea, and it's easy to deal with in *Quicken*.

The money people owe you is an asset of your business. So, in *Quicken*, you can set up an Asset account to hold your invoices. The money you owe is a liability. If you have employees, you saw in Section 10.3 how to set up Liability accounts for the PAYE and National Insurance amounts that you owed to the Inland Revenue. Similarly, you can set up a general Liability account for your other debts and enter in it the bills you have to pay. Or, if *Quicken* prints your cheques for you, you can just "write" a *Quicken* cheque for your bills as they come in. *Quicken* can use the written but unprinted cheques to produce reports on your outstanding bills, sorted by payee.

It is at this point that *QuickInvoice* comes on the scene – see Section 10.7. This program, which works in harness with *Quicken* itself, can actually set up and maintain your Accounts Receivable Asset account for you. You still have to understand what's going on, and to decide which method of accounting is appropriate to your case. Then you can hand over to *QuickInvoice*. Read the rest of this section with that possibility in mind.

To set up an Asset account for the invoices you send to your customers, click New from the Account list. In the Create New Account window, choose Asset. Call your new account AR, for Accounts Receivable. Give it an opening balance of £0.00.

Go back through your paper records and enter each of your current outstanding invoices in your new AR account. Put the date at which you sent the invoice to your customer. Put the invoice number in the Ref (for Reference) field – or use the Memo field if you need more room. Whichever you choose, be consistent in using that field for invoice numbers hereafter. Let QuickFill ensure that you type each customer's name exactly the same way every time you enter it – see Section 10.2. Enter the amount of the invoice in the Increase column, since every invoice you send out increases the amount you are owed and therefore the value of this Asset account. Put one of your income categories in the Category field – or you can click Splits to apportion the amount between two or more categories, just as you can do with an entry in other types of account. Remember, too, that you can add a class name after the category name (in or out of the Splits window) to categorise the income further. See Section 10.2 on how you can uses classes to track a particular job or project. In the future, enter all invoices in your AR account when you send them out.

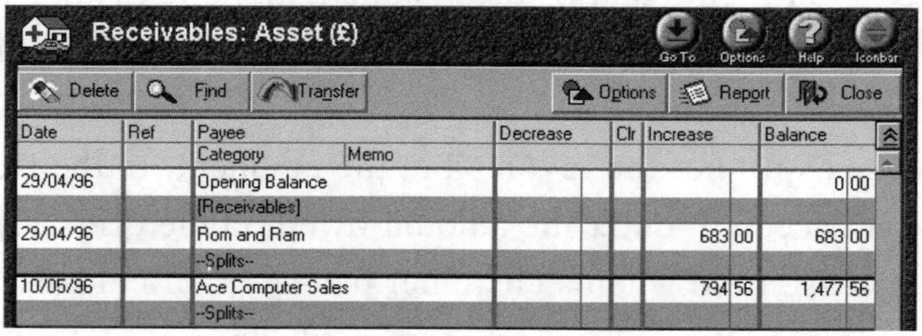

Date	Ref	Payee		Decrease	Clr	Increase	Balance	
		Category	Memo					
29/04/96		Opening Balance					0 00	
		[Receivables]						
29/04/96		Rom and Ram				683 00	683 00	
		--Splits--						
10/05/96		Ace Computer Sales				794 56	1,477 56	
		--Splits--						

Receivables: Asset (£)

Delete   Find   Transfer   Options   Report   Close

FIGURE 10.8 AN ACCOUNTS RECEIVABLE ASSET ACCOUNT

When you receive payment from a customer, enter the amount in your AR Asset account as a transfer to the account where you actually deposit the money. Use the drop-down list at the Payee field to make sure you enter your customer's name exactly as it was on the invoice.

- If your customers pay individual invoices in full, click on the Clr (for Cleared) column of the AR account to mark the payment with an "x". (Don't mark the other end of the transfer, the deposit of the money in your "real" Bank account. *Quicken* will do that when you next reconcile the account.) Use Find to search backwards for the invoice number through the AR Transaction Register. When you find the original invoice, mark that, too, as Cleared.

- If your customers pay "something on account", on the other hand, do not mark anything as Cleared. Just enter the payment, with the customer's name, as a transfer to a Bank account.

If you give discounts for early payment, you can enter a Split transaction either for the original invoice or for the payment.

Either: find the original invoice. Click Splits and then enter the amount of the discount as a negative amount on the first empty line in the Splits window. *Quicken* will automatically add another line with the remainder, so that the total of all the amounts still adds up to the amount of the original invoice. But you don't want that – you have given your customer a discount, so the amount of the original invoice has in effect changed to a smaller amount. Delete the line that *Quicken* added, and click Adj Tot so that *Quicken* will adjust the total. Click OK to close the Splits window and then click Record.

Or: you can split not the invoice but the payment. In the Decrease field of the AR Asset account, enter the amount owed on the original invoice. You use the Decrease field when a customer pays you, of course, because a payment decreases the amount you are owed. Then click Splits. On the first line of the Splits window, enter the actual amount paid as a transfer to the Bank account it actually went to. On the next line, put the amount of the discount. Assign it to an expense category for Discounts Given. Use this method if you want to keep track of how much you are "giving away" as discounts.

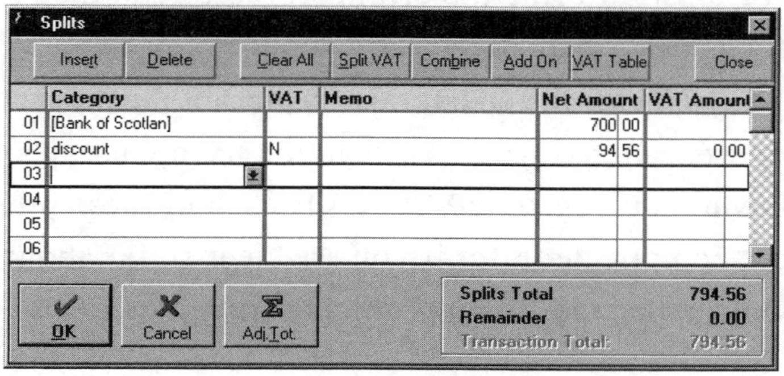

FIGURE 10.9 ENTERING A DISCOUNT IN THE ACCOUNTS RECEIVABLE REGISTER

If you operate a Sale or Return policy, record the original invoice in your AR account in the usual way. When your customer returns part of the order with payment for the rest, make an entry in the Transaction Register of your Current account for the amount you actually receive. Click Splits. On the first line of the Splits window, enter the total amount of the original invoice, and categorise it as a transfer to your AR account. Since the amount was entered as a deposit in your Current account, *Quicken* will understand that it must represent a decrease in the amount in your AR account, that is, a decrease in the amount you are owed. This will cancel out the amount of the original invoice. On the second line of the Splits window, you will see that *Quicken* has already entered the gross value of the returned goods as a negative amount. All you have to do is fill in the income category – be sure it is the same category you used for the original invoice.

If you want to set up a Liability account for Accounts Payable (instead of just writing a *Quicken* cheque for each of your bills as they come in), the procedure is exactly the same. If you are likely to receive credit from your suppliers for returned goods, it is best to have an Accounts Payable (AP) Liability account. You can enter credits as a separate transaction – in the Decrease field, of course. Or you can use Find to search back through the Transaction Register to find the original invoice and then enter the credit as a split, exactly as described above for discounts you allow your own customers.

See Section 10.6 near the end of this chapter for the information *Quicken*'s Business reports can give you now that you have your accounts in place.

If your business is registered for VAT, each of these procedures becomes slightly more complicated. But if you are clear so far about the way things work in *Quicken*, the additional problems are minor.

10.5 VAT

In theory, VAT is perfectly simple. As a business, you pay Value Added Tax on many of the goods and services you purchase, just as private individuals do. As a business, you also charge VAT on goods and services you supply. Every so often, you subtract the amount of VAT you have paid from the amount of VAT you have charged and send the balance to HM Customs and Excise.

Just as expense and income categories in *Quicken* can be designated "tax-related", so they can also be set to track VAT. When you receive an invoice from one of your suppliers, *Quicken* will automatically split the total into a Net and a VAT amount if you assign it to a VAT-tracking expense category. When you enter the gross amount of one of your own invoices to a customer, *Quicken* will do the same thing. The state of your current obligations to Customs and Excise is monitored in a special VAT Control account which *Quicken* establishes automatically.

When you need to fill in a VAT return, create a VAT Summary report from *Quicken*'s choice of Business reports. All the figures you need will be neatly gathered together there.

Wonderful. But it does involve a certain amount of preliminary planning and organisation on your part.

Your method of proceeding will depend on whether you are using accrual accounting (as explained in Section 10.4), cash accounting, or a mixture of the two. Accrual accounting is the normal way: the VAT you add to your invoices is charged from the date you issue the invoice, not the date when you receive payment. To use any other system requires the permission of your VAT office.

However, circumstances may well dictate that accrual accounting is unsuitable for your case. I knew a computer consultant in the early '90s who was a limited company in his own person, like many other independent consultants. He worked for a small software house which was having hard times during the worst of the recession. He issued regular invoices for the work he was doing. The software house paid what it could when it could, often many months in arrears. He had permission from his VAT office to calculate his VAT liability from the receipt of his money, not from the date of the invoices. *Quicken*'s flexibility made it the ideal accounting program for him. Cash-and-accrual accounting is particularly valuable in this situation, or variations of it – when receipts are late and/or dubious. There are accounting programs which cannot deal with this scenario at all.

So your first task is to decide which system is right for you, probably in consultation with your accountant. Next, you follow the appropriate path in *Quicken* and ignore the others.

When you have made your decision, you will know which of your accounts need to have VAT-tracking turned on. You can do this when you first set up an account, by saying yes when EasyStep asks if you want to track VAT in this account. Or you can choose an account from the Account List at any time in the future, click Edit, and put a tick in the Track VAT box then. When an account has VAT-tracking turned on, you will see "(V)" in the Type column of the Account List, next to the identification of the type of the account (bank, cash, etc.). Even if you load business categories when you set up your *Quicken* file, the "normal" state for an account is with VAT-tracking off. You must turn it on deliberately once you have decided which system is appropriate for your situation.

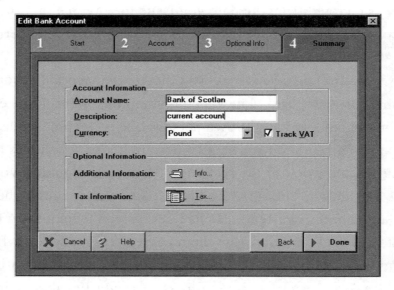

FIGURE 10.10 TURNING VAT-TRACKING ON FOR AN ACCOUNT

As soon as any account in your *Quicken* file has VAT-tracking turned on, you will find an extra column in the Category and Transfer List window, showing the VAT code for each category. When you set up a new category or edit an old one, you will find a new field in the Set Up Category or Edit Category window, in which you can enter the Usual VAT Code.

Nor will you be entirely surprised to discover that there is a new entry on the Lists menu, too: VAT Table. When you first asked *Quicken* to track VAT for a category or an account, the program asked you whether you wanted to start off with the standard UK rates for VAT. If not, you were offered a chance to make changes. If you chose the standard UK rates,

Quicken will start you off with 17.5% assigned to code "S" for Standard. Codes "E" for Exempt and "Z" for Zero-rated are set at 0%. There are seven numbered codes available for you to assign. You may want to use these if you trade with other EC member countries. In addition, *Quicken* suggests you use the code "N" for non-VAT input, such as transactions involving small companies not registered for VAT. When rules change, come back to the VAT Table, choose the affected rate and click on Edit to see the Edit VAT Rate window, where you can easily make the necessary change.

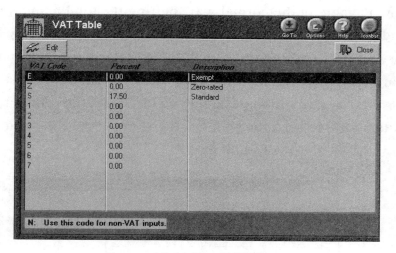

FIGURE 10.11 THE VAT TABLE

If you loaded *Quicken*'s business categories when you set up your file, you will find that the program has already assigned VAT codes to the categories. However, you should go through the list carefully and check for yourself that *Quicken* has got it right.

With all that in place, you are ready for some important decisions and questions. Which of your accounts should have VAT-tracking turned on? How do you actually enter a VAT transaction? What about special situations such as sale-or-return?

Accrual accounting – See Section 10.4 for an explanation of how this works in *Quicken*. Turn VAT-tracking on for your Accounts Receivable and Accounts Payable Asset and Liability accounts. You will not, normally, turn VAT-tracking on for your Current account, or for any of your other actual Bank and Cash accounts. With your accounts set up in that way, *Quicken* will enter the VAT amounts when you record invoices received and invoices sent out in your AR and AP accounts.

Here's how it works: you enter the invoice in Accounts Receivable or Accounts Payable in the normal way, putting the total amount in the Amount field and entering the appropriate income or expense category in the Category field. Click Record. You will hear *Quicken*'s beep in confirmation. And you will notice that instead of the category name you just entered, the word "Splits" appears in the category field. Select the transaction and click the Splits button to see how *Quicken* has divided the total amount of the invoice into Net and VAT amounts.

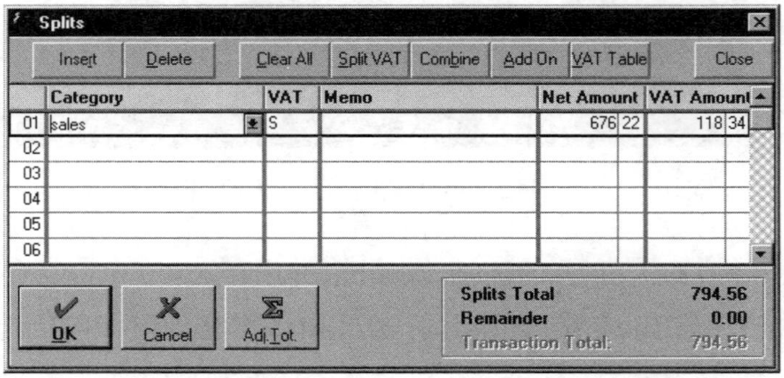

FIGURE 10.12 A VAT TRANSACTION ENTRY

What about when you receive or make payment on an invoice? That, too, will involve an entry in the Transaction Register of your AR or AP accounts. Isn't *Quicken* going to muddy the waters by splitting that as well? Answer – no. Transactions involving money will be transfers to or from your Current account. If you are using accrual accounting, VAT-tracking will not normally be turned on for your Current account. So *Quicken* will know that those transactions should not be split.

Sale-or-return complicates the elegant simplicity of this system. See below.

Cash accounting – If you have permission to use cash accounting for your VAT returns, turn VAT-tracking on for your Current account, and for any other accounts in which you enter business transactions. If you are using cash accounting, you should not need to have AR and AP accounts. If for any reason you do have them, Intuit suggests that VAT-tracking is turned off for those accounts and that you exclude them from VAT reports. For more about Business reports, see Section 10.6.

Cash and Accrual accounting – As for straight cash accounting, you will turn VAT-tracking on for your Current account. But unlike a trader who is using pure cash accounting, you will have AR and AP accounts in your *Quicken* file. You should be sure that VAT-tracking is off for those accounts. You do not want *Quicken* to make the VAT split when you enter an invoice, because if you are using this system you have permission from your VAT office to calculate VAT from the date you receive or make payment, not from the date of the invoices, which could be many weeks earlier.

Here's what you do:

- When you receive or send an invoice, enter the Net amount only, without the VAT element, in your AR or AP account.

- When you later receive or make payment on the invoices, make the entry in your Current account – not, as for the other systems, in the AR or AP accounts themselves. This time, enter the total amount of the invoice, including VAT.

- Open the Splits window. You will see that *Quicken* has separated the invoice total into Net and VAT amounts, because VAT-tracking is turned on for your Current account. Designate the Net amount as a

transfer to AR or AP, where it will cancel out the original invoice.
Assign the VAT amount to your VAT control account.

Special situations – Sale-or-return is probably the most difficult. Your treatment of it will depend on which of the three systems you are using for your VAT accounts.

Sale-or-return in Accrual accounting – See Section 10.4 for a discussion of this situation. If you are liable for VAT, you will have to turn VAT-tracking on both for your AR account and for your Current account. When you send out the goods, enter the invoice in your AR account as described in Section 10.4, allowing *Quicken* to split the total into Net and VAT amounts. When the customer returns part of the shipment with payment for the rest, enter the split transaction in your Current account as described in Section 10.4. Transfer the gross amount of the original invoice to AR, as before. Then assign the negative amount which *Quicken* has entered on the next line of the Splits window to the income category you used on the original invoice, and allow *Quicken* to split this line into Net and VAT amounts. The negative VAT amount here will make the necessary adjustment to the VAT *Quicken* calculated on the original invoice.

With VAT turned on for your Current account, you will have to take extra care to ensure that *Quicken* is splitting only the correct transactions into Net and VAT elements. There may be other invoices, not involving sale-or-return, where you deposit or transfer money to your Current account and have to suppress the VAT split manually.

Sale-or-return in Cash accounting – No problem here. You don't make any entry in your registers until the goods are returned with payment. Then you make the entry in your Cash account, which has VAT-tracking turned on, and *Quicken* makes the split as usual.

Cash and Accrual accounting – This is the tricky one, at least until you have things set up.

- From the Lists menu, choose Category and Transfer. Go to the end of the Category and Transfer List window, where you will find your accounts listed, after expense categories. Choose your AR account, click Edit, and in the Edit Usual VAT Code field, enter your code for the standard VAT rate – probably "S". Doing this means that transfers to this account will be split for VAT. It is, incidentally, *Quicken*'s ability to assign VAT codes to transfers to accounts in this way that makes it so useful an accounting tool where VAT is concerned.

- Be sure that VAT-tracking is not turned on for your AR account. That is the normal arrangement for mixed cash and accrual accounting.

- Be sure that VAT-tracking is turned on for your Current account. That, again, is the normal way in cash and accrual accounting.

- When you dispatch goods, enter the invoice in your AR account, putting the Net amount only, not the VAT.

- When the part shipment is returned with payment, make the entry in your Current account. Enter the amount actually received, and put the name of your AR account in the Category field. Open the Splits window and change the Net Amount on the first line to the total value of the original shipment (which did not include VAT, remember).

- *Quicken* will already have calculated the remainder and entered it on the next line. Fill in the income category used for the original invoice, and enter the VAT code. Click the Split VAT button to divide the amount into Net plus VAT.

Trade with EC countries – If you trade with EC member countries on the continent, you must include the totals of such transactions on your VAT return form. The *Quicken* manual suggests that you use the VAT codes 1 and 2 for this purpose, leaving the rates set at 0.00. Use code 1 for sales to EC countries, and for purchases from them that would be exempt from VAT if they took place in the UK. Use code 2 for purchases from the continent that would be subject to VAT in the UK. Then you can gather the totals together on a VAT report (see Section 10.6) and use them to fill in boxes 8 and 9 of your VAT return.

10.6 Business Reports

Reports are going to be important to you as a business user. From time to time you will need to persuade bank managers that you are a worthwhile risk. Any bank manager will be impressed by a *Quicken* Balance Sheet or Profit and Loss statement. If you are a limited company, you will need to file annual returns. Most of all, whether as a sole trader or member of a partnership, you will want to use *Quicken*'s range of reports to keep you closely informed about the progress of your business.

Some of *Quicken*'s Business reports, as you will see, provide information similar or even identical to domestic reports – money is money, after all. Others, such as Payroll and VAT reports, are for business users only. See Section 5.1 for a fuller discussion of the whole subject of reports: what is available in *Quicken* and what you can do to make reports even more serviceable. As with domestic reports, Business reports can be customised and fine-tuned until they tell you exactly what you want to know. Customising reports is fully as relevant to business users as to others, perhaps more so – if you ever feel mildly discontented with any of *Quicken*'s standard Business reports, have a look at Section 5.1 to see if you couldn't make some changes and produce exactly what you want.

And don't forget QuickReport. Select any entry in one of your Transaction Registers, and click QuickReport for a list of all the transactions involving that payee. If you are using accrual accounting methods, QuickReport can take a transaction in your Accounts Receivable or Accounts Payable accounts and show you how much a particular customer owes, or how much you owe a particular supplier.

Here is a list of *Quicken*'s Business reports:

P&L Statement – This report summarises revenue and expenses by category for your chosen period of time. The difference between revenue and expenses is your profit – or loss. This is just like a domestic Summary report, of course.

P&L Comparison – compares profit and loss for two different periods.

Cash Flow – Inflows and outgoings are summarised for each of your accounts. This is identical to a domestic Cash Flow report. This is an important one. You don't need to be using cash accounting (see above) to benefit from this report.

A/P by Vendor – If you are using *Quicken*'s cheque-writing facility to track Accounts Payable, use this report to see summaries of unprinted cheques by payee name. See Section 10.4 for more about how to handle Accounts Payable and Accounts Receivable in *Quicken*. If you are using accrual accounting and have set up a Liability account for Accounts Payable, the A/P by Vendor report will not work for you, based as it is on unwritten cheques. You will have to create your own summary report, based on your AP account. Select Payee for the row headings, and tell *Quicken* not to subtotal the figures. If you use the "balance forward" method of accounting, you will not be able to form the report by excluding cleared transactions (as there are none), but you will be able to see how much you owe each of your suppliers.

A/R by Customer – This report is based on an Accounts Receivable Asset account, as described in Section 10.4. It summarises uncleared transactions month-by-month by payee. If, of course, you are using the "balance forward" method of accounting, where your customer's payments do not refer to particular invoices, you will not have marked any transactions as Cleared. In that case, all transactions in the account will be included. You should ignore the monthly columns and look only at the balances for each customer.

Job/Project – You can use this report if you are using *Quicken*'s classes to separate accounts for different aspects of your business, as described in Section 10.2. Each job or project will have its own column. If you use classes for any other purpose besides tracking particular projects, you will want to exclude those other classes from this report. And you can get a QuickReport on any particular class by selecting it in the Class list and clicking the QuickReport icon.

Payroll – If you set up your payroll categories and Liability accounts as described in Section 10.3, you can use this report for a summary of all payroll-related transactions. You will see a column for each of your employees, and one for your Inspector of Taxes.

Balance Sheet – This report shows the balances in all your accounts as of a particular date. The difference between your assets and your liabilities will be shown as your "Equity" or net assets.

Missing Cheques – highlights any gaps or duplications in your cheque-numbering sequence.

Comparison – just like the domestic comparison report, it compares inflows and outflows for two different periods, with a third column showing the difference, either as an amount or as a percentage.

VAT detail – If you are registered for VAT, use this report for a complete list of all VAT-related transactions.

VAT summary – When it is time to submit your VAT return, use this report to gather together all the figures you need.

Quicken does not have any graphs devoted particularly to business use. You will find, however, that both the Income and Expense graph and the Budget Variance graph are extremely relevant to your situation. See Section 5.2 for a full description of these graphs and their meaning. You'll want to make full use of the forecasting tools described in Section 3.4 as well.

10.7 QuickInvoice

If your business regularly involves sending out invoices, you should seriously consider adding this program to *Quicken* itself. It comes as part of the *Quicken Deluxe* pack. It works with *Quicken* itself – in fact, it won't work without *Quicken*. What it does is this:

- Identifies your *Quicken* files as it is installed. You can, if you prefer, start a new business file in *Quicken* and direct *QuickInvoice* to work with that.

- Sets up an Asset account for your Accounts Receivable. On your instructions, *QuickInvoice* will send your invoices to *Quicken* for entry in this account. If you prefer, *QuickInvoice* can post invoices to an Asset account that you have already established.

- Sets up a Cash account in *Quicken* for sums paid by your customers in cash. This does not need to be a "real-world" account. You can make transfers from it to your Current account as you pay cash in.

- Maintains an item list of the goods and/or services you provide, with the rate applicable to each. Each is identified with an income category in your *Quicken* accounts. Discounts which you allow can also be set up as items, allowing *QuickInvoice* to calculate the amount automatically.

- Maintains a list of your customers or clients, with the terms of business you use in dealing with each of them. This is a double list, maintained in the form (probably alphabetical) that is most convenient for your records and also in the form in which names are entered on the invoices.

- Posts invoices to your *Quicken* Accounts Receivable account and also, if appropriate, to your VAT control account.

- Maintains a complete, chronological list of all the invoices you have ever sent using the program.

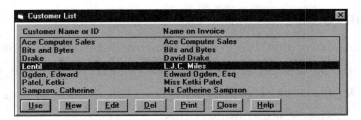

FIGURE 10.13 A CUSTOMER LIST IN *QUICKINVOICE*

You must still decide whether cash or accrual accounting, or a combination of the two, is appropriate for your situation, and you must still do the accounting when you receive payment from your customers. On these subjects, the *QuickInvoice* manual covers much of the ground already covered in this chapter, and in the *Quicken* manual itself.

QuickInvoice installs as easily as any other Intuit product. You must instruct the installation routine to put the program in the same directory as your *Quicken* files – probably C:\QUICKENW. When the installation process is complete, you will find that there is a *QuickInvoice* icon on your *Quicken* iconbar, and that *QuickInvoice* is now one of the choices in the Activities menu.

When you start *QuickInvoice* for the first time, you will have to set up your company, and give the names of the Asset account and the Cash account in *Quicken* that *QuickInvoice* is to use.

The choice you must make here between "Service" and "Professional" will affect the look of the printed invoices, but not those you will see on-screen. The Service invoices have columns to show rates and prices per item, while the Professional ones show only a description and an amount.

Next, you need to make an item list. If you have been keeping business accounts for any length of time, this should be easy. You know what goods or services you offer, what you charge for them, how you account for your income, and what VAT rates apply. If you are new to business accounts, you may need to take some time at this point to think things out.

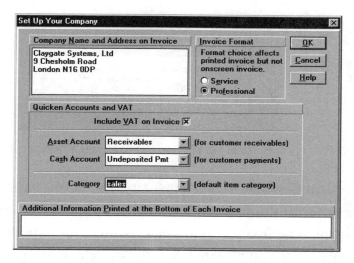

FIGURE 10.14 THE SET UP YOUR COMPANY WINDOW

You do not, of course, need to have a "list" of items at all. If you are an accountant or a window-cleaner, there may be only one item: your own time. On the other hand, a cabinet maker might want to itemise the different types of furniture on offer, with prices for each. As you would expect from your knowledge of *Quicken*, prices and rates can be changed as you are typing in individual invoices.

You can then set up a customer list, if you like – from the Lists menu, choose Customers. Or you can do it as you go, letting *QuickInvoice* draw information about your customers from the invoices themselves. Your own knowledge of your business will determine procedure here. If you have an established base of regular customers, it would be a good idea to take time at the beginning to make the list.

You should click on Preferences in the Edit menu and make any necessary changes in the way your invoices are to be laid out and printed.

Now you're ready to write invoices. You have everything in place, so the process will be very easy. Customers and their details, items and their details, can all be drawn from the lists you have already set up. Notice how

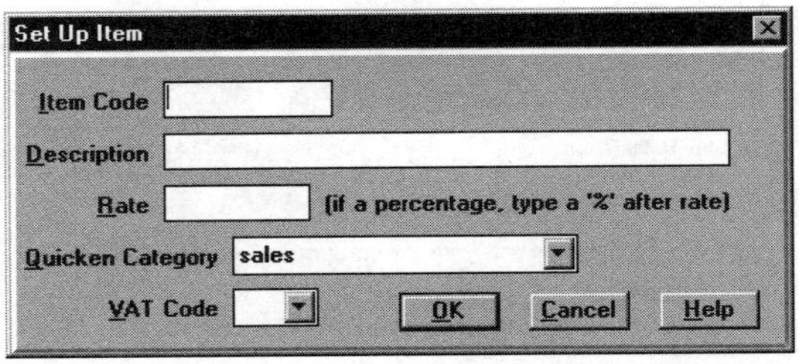

FIGURE 10.15 THE SET UP ITEM WINDOW

the invoice-writing window has, unusually, two scroll bars. The smaller one allows you to scroll through the line items on the current invoice; the taller one scrolls from one invoice to another. Notice, too, that the invoice form provides a space for you to enter the *Quicken* class you may be using to keep jobs or projects distinct, as described in Section 10.2.

Like cheques in *Quicken*, you can save up invoices in *QuickInvoice* for later printing. The program allows you to use plain, continuous stationery; your own headed paper; or lined forms supplied by Intuit.

Tip

Do not post invoices to Quicken until they have been printed and are ready for dispatch. Corrections are easier when you do not have to go across and make them in the other program as well.

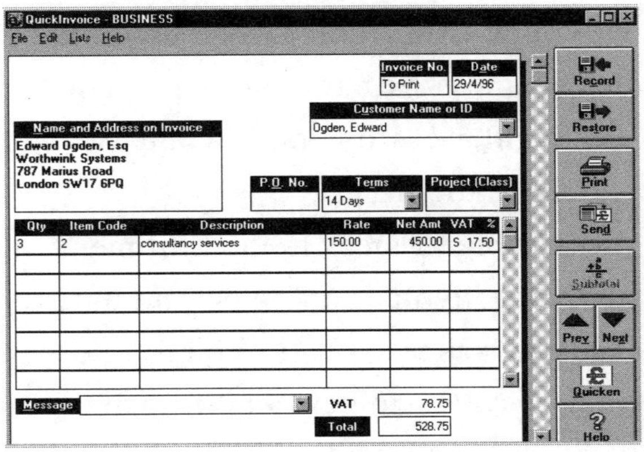

FIGURE 10.16 FILLING IN AN INVOICE

CHAPTER 11

Under the Bonnet

This is the housekeeping chapter, where you'll learn about tedious but necessary operations like making backups of your valuable financial data, setting passwords to protect your files, and making archive copies when your files get too big. If you're working from home and don't like to think about the mechanics of computing, there's a lot here that you can skip. One section, however, is vital for everyone: backups. Don't skip that, whatever you do. And if you're using *Quicken* for business accounts, you can't afford to miss the sections about security and archive files.

11.1 Backups

The hard disk of your computer is the internal storage medium where the *Quicken* program itself and your data files reside when the computer is switched off. Hard disks are a lot more reliable than they used to be. If you're fairly new to computing, you could be lulled into thinking that they are completely reliable. They're not. And every time you use *Quicken*, your data files become more valuable.

Back in the days of *Quicken* for DOS, the program itself could be set to remind you to make a backup every time you closed it down. Today's *Quicken*s – both *Quicken 4* and *Quicken 5* – will remind you every so often, but not every time.

The *Quicken* manual is emphatic about the need for regular backups. If you ever do have a hard disk failure, you will never again need reminding. You might as well take the lesson to heart before the hard disk fails – it's a lot less painful that way. I have the backup icon on my iconbar, and use it most days, certainly after any *Quicken* session that involves more than a couple of transactions.

It is essential to make backup copies onto a floppy disk, not on the hard disk itself. Get hold of two new floppy disks, format them if necessary, and label them "Quicken 1" and "Quicken 2". The manual recommends using them alternately. I would get confused if I did that. I prefer to keep the disk called Quicken 1 on my desk, where I can reach it at the end of a session without having to stand up and search the room. I keep Quicken 2 in a disk storage box within sight but not within reach – I use it on Saturdays. If your computer is capable of running *Windows 3.1* or *Windows 95* (essential for running *Quicken*), you almost certainly have a disk drive that uses high-density disks. Although the *Quicken* manual tells you how to proceed when your files get so big that it takes two disks to back them up, you will find in practice that you can go on almost indefinitely doing the backups on one disk only. But do keep the backup disks for use with *Quicken* only.

To make a backup, insert the backup disk in the floppy drive and choose Backup from the File menu. If you have only one floppy disk drive on your computer, and keep all your *Quicken* accounts in one *Quicken* file, you may eventually find it a bit tedious to be asked every time which file you want to backup and which drive to use. You can tell *Quicken* to skip that bit. To do so, you have to put the backup icon on the iconbar – a good idea anyway. For detailed instructions about the iconbar, see Section 4.1. As you are installing the icon, you will be asked whether or not you want to skip the initial dialogue.

When disaster eventually strikes, reinstall *Quicken* on your new computer. Then insert the disk with your latest backup copy in the disk drive and choose Restore from the File menu. In the Restore Quicken File window, you will have to choose the drive where the backup files are to be found (probably A:) and the name of your data file. *Quicken* provides lists on-screen to help with the choice. If you have only one *Quicken* file, and no *Quicken* experience before *Quicken 4*, the program will have named the file "QDATA". But you may have brought differently-named data files with you from earlier versions of the program, as I did; or you may have more than one file, perhaps because you run more than one business. In that case you will have to choose. Then click OK – *Quicken* does the rest.

11.2 Using Quicken on Two Computers

It is very likely that you will want to use the program on more than one computer – perhaps bringing business accounts home to work in the evening, or carrying your files with you on a portable computer to update while you are travelling. Expenses are a good deal easier to track if you can do them daily instead of having to make sense of a wallet-full of receipts 10 days later.

If you're using *Windows 95*, and if you can connect your portable computer to your desktop computer by cable or over a network, there's a great new way to manage files on two computers at once by using the *Windows* "briefcase". You use it to copy files from the desktop to the portable, and later to update the desktop files from the portable. The more earth-bound of us will have to stick to older methods.

If you use any other *Windows* programs, you will know that there are two commands that usually appear on the File menu: "Save" and "Save As...". "Save" copies the file you are working on to its place on the hard disk, either while work is in progress or when you decide to knock off for the day.

"Save As…" lets you copy the work again with a different name or in a different place, usually a floppy disk, as a backup copy.

So when you discover that the *Quicken* File menu offers neither "Save" nor "Save As…", you may feel a moment's surprise. *Quicken* doesn't need a "Save" command because every transaction is saved to your hard disk as soon as you click Record. You have nothing to fear from power failures or the cat tripping over the flex.

And the place of "Save As…" is taken by *Quicken*'s Backup command, which you will find on the File menu. As well as making security backups, this command is the one to use if you want to use *Quicken* on a second computer. Install *Quicken* on your portable or your home computer just as you did the first time. Insert a backup disk you made on the other computer, and choose Restore from the File menu, as you would do if your data files had been lost in a disaster. Choose the disk drive and file name from the Restore *Quicken* File window.

When you restore a file to a computer that already contains data files with the same name, the restored files overwrite the ones that were already present. This means that, if you are repeatedly switching between two computers, you will have to be distinctly careful not to restore an old backup file over a new data file.

___

Tip

The best way to proceed is to have one disk, and one disk only, as Quicken's link between your two computers. That will be your "transportation" disk as well as part of your security system. Then be sure always to back up Quicken, after every session on either computer. That way, the transportation disk will always contain the latest version of your data. You should still have a second backup disk, kept in a separate place. Once a week or so, make two backups in the same session, one to each disk.

11.3 Closing Out the Financial Year

The *Quicken* manual tells you that you don't need to close out a year. You can go on adding transactions to your data files virtually forever.

When I first met this claim, I was distinctly sceptical. My pre-*Quicken* accounting program became heavy and slow when it had six months' figures on board, and gave up completely after nine months, so that I had to split a year's accounts into two files.

Now I am ready to think again, for I have found *Quicken* to be as good as its word. My data files span nearly four years – they have come along with me from *Quicken* for DOS to *Quicken 2 for Windows*, on through *Quicken 3*, and *Quicken 4* to *Quicken 5*. I have 14 different accounts. Several of them no longer contain any money, but they are there on the list and available for inspection if I ever want to look back. I keep detailed Cash accounts. I often make entries in the Memo field. And yet my backup files for all of this would fit on one high-density floppy disk, with room to spare, while I was still using *Quicken 4*. As soon as I switched to *Quicken 5*, I found I needed a second disk. But *Quicken*'s on-screen instructions are clear and the procedure is relatively painless, so I still have never closed a financial year as far as my own accounts are concerned. And I have never noticed any sign of effort in the program itself as it deals with the Transaction Register of a busy account with data going back to the autumn of 1992.

So it's true: you don't need to close out a year. And it's also true that there are advantages in having a lot of data available. You can make comparisons between what you spent this year and last. You can look at your spending quarter-by-quarter, often more revealing than a month-by-month comparison. You can look back at the big events in your financial history, rather like turning the pages of an old diary.

You may still feel that you would like to draw a line under ancient history. *Quicken* has various ways of letting you do so:

Password Protection – You can set a password to protect a whole data file, if you are afraid of prying eyes. You can also set a password to protect all data before a certain date. It is a good idea to do this after making an income tax or VAT return. You know the password, after all – so if you really have to, you can still go back and change the data. But with the password set, there is no danger of an inadvertent change being made in day-to-day use.

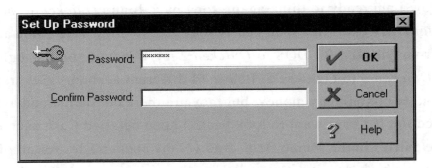

FIGURE 11.1 THE SET UP PASSWORD WINDOW

From the File menu, choose Passwords. You can then choose whether to set a password for the entire file, or only for certain transactions. If you choose "Transactions", you will then have to specify a date. All transactions before that date will be "locked" by the password. And, of course, whichever choice you make, you have to type in your password. Password-choosing is a surprisingly difficult art. For improved security, include some non-alphabetical symbols. I use the cat's name, but I spell it Pou$$in. Whatever you choose, for heaven's sake don't forget it.

To change the password, choose Passwords from the File menu again. You will see a window in which you have to type the old password again, and then a new one. And if you decide that this security business is a nuisance after all, just leave the New Password field empty. Password protection will be removed.

Archive Files – Use this command to create an archive copy of your data up to a certain point; you will probably choose the end of a tax year. Your current file is unchanged, so you can continue to enjoy the advantages of having several years' data available. The archive file provides an extra record. From the File menu, choose Year-End Copy. Choose Archive in the Year End Copy box, and then click OK. In the Archive File box that follows you will have three decisions to make:

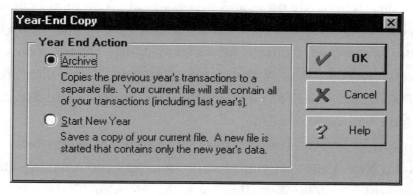

FIGURE 11.2 THE YEAR-END COPY WINDOW

1) The cut-off date. All transactions before the date you choose will be copied to the archive file. UK users will certainly choose last April 5 for this date – the last day of the previous income-tax year. I would suggest not using this option until at least the end of May, to ensure that all lost-sheep transactions have had plenty of time to find their way home.

2) A name for the archive file. *Quicken* will suggest a name for you, based on the name of your data file and the last two digits of the previous calendar year. My *Quicken* suggestion might be JMM95, for instance. But you don't have to accept the suggestion. You might prefer something like TAX95-6.

3) The location of the archive file. The program suggests putting it in your *Quicken* directory. You might as well.

Once the archive file has been created, I would suggest you open it and do two things:

1) Set a transaction-date password, as described earlier in this chapter. Choose today's date, so that all transactions in the file will be protected.

2) Back up the archive file. I would suggest dedicating another floppy disk to this purpose, not the one you use for regular backups.

Your current file will be unchanged, remember, so you don't really need to keep the archive file on your hard disk at all. You might consider deleting it. If you want to do that, from the drop-down menu under File choose File Operations and then, from the next menu, choose Delete. You will see a list of the *Quicken* data files in the current directory. Select your archive file and click OK. Deleting a file is a serious matter. *Quicken* will ask you to type the word YES before it proceeds.

You can, of course, restore your file from the backup whenever you like.

Start a New Year – If you're still not happy about having old data in your current files, *Quicken* allows you the traditionalist's choice. From the File menu, choose Year-End Copy, and this time click Start New Year instead of Archive. You will have to make the same three decisions about date, file name and file location.

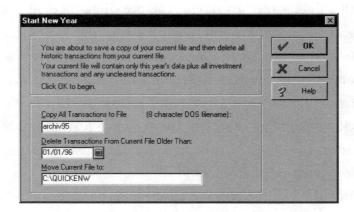

FIGURE 11.3 THE START NEW YEAR WINDOW

Quicken will make a copy of your data up to the cut-off point you have chosen, just as before. This time, it will do something else as well: it will delete from your current file all cleared transactions before your chosen cut-off date. Your Investment account is unaffected. No transactions whatever are deleted from that.

If you want to use this option, it is a good idea, again, to wait until at least six weeks after the end of the tax year. My own preference is to wait until I have completed my income tax return, usually some time in June. That way, there shouldn't be any outstanding uncleared transactions for the time period to be archived.

Obviously, this option will not be much use if you don't reconcile your Bank accounts – because cleared transactions will not be marked. And if you maintain a Cash account, which is of course never reconciled in the normal way, none of its transactions will be filtered out by this procedure unless you have marked each one in the Cleared column yourself. If you're going to do it, the best way is to click on the Cleared column twice as you enter each transaction. The first click enters a "c" for "cleared", the second, an "R" for "Reconciled". For a discussion of cash accounting, including the question of whether to mark transactions as reconciled, see Section 2.3.

11.4 File and Data Management

By now you certainly realise that a "file" in *Quicken* does not mean what the word usually means in computer-speak. A *Quicken* file consists of several separate files on your hard disk. Each of the computer files has the name of your *Quicken* file, plus a three-letter suffix – QDATA.QDB, QDATA.QMD, QDATA.QSD and so forth. (The suffixes are different for *Quicken 4* files.) It is therefore both easiest and safest, when you want to do anything directly to your *Quicken* files – deleting, renaming, or copying them, for instance – to do it from within *Quicken* itself.

New Files – You should stick with one *Quicken* file if you can, to take advantage of all the powerful facilities for exchanging data between accounts and building up a complete picture of your financial life. But there may be times when one file simply won't do. If you run two or more businesses that are separately registered for VAT, it is essential to keep the accounts separate. If you keep accounts for a club or charity, they belong in a different file from your domestic accounts. To open a new file, choose New from the File menu. After that, the procedure is exactly the same as when you installed *Quicken* and set up your first file.

Opening a File – Whenever you open the program, *Quicken* will automatically load the file you were working on last. To choose another one, click File in the menu bar. The last four *Quicken* files you have used will be listed at the bottom of the drop-down menu. Unless your financial life is really complicated, you'll find what you're looking for there. But if four isn't enough for you, choose Open from the File menu to see the complete list.

Renaming a File – When you set up your first file, *Quicken* called it QDATA. If you'd like something livelier or more personal, choose File Operations from the *Quicken* File menu, and then choose Rename. You are limited to eight letters for a file name, unless you're using *Windows 95*. *Quicken* won't let you give your file name an extension (those three letters that come after the dot). It does that itself.

Deleting a File – Again, choose File Operations from the File menu. This time, choose Delete. Once you've done it, you've done it; there's no going back. *Quicken* will ask you to confirm by typing YES that that is really what you want to do.

Copying a File – You can create a new *Quicken* file by copying all or part of an old one. This is, in fact, exactly what you are doing when you archive old data as described earlier in this chapter. *Quicken* also provides a Copy command with the other File Operations on the File menu. This command gives you great freedom to copy just what you want to a new *Quicken* file. As well as providing a name for your new files, you have three decisions to make:

- the date range for the transactions to be copied. *Quicken* suggests a date range which includes all the transactions in your file. Leave it like that if you want a complete copy. If you want to copy only the structure of your file, and none of the transactions, set a starting date after the date of the last transaction you have entered. Your accounts, category list, class list and icons will be copied, but no transactions.

- whether to include prior uncleared transactions. If your work with the new file is going to involve reconciling accounts, you will want to leave the tick in this checkbox. If you are in any doubt at all, leave the tick.

- if you have an Investment account, whether to include prior investment transactions.

Copying Data between Accounts – It happens sometimes, especially if you maintain a Cash account, that you suddenly realise you are typing transactions into the wrong account. If things haven't gone too far, the easiest solution is probably to move them one by one. Select a transaction that is in the wrong place and then choose Copy from the Edit menu. (The Edit menu on the menu bar and the one on the Transaction Register both offer Copy.) Go to the account where the transaction belongs – it could even be in another file – and create a space for it in the Transaction Register by going to the end of the register or by clicking Insert. Then choose Paste from the Edit menu, and finally click Record. If you don't create a space in the Transaction Register before you click Paste, the copied transaction will replace the one in the register. If you do that by mistake, remember the Restore button. Click that rather than Record and all will be well.

If you have a more serious need to copy data from one account to another, or from one *Quicken* file to another, you can make use of the special Quicken Interchange Format (QIF) files to do the job. From the File menu, choose Export. You will see the QIF Export window. Provide a name for your QIF file in the field labelled QIF File to Export. Choose the account you want to copy from, and specify a range of dates. You cannot specify individual transactions any more precisely. You can then choose whether to export transactions only, or to include Accounts, Categories, and Memorised Transactions as well. If you choose Categories, that includes Classes. Click OK when you're ready.

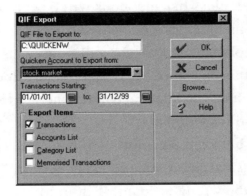

FIGURE 11.4 THE QIF EXPORT WINDOW

Then go to the file you want to copy the transactions into, if it's not the current one. Choose Import from the File menu. In the QIF Import window, provide the name of the QIF file you just created; choose the account to receive the copied transactions; and, again, choose whether to import the Accounts list, the Category list, and Memorised Transactions.

If you are going to go on with this procedure and copy over transactions from another account that include transfers to and from the first account, tick the Special Handling for Transfers box. If you don't, transfers will be duplicated in both accounts by the time you are finished.

CHAPTER 12

On-Line Banking and the Internet

What about the future? This final chapter takes a look at the world beyond your desktop – specifically, at the possibilities of on-line banking in conjunction with *Quicken*. At the very end you will find a few words on that subject of perennial interest, the Internet.

12.1 On-Line Banking

Quicken users in the United States have been able for years to pay their bills directly from the program. To do so, they need to have a modem to connect the computer to a telephone line, and an account at the bank which is running the scheme. This facility is not yet available to British users, not because of any lag in technology over here, but because British banks have been much more cautious over questions of security.

However, if you like the idea (as I do), the UK possibilities are now so good that you probably won't mind the slight amount of extra typing involved in using not *Quicken* itself but a separate program to connect with your bank.

The Bank of Scotland has been running its Home and Office Banking (HOBS) system for years, but so quietly that few people outside of Scotland are aware of it even now. It took some time for technology to catch up with the bank. But things are changing:

- the price of a fast modem has come down to something around the £200 level;
- the popularity of the Internet has turned everyone's attention to the advantages of being on-line;
- and the bank has replaced its slow, clunky DOS software with a streamlined, 1996 *Windows* version.

Other banks by now are jumping on the bandwagon. The systems are all pretty much the same. I will describe the Bank of Scotland's HOBS because it was the British pioneer of on-line banking and because it is the system I have used myself for some years.

There's one possible difficulty: the main point of on-line banking, at least for individual users, is to earn the maximum amount of interest on your cash by keeping it on deposit until the last moment, transferring it to your current account only when it's actually needed. And that won't work unless you have some spare cash. If you're overdrawn every month, and don't have a savings account, HOBS is not for you.

To use HOBS, you will have to have both a current account and a so-called HOBS investment account with the Bank of Scotland. The HOBS account pays interest slightly under the best the bank offers on other deposit accounts. It offers instant access to your funds with no penalty – the system wouldn't work otherwise. You can have other accounts of various sorts as well, and use HOBS to view balances and manipulate funds in all of them. Husband and wife or other joint account holders can have a joint HOBS account: each will have a separate user number and password.

To use the system to maximum advantage, you will want to use it to pay bills as well as transferring money in and out of your current account. In order to do that, you must tell the bank in advance the details of your "accounts" with your principal creditors — the gas board and the electricity board, British Telecom, the authority which claims your Council Tax and the board which gets the water rates; your mortgage-holder and your insurance company. The Inland Revenue is particularly keen to be paid electronically. You'll probably be able to think of others to add to the list. For each of them you fill out a form, authorising the bank to make electronic payments. You give the bank a copy of an old bill so that they can add details of your creditor's bank account. In most cases you'll also have a lengthy "customer identification number". That will be noted as well. (My local authority changes my identification number every year as it starts to collect a new lot of Council Tax. It's a nuisance, because the bank has to be notified to make the change. But that sort of irritating oddity is rare, in my experience.)

Security is tight, and you won't be able to use the system until it has been set up. The software itself comes on a single disk, and is simplicity itself to install. You could put it in the *Quicken* group, if you're using *Windows 3.1*, or have a separate HOBS group for it. The bank will tell you your HOBS identification number and a separate user number. You need to choose passwords to get into the Bank of Scotland network, and from there into the HOBS system. It's not quite as bad as it sounds, because the software can be set up to enter most of the numbers and passwords automatically. The more sensitive ones will be entered invisibly, so that they do not appear on your computer screen. The first time you log on to HOBS, you will notify the system of the passwords you have chosen. Then you have to wait a frustrating day or two before you can get started in earnest.

Take a look at the HOBS screen while you're waiting. The blank space in the middle is where you will conduct your dialogue with the bank while you are on-line. To the right is a calculator (a really thoughtful touch) and a digital counter to show you how long you've been on the telephone. Calls to HOBS from anywhere in the United Kingdom are charged at the local rate. Still, it's handy to know how long the current call has lasted. At the top of the screen, under the standard *Windows* menu bar, are two rows of icons.

In the first row, pausing over one of the icons will produce a "bubble" with a quick explanation — a device used by more and more programs these days, including *Windows 95* and *Quicken* itself. The second row does not incorporate this feature. The top row is largely concerned with the technicalities of getting connected and, later, disconnected; and down-loading screens. The lower row has the icons you'll use to access different HOBS functions when you're on-line.

The new software has a lot of useful bells and whistles. More of that in a moment. For day-to-day use, the main thing you want to do is check the balances in your accounts and make transfers from one to another to make the most of interest-earning possibilities. First of all, start *Quicken* running, and go to the account register for your Current account. Then start HOBS, and click on the telephone icon at the extreme left of the upper toolbar. That will connect you to the Bank of Scotland network. When you have successfully negotiated that step, your next choice will probably be the HOBS icon in the middle of the second toolbar. That will take you past some more security checks into the HOBS system itself.

Tip

If you're using Windows 3.1, the quickest way to switch between active programs is to use the keyboard, not the mouse. The key combination Ctrl-Esc produces a list of the active programs. Select the one you want using the arrow keys, and press Return. If HOBS and Quicken are the only programs running, the Alt-Esc combination cycles between them and the Program Manager (which counts as a program, and is always running when you have Windows loaded). That's quicker yet. In Windows 95, of course, all you have to do is click on the name of the program you want in the taskbar at the bottom of the screen.

Click on the icon showing a little stack of leaning coins. That will take you to an index of all your accounts, and show you the balances at once. You can then choose to see Today's Items, or a statement of recent activity in the account. If need be, you can keep on choosing "earlier items" from the menu until you have seen a statement of a full three months' activity in any of your accounts.

Check back with *Quicken* and note the balance in your Current account – I'm assuming your *Quicken* accounts are up to date. Then go back to HOBS and look at the balance there. It is very likely to be different.

You'll soon figure out the reason for the difference between *Quicken* and reality as represented by the bank's ledgers – it's because the cheques you write can take quite a long time to make their way home to roost. That gives you a chance to exploit the system, in a mild way.

HOBS doesn't work in what the computer boffins call "real time". What you see on-screen is the state of the ledgers at the official end of the preceding day. They were updated in the small hours of the night, during a period when the system was temporarily unavailable. When you choose to see Today's Items, you'll see listed any of your cheques which turned up yesterday and which the bank intends to pay out today.

That's what gives you your chance. The bank doesn't pay out cheques the instant they arrive. Instead, it logs them on as Today's Items for the next business day. If you dial into HOBS faithfully every day, you can wait until a cheque appears in the list of Today's Items before you move the money to cover it into your current account. Switch payments are different – they almost always go out on the business day after the transaction, whether or not they are listed with Today's Items. And cashcard withdrawals don't wait even that long. They are debited to your account at once – or the moment the bank opens again, if you're withdrawing money at night or during the weekend.

To make a transfer, click on the icon in the second row of money bags connected by an arrow. You will then choose the accounts to make the transfer from and to. You'll have plenty of chance to correct any mistakes before you finally send your instructions to the bank. You'll notice that you must type the pounds and the pence of your transfer on separate lines – that works for bill-paying, too, and reduces the chance of making a mistake.

When you have made a transfer, go straight back to *Quicken* and make the appropriate entry in the account register there. When you're using HOBS every day, the number of transfers can get quite high. Things will get muddled if you don't enter each one promptly.

It's important, and useful, to notice that your transfers and payments don't have to happen on the day you make them – you can schedule them for anything up to a month ahead. So when your telephone bill arrives, you can tell the bank to pay it in (shall we say?) 10 days' time, and make a transfer of funds to your current account for the same day, and then file the bill and forget the whole thing, while your funds earn 10 days' more interest. I have the sort of Visa card which automatically collects the full amount due from my current account by Direct Debit. So when the bill arrives, I reconcile it with my *Quicken* accounts and then tell HOBS to make the necessary transfer of funds to the current account on the due date.

The system has a number of other useful features. I think you'll find, once you start using it, that the most important advantage of all is being able to monitor the state of your accounts. I sent that cheque off to the bank – did it get there? Did the pay cheque go in all right? Was last month's mortgage payment for the right amount? And so forth.

Here's what you can do using each of the icons in the second row in turn:

- The leaning stack of coins accesses your accounts.
- The one marked SS/DD produces a list of your Standing Orders and Direct Debits. You can't change them yourself directly, but you can send instructions to your branch – see below.
- The light bulb lets you change your HOBS password, or change the way accounts are accessed. Normally, you see a screen on which four

accounts are shown. You can ask to see Today's Items or a statement for any one of them, or you can choose to see more accounts (if, of course, you have more) by choosing option 8 from the menu below. If you have a lot of accounts, this can become slow and irritating. Use this icon to tell HOBS that you'd rather not see a list at all, but access your accounts by typing in part of the account number.

- The little hand is for service requests – you can type in a message for your own branch.
- The cheque-form icon is for making payments.
- The money bags indicate transfers between accounts.
- The dollar sign accesses your foreign currency accounts. *Quicken*'s ability to handle foreign currencies works particularly well with this feature of HOBS.
- The key lets you change your passwords. You'll have to change your HOBS password once a year – the system will remind you when the time comes.
- The HOBS symbol lets you log into HOBS from the Bank of Scotland network. The network is where you first arrive when your modem connects.

There is a certain amount of overlap in the remaining icons. Choose the ones which lead most directly to the services you want:

- The Bank of Scotland logo produces the "bank index", from which a number of other functions can be selected, including the noticeboard and logging off.
- The finger board icon produces a list of other services, including information about interest rates and bank charges.
- The notice board icon leads, not surprisingly, to a notice board. You'll find information here about any unusual events which affect the system, including mysterious Scottish bank holidays.

- Three overlapping pieces of paper take you to the screen about other Bank of Scotland products and services. You can send for any brochures which sound interesting directly from this screen.
- The form with a pound-sign at the bottom produces a list of bank charges.
- The image of the globe leads to a list of the bank's current exchange rates.
- Finally, the image of an interesting letter arriving through a letterbox does not, alas, mean that the HOBS system can be used to receive email. It just offers another opportunity to send a message to your branch, or to the HOBS Help Desk.

I have always found the Help Desk helpful, incidentally – and not at all difficult to reach when needed.

The system also allows you to save screens and look at them off-line. This can be a very useful telephone-bill-reducer when you have a stubborn problem to deal with.

There are two methods of approach, depending on whether you want to print the information or just to look at it on-screen.

For future printing, click on the spool icon in the top row to add the current screen to the spool. If you prefer, you can select text for addition to the spool, instead of the whole screen. The spool icon is the one in which a floppy disk is shown with what might well be a video camera on top of it. Click on the printer icon to print the contents of the spool at any time (but preferably after your modem has hung up). After they have been printed, HOBS will ask you whether you want to empty the spool by deleting the contents. You don't have to – you can save them for the next session, and beyond, if you prefer.

To save screens for future viewing, click on the icon showing a floppy disk surrounded by arrows to add the current screen to the carousel. Later, when you want to view the screens you have saved, choose the icon showing the arrows without the disk. Keep clicking until you see the screen you want as the program cycles through all the ones you saved.

Both the spool and the carousel can be emptied by choosing the appropriate option from the File menu.

12.2 The Internet

Once you've got a computer and a modem, of course you'll want an Internet connection. The most difficult aspect of the 'Net is choosing a service provider and getting connected. Ask around, and read some magazines. Be sure to choose a service provider who offers connection at local-call rates from wherever you happen to be. You're going to be spending a lot of time on the telephone.

You'll soon discover that the Internet itself is the best teacher. Once you've found one interesting 'Net site, it will contain links to others. You'll make cyberfriends who will give you tips about interesting sites to explore. Almost all magazines and newspapers these days mention Internet addresses, and may actually be on-line themselves. You might like to start with http://www.ft.com, where you can find all the share prices published in the Financial Times. A selection of the articles from the current issue of The Economist are at http://www.economist.com.

Try doing a search for terms like "money" or (better) "personal finance". Searching the 'Net is easy if you're using one of the popular browsers like Netscape – and you certainly will be. One word of caution: most of the material on the Internet is American. In financial matters, you'll probably want to focus on the UK. You'll find plenty to interest you, as long as you're aware of the need to be selective.

The possibilities of the Internet are virtually limitless. For the moment, however, you're most likely to be using it for information and (let's face it) fun. Practical applications like shopping, share-dealing and banking are on their way, but for now those things are best done with a direct connection, like the HOBS system described above.

Tip

Don't forget British Telecom's reduction for frequently-used telephone numbers. You've probably seen it advertised, but you may not have realised it applies to numbers your modem dials as well. The idea is that you pay British Telecom a modest one-off fee which allows you to designate five telephone numbers. Thereafter, all calls to those five numbers are subject to a 10% reduction in the charge. When you're phoning your on-line bank five times a week, and your Internet service provider three times a day, that adds up to a substantial saving.

INDEX

E

F

G

M

N

O

P

Q

W

Y

U

V

SERIES TITLES

The Complete Guide to Sage Sterling and Accounting
by Stephen Jay

The Complete Guide to Sage Sterling for Windows
by Stephen Jay

The Complete Guide to Payroll using Sage and Other Systems
by Stephen Jay

The Complete Guide to Quicken UK using version 4
by Jean Miles

The Complete Guide to Quicken 5 - UK
by Jean Miles

The Complete Guide to Visual Basic 4
by Arthur Tennick

The Complete Guide to Java
by Andrew Cobley

The Complete Guide series of books is developed by the leading British computer books publisher, Computer Step. These comprehensive books provide all you need to know for a total solution. They are available from your local bookshop now, or in case of difficulty, contact Computer Step at:

5c Southfield Road Southam
Warwickshire CV33 OJH
Tel 01926 817999 Fax 01926 817005

NOTES

NOTES

NOTES